Island Cup

BY THE SAME AUTHOR

*Seven Dirty Words*
*The Hardest Working Man*
*Jeans*

# Island Cup

*Two Teams, Twelve Miles of Ocean, and
Fifty Years of Football Rivalry*

## James Sullivan

## BLOOMSBURY

New York    Berlin    London    Sydney

Published by Bloomsbury USA, New York

All papers used by Bloomsbury USA are natural, recyclable products made
from wood grown in well-managed forests. The manufacturing processes
conform to the environmental regulations of the country of origin.

LIBRARY OF CONGRESS CATALOGING-IN-PUBLICATION DATA

ISBN: 978-1-60819-527-5

First U.S. Edition 2012

1 3 5 7 9 10 8 6 4 2

Typeset by Westchester Book Group
Printed in the U.S.A. by Quad/Graphics, Fairfield, Pennsylvania

For Carolyn, teacher

"Football is an incredible game.
Sometimes it's so incredible, it's unbelievable."

—TOM LANDRY

# CONTENTS

*Kickoff*

# THE NAPOLEONIC WARS

THIS KID WAS something special. All year long, he'd carried the football team from Martha's Vineyard on his shoulders, scrambling from the quarterback position for two or three touchdowns every game. When he gained the edge and sprinted up the sideline, he seemed electrified, struck by lightning. Defenders who thought they had an angle on him were left chugging out of bounds, craning their necks to watch him score.

He had a million-dollar smile on his face and a new haircut on his head, with jagged racing bolts shaved into the sides and a large star etched in back. He did well enough in the classroom, taking a handful of honors courses. When he was named homecoming king during halftime of the Vineyard's ugly loss to Somerset, he had the poise to express his embarrassment that it had to take place during such a poor showing. Randall Jette, one of the best high school football players in the state of Massachusetts in 2010, even had a marquee-ready nickname: the "Jette Stream."

Now the final game of the season was under way. The Vineyarders had received the opening kickoff, and they were feeling their way downfield. Senior running back Brian Montambault fought for a couple of first downs, and the team in purple—by legend a remnant of a long-ago donation from the purple-clad Crusaders of Holy Cross, where a school superintendent on the Vineyard had once gone to college—was marching toward midfield.

On the other side of the ball were the Vineyarders' archrivals, the blue-and-white Whalers of Nantucket. The two teams practiced and played on islands off the southern shore of Cape Cod, where the proud, stubborn, self-sufficient locals referred to the vast wasteland on the other side of the ferry terminals as "America." The two islands were forever linked; once, in the late 1970s, they banded together in a half-serious attempt to secede from the state after legislators had proposed an unfavorable redistricting. Yet like feuding brothers, they coexisted in a perennial state of high pique toward each other. For fifty years they had brawled, taunted, and scuffled over one of the country's best, and strangest, high school rivalries.

Most people from Nantucket knew next to nothing about their counterpart island. You went over on a chartered ferry once a year for the so-called Island Cup game. You drove off the dock at the Steamship Authority in Vineyard Haven and followed Edgartown Road straight to the high school. The edges of the properties along the road were lined with hundreds of hand-lettered signs designed to make you feel not quite welcome: MV RULES! and WE STILL EAT WHALE MEAT.

What's the Vineyard like? It's nothing but an eyesore, Nantucketers have insisted for generations. All they've ever seen are the ferry landing and the scrubby bushes along Edgartown Road. Families from the Vineyard have equally little regard for their neighbors to the east, where the football field abuts a cemetery and the team has been known to erect funeral crosses marked with their opponents' names.

On the field, Randall Jette ran the option. His speed, quickness, and uncanny ability to elude tacklers made the team's offensive playbook relatively easy to design: more often than not, Jette rolled to the right, with a halfback on his flank. If a defender broke free of his blocker and lined Jette up, he'd pitch the ball to his trailer. If the blocks were there, he'd tuck the ball under his arm and burst upfield.

Nantucket's left end was one of the visiting team's key players, a looming six-foot-six-inch man-child named Terrel Correia. A sophomore, he was, absurdly, still only fifteen. Coaches drooled at the prospect that the kid might be even bigger and stronger by his junior and senior years. "You should see his younger brothers," said Steve Murphy, a former Whaler player now coaching the island's Boys Club team of junior high schoolers, at a Nantucket home game a few weeks before.

Correia had been coached hard all week. Randall was his, they said. Keep him inside! Contain, contain, contain. Whatever it takes, *do not* let the kid get outside.

Nearing midfield on the opening offensive series of the game, the Vineyarders were methodically testing the opponent's defense with basic run plays. This time, Jette hung back, keeping the ball after the snap. He strung himself along toward the near sideline, in the direction of the Vineyard's two thousand or so eager fans. All season long, he'd played as if his internal clock was set on half speed. Plays that seemed like a chaos of collisions to everyone else on the field unfolded like dream sequences for Jette, slow and inexorable, as if he could manipulate the players on both sides through sheer will. He'd glide, biding his time. Then, boom! A patch of green would suddenly present itself, and he'd cut toward it and be gone.

Correia, though, had him in his sights. With his height, he had *everyone* in his sights. But he'd flinched inside, however momentarily, when Jette faked a handoff before he started to move. Now he was lunging toward the outside, but he had two Vineyarders blocking his path. As bodies clashed and feet pounded the turf, Correia's long arm took a swipe at the purple jersey from between the two blockers, like something from beyond the grave. But Jette was already outside his grasp, blazing to the sideline and upfield. To the 30, the 20, the 10. Touchdown, Martha's Vineyard!

The packed stands on the Vineyard side erupted in delighted cheers. The drivers of the fire trucks parked behind the end zone nearest Edgartown Road cranked up their sirens and sounded their fog-cutting horns. From the far corner of the field, the toy cannon fired with a resounding crack, startling even those who'd been coming to games for years and were well aware of the tradition.

Senior Dhonathan Lemos, an affable, heavy-legged Brazilian kid who had played soccer until his junior year, split the uprights with ease on the point-after try. Over by the huge inflatable football, which identified the Island Cup game as the newest addition to the Great American Rivalry Series, the scoreboard lit up the number 7 on the home side.

Nantucket, once the dominant team in this inter-island rivalry, hadn't won a game against the Vineyard since 2002, and few of the games in the interim had been close. Was the team resigned to another rout?

There was a time when the Whalers made Thanksgiving miserable, year in and year out, for the boys in purple. Nantucket won eleven of twelve head-to-head matchups from 1966 to 1971, when the teams still played each other twice each year. Between 1972 and 1990, the blue and white won fourteen of nineteen.

But the tide began to turn in the early 1990s. Down 12–0 late in the fourth quarter in 1992, big-game Vineyard quarterback Jason Dyer, who was now an assistant coach for the team, engineered an exhilarating comeback on the opponents' home field. Before the Vineyard put any points on the board, one of the announcers handling the game for the Vineyard's local television station, MVTV, sagely predicted that it would be hailed as a pivotal moment in the history of the rivalry. "This is a game that will be remembered for an awful long time, either way," he'd said.

When the Vineyard roared back to victory, fourteen-year-old John Aloisi, a Nantucket freshman, was stunned. The youngest of four, three boys and a girl, he was clearly the most gifted athlete in his family. After years of getting trounced in one-on-one basketball by his brother Matt, John had begun to dismantle his older sibling under the backboard. Matt graduated in the spring of 1992. The eldest brother, Sam, had been on teams that won three straight games against the other island, two by shutout, in the late 1980s. Their father, also named Sam, assisted Vito Capizzo, the island's legendary coach, for several years, and their uncle on their mother's side had been a Nantucket quarterback in the 1960s. After the upset, John was despondent, for his family and his entire community.

A born leader, the youngest Aloisi would deliver sweet

payback, quarterbacking the Nantucket team the next three years to Island Cup wins and three straight Massachusetts Super Bowl appearances. Nantucket won the rivalry game again in 1996, after Aloisi left for Holy Cross. That four-year stretch was perhaps the most impressive in what had already been an amazing reign for Coach Capizzo. Few could have seen then that these would also be the last great years of his program.

IN A HALF century of antipathy, the hardy souls who live year-round on Nantucket and Martha's Vineyard have seen some incredible things on the football field. Under Capizzo, Nantucket—usually the smallest high school in the state to play football—has gone to nine Eastern Masachusetts Super Bowl championship games, winning three. Since the arrival of Donald Herman in the late 1980s, the Vineyarders have won five Super Bowls of their own, in eight tries. Both schools have produced several Division I college players and many more in the NCAA's lower ranks. Some went on to key coaching jobs of their own. A gifted few have even tasted the pros.

And the students who played the game have had some extraordinary life experiences off the field, for better and for worse. Players went to war; not all of them came back. A few made fortunes. Others have done prison time. Some of them traveled the world. One, an underwater photographer, worked with Jacques Cousteau. Another became a television comedy writer.

But those are the exceptions. The largest group of these football players came back to the islands, or never left. Their family names are on the island farms, the fish markets, the rubbish-removal and septic companies, the florists and gas stations and office-supply shops. A lot of them found work as carpenters; many more became teachers and cops.

Though Nantucket and Martha's Vineyard have similar reputations as playgrounds for wealthy white Americans, the truth of the places is more accurately represented by the rosters of their football teams. Over the years the Whalers and the Vineyarders have featured boys of polyglot heritage: New England descendants of the original English and Irish whalers and fishermen, of course, but also later generations of native Wampanoag tribesmen, pioneering black families from a historic summer enclave on Martha's Vineyard, and immigrants from Cape Verde, the Azores, Brazil, and many other Portuguese-speaking lands.

Some of the island teams over the years have been scarred by tragedy. One star quarterback was paralyzed in a car accident as he prepared to embark on his college career. Another lost his life on the day of one of the most exciting games between his former team and its archrival. His old teammates still credit him with causing the opponent's missed field goal—his last act, they claim, as he left this earth.

Both islands have seen several football coaches, and dozens of assistants, come and go. The players, of course, change from year to year. But the two men who have wrestled greatness from these unique programs together form a case study in serendipity. In places where most families have remained for a century, or even two or three, Vito Capizzo and Donald Herman were both "wash-ashores," brought in as twentysomethings to teach the local children a game. Separated by a generation, a few miles of the Atlantic Ocean, and the vast chasm of this rivalry, these two men are inextricably linked. It was the younger Herman's arrival on the Vineyard that goaded Capizzo, by then already a local legend, to extend his own career an extra decade—a few years too long, some say.

These two coaches are olive-skinned imports in two of the last bastions of old New England tradition. Both had roots on far-flung islands. Capizzo, now in his seventies, still speaks in the choppy rhythms of his Sicilian birth. Herman, born to Jewish parents, still carries the southern drawl he learned in his native Savannah, where he lived for a time on Wilmington Island. Even their matching thick, dark mustaches seem to follow some obscure Island Cup bylaw.

Neither man was big enough to excel as a player beyond high school, but both were schooled in the time-tested philosophy of power football. Finesse was never a significant part of their vocabularies, and they sometimes treated their players in ways that might get them fired today. One person familiar with both men suggested, only half joking, that the title of this book should be *The Napoleonic Wars*.

Vito Capizzo and Donald Herman had one more thing in common: they won. They made a habit of winning, and in two small, isolated, close-knit colonies, the habit was infectious. For years, the only obstacle that stood in the way of another banner season was the other island's coach. Generations of boys on both islands grew up dreaming of playing football for these two men—for better and for worse.

UP ON THE wooden observation tower behind the Nantucket bench, assistant coach Beau Almodobar followed the arc of the Vineyard's kickoff from right to left and watched it land in the arms of Nantucket senior DuVaughn Beckford. With his braided hair dangling past his shoulders, splayed across the back of his white visitors' jersey, Beckford was probably Nantucket's flashiest player. As a receiver, he'd carved out plenty of big gains, connecting often with junior quarterback Taylor Hughes, who could throw darts. On defense, Beckford had a magnet for the ball, and he unloaded some explosive hits for such a slender kid. But he also had a tendency to miss assignments. The Nantucket coaches often found themselves exasperated by his uncertain command of his talent.

On the return, Whalers blockers chucked the onrushing Vineyarders toward both sidelines, parting the space between the hash marks for Beckford. In an instant, the hole was huge. The lanky six-footer bolted to midfield before he was brought down. "See ya!" blurted Almodobar, a bit prematurely, into his headset, jumping up with his arms dangling over the tall railing. A cold wind whipped thirty feet above the playing field, but he was too keyed up to notice.

Beckford's long scamper replenished the visitors' adrenaline as quickly as Jette's touchdown had sapped it. With the ball, the team began marching downfield. On the first play from scrimmage, Hughes zipped a pass to Correia running a crossing pattern, and the big boy turned upfield and rumbled to the Vineyard's 37-yard line. A well-executed trap play designed for Hughes netted another 8 yards. After two runs for negligible yardage, it was fourth down. Senior fullback Mike Molta, a captain and the team's inspirational leader, put his head down and powered up the middle. Collared by a Vineyard tackler just after crossing the line of scrimmage, his feet flipped out from underneath him, and he landed flat on his back.

"It's gonna be tight," Almodobar blurted into the mouth-piece of his headset. "I don't think we got it."

But when the attendants jogged out with the chains, the yard marker came to rest right in the center of the ball. First down. "Wow!" cried the assistant coach.

After a Hughes pass—a carbon copy of the drive's first play—clanged off the hands of his big tight end, Beckford gained good yardage on a sweep to the right. A Hughes keeper moved the ball farther downfield. "Rip red! Fox two!" Almodobar screamed into his headset, suggesting a play for the team's no-huddle set to Bill Manchester, the offensive coordinator. Hughes took the snap and began shuttling sideways along the back of his line, looking for an opening. "North-south!" Almodobar im-plored from above the field, anticipating the open hole. Hughes covered the ball with both forearms and lunged for the goal line, where he was met by a cluster of Vineyard defenders.

*Chapter One*

# FISH OUT OF WATER

NEW ENGLAND PATRIOTS coach Bill Belichick owns property on Nantucket, out east, in the quiet, tidy little village of Siasconset—'Sconset to the locals. When the three-time Super Bowl champion jets in to the island, he keeps to himself.

He's heard of Vito, though. Belichick was asked once if he knew Vito Capizzo, the pipe-smoking, rosy-cheeked Italian who coached Nantucket's varsity football team for forty-five storybook seasons.

"Doesn't everybody?" the mastermind replied.

Nineteen sixty-four, Capizzo's first season on Nantucket, came and went without a single win. The previous coach had been a college basketball star who tolerated football only because he had no choice.

By 1966, the Whalers were good enough to go undefeated. For the next three decades, Capizzo's teams were rarely out of contention; during the coach's most fertile stretch, Nantucket went 177–34–1 over twenty seasons. Some years, Nantucket High School enrolled just a hundred boys; sometimes as many as three-quarters of them were enlisted in the football program. And in the team's spirited, sometimes vicious rivalry with Martha's Vineyard, Capizzo's teams dominated: they won 31 of 53 (including two ties) during the long reign of the "Godfather of Nantucket."

Capizzo was about as old-school as they come. He and his family moved to Massachusetts from Salemi, Sicily, when Vito was ten. They left behind a couple of bad influences in Salemi— the Mafia, Capizzo says, and the socialists. Settling in America, Vito played football and captained the hockey team for the high school in Natick, an athletics-crazed community that produced All-State quarterback, shortstop, and hockey center Walt Hriniak (a future big-league batting coach) and, later, Doug Flutie, the football magician. Despite Capizzo's average build, "he was a very good lineman," says Jim Stehlin, whose first year as an assistant to incoming Natick coach Dan Bennett was in 1958, Vito's senior year. "He was aggressive, a very coachable-type person. He listened intently, and that, I think, created an interest that he might want to go into coaching." Bennett, a standout player at Tufts University and a former Marine officer, ran a "tremendous program," says Stehlin, "very well organized, tradition-moded. The basic techniques, the fundamentals, he was such a good teacher of that. I'm sure Vito got that package from Natick."

Bennett, who died in 1973, compiled a 102–34–8 record at Natick. "Natick had such a winning tradition. I certainly profited from it," says Stehlin, who put up an impressive record himself, winning almost twice as many games as he lost in two decades as head football coach at Newburyport High School. The Capizzo boys—including younger brothers Gus, now an insurance agent, and Frank, a cardiologist—and their parents "were all hardworking people," Stehlin recalls. "They had a tremendous desire to succeed, all of them."

In 1959 Vito Capizzo went to Alabama to play football for Paul "Bear" Bryant. Maybe 175 pounds in cleats, Capizzo never made it past the practice squad. "I tried," he says. "I didn't have the size or the speed." He practiced under linebacker coach Gene Stallings, who went on to coach the NFL Cardinals and, as a successor to Bryant, an undefeated Crimson Tide team that won a national championship in 1992. Bryant, the legendary figure whose brutal training programs were designed to separate "the champions from the turds," was a living deity in Alabama. "In Alabama, an atheist is someone who doesn't believe in Bear Bryant," said a rival coach from Georgia. The eleventh of twelve children born to a poverty-stricken Church of God family in backwoods Arkansas, Bryant drew his disdain for injury and illness from his family's devout conviction against seeking medical attention. Before taking the coaching job at his alma mater, Bryant conducted notoriously grueling summer sessions for his Texas A&M team at a bleak training facility in Junction, Texas. One of the coach's pet drills over the years was known as "Kill or Be Killed." Alabama lineman Christ Vagotis recalled Bryant's pitiless methods for author Mark Kriegel: "It was commando training. In the off-season we went to 'football class.' They put on the heat until this little room was about 120 degrees. Then you had to rassle each other to get out. If you lost, you stayed. The only way to get out of that room was to win."

"Bear was a dictator, like Mussolini, really," Capizzo told *Sports Illustrated* in 1996. But Stehlin, who saw Capizzo regularly over the years at coaches' clinics and interscholastic board meetings, has heard his former player speak of his experience at Alabama many times: "College football in New England has never been near the level of the Southeastern Conference. Vito used to talk about how big the mystique of Bear Bryant was. He spoke so well of just being around such a football environment. I'm sure that's where his love of coaching was really fostered."

It was the dawn of the civil rights era in the South when Capizzo arrived. On the Alabama campus, Governor George Wallace stood in an auditorium doorway and vowed to block any integration effort. But Bryant was in favor of integration, mainly for what it would do for his program. "Those soul brothers could run like deer," says Capizzo, who delivers his Archie Bunker commentaries with a twinkle in his eye. (This is a coach who for decades ridiculed soccer as a "Communist" sport.) While taking summer classes, he roomed with a young Alabama player by the name of Joe Namath. The Alabama coaches asked Capizzo to keep an eye on the newcomer, who carried a reputation as a ca-rouser. Namath, of course, was the spectacularly gifted quarter-back who became the NFL's first swinging media superstar after parlaying his collegiate exploits into a dazzling, much-discussed pro career that was as much about his conduct off the field as on it. They didn't call him "Broadway Joe" for nothing. "As soon as you were in Joe's presence, you were young and famous," old friend Tim Secor, who owned a bar called the Tittle Tattle, told Kriegel for his book *Namath*.

Falstaff beer was 99¢ a six-pack in Alabama in the early 1960s, and Capizzo had more than a few adventures with the playboy quarterback during their summer stint as roommates. One time, Capizzo recalls, they piled into Namath's '47 Plymouth and drove to Louisiana, where the star player had a girlfriend. "Some bimbo's house," says Capizzo, flashing a mischievous smile. Years later, when he contacted his old roomie to lobby on behalf of players he wanted to send to Broadway Joe's football camp, which was based in Vermont, the two were still slinging good-natured slurs at each other. "Tell that Polack I'm only paying a hundred fifty bucks," Capizzo told an administrator, disregarding the fact that Namath's family is Hungarian.

"Tell that cheap wop to call me," Namath shot back.

Wearing a ring from Alabama's undefeated national championship season in 1961, Capizzo got a coaching job at a high school in Tuscaloosa, handling the defense and the kicking team. After five straight losses, the head coach suffered a nervous breakdown, or so Capizzo tells the story. He took over and won the last five games of the season.

By then he'd started spending summers back in Natick, where he worked as a lifeguard. The plan was to move north for good with Barbara Henderson, the shy young schoolteacher from Georgia ("she's a Rebel," as Capizzo loves to say) he'd met and married.

While searching for jobs, Capizzo got a postcard from the Department of Education with a long list of teaching and coaching vacancies in New England. When he applied for a job in Nantucket, he thought it was Nantasket, the name of a beach in Hull, Massachusetts, at the mouth of Boston Harbor. (It's one of his favorite stories.) They visited on Labor Day weekend. "The place was hopping," says Barbara, who would become an accomplished painter of landscapes and still lifes. They went to Natick to see Capizzo's parents and pick up a few things. When they returned, Nantucket was fogged in, and the place had been deserted for the off-season. "Where did everyone go?" Barbara wondered.

Don't unpack, her husband said.

But the job would quickly prove to his liking. Can you handle discipline? the superintendent of schools asked when he arrived for his interview. You're damn right I can! Capizzo replied.

Basketball, not football, was the big game on the island when he arrived. "When he started coaching here in 1964," wrote the *Boston Globe*'s Stan Grossfeld in a 2009 feature on Capizzo's retirement, "the players wore leather helmets, the plays were drawn in the sandy soil, and there were more dogs" at the field than spectators.

Dave Otto, the basketball coach, had played college ball for the Dayton Flyers, and he was good enough to earn a tryout with the Boston Celtics. Dick Glidden, the Nantucket junior varsity's point guard as a freshman during Otto's third and final year on the island, remembers Otto racking up 57 points against a team from the former Otis Air Force Base on the Cape in a pickup game. "If he'd stayed, we would have become a big basketball power," says Glidden, now an attorney. "He hated football, but he had to coach it."

As was then the custom at the high school, when Capizzo took the job as head football coach, he became the basketball coach, too. "Vito hated basketball as much as Otto hated football," recalls Glidden.

During that first football season under Capizzo, most of the seniors quit. Let 'em go, Capizzo felt. They hadn't learned much about the game under Otto, and now they were set to graduate. What use would they be to him? Instead, he concentrated on preparing the underclassmen—all seventeen or so of them—for their junior and senior years. That year the team went winless, with one scoreless tie. The Whalers won their first game under Capizzo the following season, against Apponequet Regional

High School, but lost all the others on their schedule. By then, though, Capizzo had schemed a way to toughen up his players.

The Tom Nevers Naval Facility was built on Nantucket in the mid-1950s, on land that had been used as a bombing range during World War II. After the election of John F. Kennedy, the base featured a bomb shelter built to protect Hyannis Port's most famous resident in the event of a nuclear attack. The complex stood behind imposing iron gates, which opened every Tuesday, releasing a troupe of young Navy men to the high school to scrimmage Vito's boys. Capizzo called them "ding-dong sessions." For the high schoolers, the prospect of lining up against grown men took some getting used to. "I remember Stevie Lamb would come in every week and ask, 'Is the scrimmage on?'" recalls Glidden. "If we said yes, he'd go right in the men's room and throw up."

The Navy had an enormous, ferocious-looking nose tackle, a guy who looked like he chewed the tops off beer cans, a southerner who was, according to the lore, probably six-four, 240. "Black as coal," says Glidden, "with a big black beard and, for some reason, one black glove." In one scrimmage, Glidden, by then the team's quarterback, put his hand underneath his center to take the snap, and he realized the back of his right hand was suddenly warm and wet. His center had pissed in his pants.

"I sometimes wonder why I wasn't arrested," Capizzo once told a reporter from the defunct sports daily the *National*. "But my kids learned to run the ball, out of genuine fear."

Only around twenty-five hundred people lived year-round on the island in those days, and the old whaling port had not yet become the picture-postcard destination it's known as today. Modest homes on one-acre lots sold for five or six grand. A lot of the kids were rough around the edges, and the faculty wasn't angelic, either: one assistant coach at the school ran off with a cheerleader.

NANTUCKET'S FIRST TRUE rival was not the Vineyard but Provincetown, the hard-bitten fishing community out at the northern tip of the Cape. Basketball games between the two schools in the 1950s and '60s were bruising, sometimes bloodthirsty contests. The Vineyard, meanwhile, had small high schools in each of the island's main towns—Tisbury (known today as Vineyard Haven), Oak Bluffs, and Edgartown. They didn't travel off-island for their athletic programs; they played each other. Those rivalries, at the time, were all that mattered to the kids on the larger island.

"It was intense," recalls Wayne West, a talkative tenth-generation Vineyarder (his family has been on the island since 1660) who drives a cab for Edgartown's Stagecoach Taxi. Weekends during his childhood revolved around the townie matchups at the old boxing arena in Oak Bluffs, where one of West's uncles—a future cook who was "all of five foot three"—went undefeated in his youthful career as as prizefighter.

There was a distinct history of battle-readiness on the island. In the early 1990s the high school toyed, however briefly, with the idea of changing the team name from the generic Vineyarders to the Vikings. Some island residents liked to believe that Martha's Vineyard was the mythic Vinland of the medieval Sagas of Icelanders. The ancient tales planted the notion, still debated today, that Norse explorers may have set foot on the Vineyard as early as the first millennium. For years, Vineyarders had rumored that their home was once visited by the Norse explorer Leif Ericsson, who, scholars say, may have "found" North America five centuries before Christopher Columbus. In the 1920s, one author claimed that the Norseman came ashore in the year 1001 on Noman's Land, the tiny, uninhabited island three miles south of Aquinnah, where he supposedly carved his name on a runestone. The legend has been debunked and revived several times since.

From the 1700s the Vineyard was known as one of the first deaf colonies in America. Descendants of the forested region in the south of England known as the Weald likely brought hereditary hearing loss to the island sometime after the arrival in Massachusetts of the first Puritans. The problem persisted for centuries, especially in the mid-island town of Chilmark, where the incidence rate was said to be one in twenty-five by the mid-ninteenth century. Over time, islanders developed their own sign language, which was used by most of the population, deaf or not, until the early twentieth century. The local wisdom of Martha's Vineyard Sign Language would prove critical to the development of the official American Sign Language.

Vineyard kids of the 1950s believed the rumors they heard— that the deaf-mute population was the result of inbreeding up-island. "Nobody liked to associate with the people from up-island," says West, who played football at the regional high school after the school district consolidated for the 1960–61 school year. "A lot of people thought that cousins were marrying cousins. You imitate what you hear from your parents." But if some of his friends' parents were derogatory toward the deaf-mutes, his own mother and father wouldn't tolerate it: his mother had been born and raised in Chilmark herself. "You might want to cool it," his father warned the boy when he made an unwise comment. "You're related to most of those people."

On both islands, it sometimes seems as though everyone is related—it's all Coffins and Holdgates, Araujos and Moreises and McCarthys. Tristram Coffin, who left Devon, England, in 1642, became one of the first landowners (and chief magistrate) on Nantucket by the 1660s. At one point he and his sons were said to own a quarter of the island. One of his descendants was the abolitionist and women's advocate Lucretia (Coffin) Mott. Whaling captain Seth Coffin was noted for conducting the amputation of his own leg after it was crushed in an accident at sea, and Owen Coffin was the seventeen-year-old sailor who was cannibalized after the whaleship *Essex* sank in 1820. The episode, chronicled in Nantucketer Nathaniel Philbrick's best-seller *In the Heart of the Sea*, inspired Herman Melville's classic novel *Moby-Dick*, which features an innkeeper named Peter Coffin on its first page.

And the rich Coffin lineage extended all the way to the island's high school football program. Tristram Coffin's direct descendant Dick Coffin coached the Nantucket football team throughout the 1950s. His son, Bernie, now a real estate agent, was a halfback and team captain in his father's last season as head coach.

Bernie's counterpart at halfback on the 1960 football team on the Vineyard, the first year of the island's regional high school, was Lloyd Mayhew. Just as the name Coffin connects Nantucket to its earliest days of European settlement, the Mayhews are the first family of the Vineyard. Thomas Mayhew Sr., a native of Tisbury, England, settled in Medford, Massachusetts, before purchasing the island that he named Martha's Vineyard. Mayhew paid £40 and two beaverskin hats for the offshore land that included Nantucket and the Elizabeth islands. He appointed himself governor of the new settlement, sending his son, Thomas junior, and a few dozen families to inhabit the place and begin farming and whaling ventures there. Like the Coffins, the Mayhews continue to thrive. The wife of Vineyard coach Donald Herman, the former Pam Mercer, is a Mayhew.

The late Dan McCarthy was the first football coach at the regional high school on Martha's Vineyard. His sons, Mike and Mark, played; Mike McCarthy, who was the eight-year-old water boy for the 1960 team, grew into a record-setting running back for the Vineyarders. His own sons, Ryan, Eric, and Mikey, all excelled for the team under Donald Herman, and they had several cousins who suited up as well. The high school's football facility is now called the Daniel G. McCarthy Memorial Athletic Field.

"I was too young to ever meet him," the young Mike McCarthy told the *Vineyard Gazette* in his senior year, 2008. "But to me it's an honor to go out there and play on a field with his name on it. Sometimes when I play I think of everyone [in my family] who has played for the team. And I think I play better at home because of that."

The same holds true on Nantucket, where Capizzo's team once went through a fifteen-year stretch in which they lost just five home games. Coaches from the mainland have never been particularly enthusiastic about adding either island to their schedules. Back when Nantucket counted only six thousand or so year-round inhabitants, as many as half of them could be found at the football game each weekend. Sometimes a thousand or more traveled off-island to the away games. And Capizzo enlisted the help of the entire community. Taking a cue from another legendary coach, Paul Brown, Capizzo brought tiny blue footballs to the hospital whenever he heard that another local mother had given birth to a boy. Baby girls received pompoms. (Brown, a key figure in the development of the NFL, famously made a habit of giving newborn boys little footballs in his hometown of Massillon, Ohio, when he established the great high school football tradition there in the 1930s.) "You play Nantucket and you're not just playing eleven guys on the field," Southeastern coach Joe Dawe, then a Mayflower League competitor, told *Sports Illustrated* in 1996. "You're up against mystique and tradition. You're battling a town, a community, a whole island."

FOR HALF A century the islands of Nantucket and Martha's Vineyard were locked in battle. In the early years, when the high school football schedule was sometimes just six games long, they played each other twice each season. The teams' mutual contempt has only grown in the ensuing years, and in 1978 it was finally memorialized with its own trophy.

Capizzo has always seen the Island Cup game as the product of his own brilliant football imagination. "I created a *monstah*," he'll say every time the subject comes up. But plenty on the Vineyard insist it was their idea.

"I have a cancelled check from a trophy place in Falmouth," says John Bacheller, who was the Vineyard head coach in 1978, the first time the winning team received the Island Cup.

After showcasing the trophy in its school's display case, the winning team would be expected to bring it to the next year's game. In theory, the Cup was once again up for grabs. In the reality of the early years, it would be going home with Nantucket again.

The taunting was outrageous, says Bob Tankard, a retired middle school principal who coached the Vineyarders' varsity for almost a decade. "If you could take all that trash talk and put it in one place, it'd be bigger than the New York dump."

And the coaches weren't exactly models of restraint. Capizzo was in the habit of sending his Vineyard counterparts complimentary boxes of pastries—cream puffs. From his perspective, that's what the Vineyard's schedule amounted to.

"He'd do anything to beat you," says Bacheller, who put in a total of twenty seasons on the Vineyard sideline, including a few as head coach in the late 1970s. Capizzo called the silver-haired former assistant principal the "Gray Fox," just as the Nantucketer would later call Coach Herman the "snake in the grass." One year the Vineyard players, staying in a hotel on Nantucket, were kept awake much of the night by Nantucket fans making a racket outside. Visiting teams on Nantucket were often told there was a broken sprinkler pipe on their side of the field. "You'd be standing in an inch and a half of mud," Bacheller recalled. So the Vineyard retaliated. At a Cup-week rally they threw a wooden box on the bonfire. It's a casket with Vito inside, the players were told.

Beginning in 1978, the Whalers won the Island Cup game seven years in a row, including four shutouts. Nantucket became so accustomed to taking home the trophy that in 1985 Capizzo told one of his assistants to leave it in the car. "We ain't gonna lose," he said.

But they did lose, by 10 points—the one time Tankard would beat Nantucket as head coach. Capizzo sent the Cup over to the other island the following Monday on a plane. "He didn't want to hand that trophy to me," recalls Tankard. "I said to myself, 'You punk!'"

In those days, the head coaches of the Mayflower League met on the Monday before Thanksgiving, two days after the Island Cup. (Given the travel logistics, the game is typically scheduled the weekend before most traditional rivalries.) Capizzo relished the chance to rub the Vineyard's nose in their losses. "Gee, you played us real tough," he'd say sweetly. "You're really coming along." The year his team lost to Tankard's, Capizzo skipped the meeting.

*Chapter Two*

# WHAT'S HOMECOMING?

Each time another *American Idol* dreamer warbles an uncertain rendition of "The Star-Spangled Banner," Donald Herman holds his left hand over the right side of his chest. That's where his heart is. Herman was born with situs inversus, a rare congenital condition in which the internal organs are inverted.

"I'm special," he says with a laugh.

Though he'd noticed his heartbeat on the right side early on in his childhood, Herman's mother downplayed it. She figured the family doctor would have pointed out such an anomaly. The condition was discovered when Herman, then sixteen, took his first part-time job in a restaurant, where employees were required to have an X-ray taken for tuberculosis. His father was "healthy as a damn horse," says Herman, whose drawl hasn't faded in a quarter century up north. The son never saw the old man take an aspirin; when Samuel Herman had a headache, he rubbed Ben-Gay on his forehead. But the elder Herman had been born with a heart defect, and he'd endured a bout of rheumatic fever as a child. When Donald was a junior in college—studying

anatomy, oddly enough—his father underwent emergency surgery to replace a valve in his heart with a pig's. Three years to
the day, he had a second surgery, another replacement valve. He
needed a third replacement three years after that. This time, the
surgeon used a metal valve. The family still jokes that Samuel
Herman, being Jewish, rejected the pig.

Within a month of the third procedure, Samuel was flown to
Birmingham for his fourth open-heart surgery in a decade: the
stitching on the new valve had torn loose. After this the valve
functioned properly for several years, until the end of Samuel
Herman's life.

Donald Herman grew up in Savannah, Georgia, where he
played football, winter soccer, and baseball in high school.
The family lived in the Ardsley Park section of the city, where
the boy played pickup sports constantly. There was a town park
right near his house. "The park was more or less my babysitter,"
he says. When Donald's big brother, Bobby, eight years older,
switched from public to private high school as a junior, he was
required to sit out a year of football. To occupy himself, he
coached Donald's youth football team.

Both of the Herman parents were avid sports fans. Samuel, a
Duke University graduate who had been a Savannah citywide
tennis champion in high school, owned his own bedding business. When his younger son's teams needed rides to out-of-
town games—they had no access to buses—Samuel often left his
employees in charge, hauling Donald and several teammates.
Donald's mother, Archee, an only child named after her father,
was a devoted booster of her son's teams. A little lady who loved
to stuff her children and their friends with home cooking, she

had plenty in common, her son says, with Marie Barone, the fussy mother on *Everybody Loves Raymond*. Archee loved her football. "You don't usually associate mothers with being very knowledgeable about football, but she was," says Herman. "She knew a lot about the game—exactly how, I'm not sure."

Besides the Hermans' beloved Georgia Bulldogs, there were the Atlanta Falcons—"the local shmoes," Herman recalls. After joining the NFL as an expansion franchise in 1965, it took the team six seasons to compile a winning record. Samuel Herman was a big Vince Lombardi fan; in time Donald adopted the Dallas Cowboys as his own favorite. In baseball, his favorite player was the Red Sox left fielder Carl Yastrzemski, whose signature model bat, thirty-four ounces, Herman used on the high school baseball team.

The three Herman kids—sister Barbara is the middle child—attended the Temple Mickve Israel synagogue in Monterey Square, which was featured in the book *Midnight in the Garden of Good and Evil*. When a television crew shooting a movie about the Lincoln assassination came to the square to shoot a scene, police asked neighbors to move their cars and remain in their houses all day. The crew dumped truckloads of dirt on the paved streets to simulate the 1860s, bringing in horses and wagons and hoop-skirted ladies. "It was intolerable," antiques dealer Jim Williams told author John Berendt. On behalf of his irritated neighbors, Williams hung a Nazi banner an uncle had brought back from the European front in World War II, to ruin the filmmakers' scene. Because the temple was directly across the square, the incident became an instant piece of Savannah lore.

"I remember seeing that swastika walking out of service,"

says Donald Herman. In fact, he owns a few pieces of German memorabilia himself—artifacts his father brought home after serving as an Army captain in Europe after D-Day.

An outstanding second baseman who was already showing his tendencies as a field general, Herman went to Armstrong State College (now Armstrong Atlanta University) on a partial scholarship for baseball. After playing fall ball in his sophomore year, he was forced to quit due to injury. His shoulder, which he'd first blown out as a fourteen-year-old pitcher, was a mess. He graduated from Armstrong and moved with a couple of buddies out to Wilmington Island, a Savannah suburb connected to the mainland by a long bridge.

Donald was in his second year of teaching and coaching at Jenkins High School when his sister-in-law set him up on a blind date. At a family dinner one Sunday, Bobby's wife, a schoolteacher, told Donald about a young woman who'd been hired to teach at her elementary school. Pam Mercer had come to Savannah from her native Martha's Vineyard to take a teaching job. Upon graduation she taught, coincidentally, at Mercer Middle School. After the death of her mother, she left Savannah to look for work back in Massachusetts. Unable to find a job, she accepted an offer to return to Georgia to teach elementary school.

When Bobby's wife showed Pam a photo of her brother-in-law, the native Vineyarder was underwhelmed. Donald still gets a chuckle out of telling that story. But she heard good things about the Savannah boy, and she agreed to meet him. They were introduced on the sideline during a Jenkins football game. It would be one of the last times Pam, who detests the sport, would set foot on the field. That night, Herman and his roommates threw a party, and Pam came. "Three months later I asked her to marry me," he says.

Herman already knew he wanted to join a public school system in a community where he could build his own football program from the ground up. There were fourteen high schools in Savannnah at the time, both public and private. The private schools recruited; in the public schools, the athletic talent was spread across the city. "I'd been looking to leave Savannah for quite a while," he says. He began scouring the employment ads in Massachusetts so Pam could move closer to home. He landed interviews in the towns of Millis, Stoughton, and Wayland, and at King Philip, a regional high school in Wrentham. But the schools had no openings for phys ed teachers; one found him a job at another school, an arrangement that didn't interest him.

Finally, Herman and his wife heard from a cousin of Pam's who was serving on the school committee on the Vineyard. A gym teacher was leaving, and Bob Tankard, the football coach, was stepping down. "I was actually hired for a one-year position," Herman told the *Martha's Vineyard Times* before the 2010 Nantucket game, which would close his twenty-third season on the island.

The young couple moved with their first child, eighteen-month-old Eric, to Pam's native slab in the summer of 1988. Their second son, Adam, was born within the year. The baby, Gail, followed in 1992. Herman quickly established himself as the man who could ensure the long-term health of the Vineyard's football program. After losing his first Island Cup game, his teams won three of the next four. That success infuriated Capizzo and made an already unique rivalry an object of national attention. The game would be featured in *Sports Illustrated* and

*USA Today* and on NBC Sports. After Herman's arrival, with both programs flourishing, the trophy routinely represented all the marbles: the winner took home island bragging rights, clinched the Mayflower League title, and earned a berth in the Eastern Massachusetts (EMass) divisional Super Bowl.

"It was one of those meant-to-be things," says the native Georgian, "and I wouldn't want to be anyplace else."

HERMAN WAS INDOCTRINATED into the peculiar cult of football on the islands straightaway, when he interviewed for the Vineyard coaching job. "Who do you play for homecoming?" he'd asked.

"What's homecoming?" came the reply. Every football season on the Vineyard built inexorably toward the season-ending Nantucket game, not some halfhearted alumni gathering in mid-October.

He gets it now. "There are three certainties in life," he loves to say. "Death, taxes, and the Island Cup."

The players who have suited up for the two island football teams share much more than a few old scars and memories of their glory days. Though they're programmed to despise the colors of the other guy's uniform, when they meet away from the field they realize just how much they have in common. Nantucket's Bill Manchester and Vineyarder Louis Paciello, who played against each other in the Island Cup game in the 1980s, both went on to attend Springfield College, where they became roommates and great friends.

Nantucket's Billy Santos, a cocaptain who graduated in 1977, today runs his family's rubbish-removal service. When he went off-island to attend Plymouth State, he almost quit during the first week of school. At an assembly, a school administrator asked the new students to look around. Some of them wouldn't survive until graduation, he said. Santos walked out of the assembly thinking, Damn right. I'm out of here *now*.

Just then, he heard someone calling his name: "Santos?" It was Paul Kearns, a former Vineyard cocaptain and standout basketball player who was a little older than Santos and had already spent a year in prep school. "Wanna grab a beer?" he asked the newcomer. When Santos—"Toes-man," as Vito called him— told Kearns he couldn't stand his roommate, Kearns arranged a switch so the two islanders could share a dorm room.

"He took me right under his wing," recalls Santos. Kearns left Plymouth State after his first year, but Santos stayed all four years.

Yet when the game is on, there is no love lost. The island rivalry is Army-Navy, Ohio State–Michigan, Georgia-Florida, says Donald Herman. "It is Harvard-Yale without the ivy," wrote Ron Borges, a Boston sportswriter who played center (and kicked with a square-toed shoe) for the Vineyarders in the mid-1960s. "It is USC-UCLA without the roses."

It's also something else entirely. What the game has like no other game is the isolation. It's a forty-five-minute ferry ride to the Vineyard from the little Cape Cod hamlet of Woods Hole. In the summer, when the population of the island balloons from fifteen thousand to six or seven times that many, the boats run constantly, between the piers at both Vineyard Haven and Oak Bluffs. In winter, the Oak Bluffs terminal shuts down.

For decades, taking the ferry to Nantucket was a tedious commitment—more than two hours crossing Nantucket Sound. The Vineyard sits just a few miles off the south shore of Cape

Cod, but Nantucket, the onetime whaling capital of the world,
lies much further out to sea—about twenty-five miles from
the ferry landing in the rough-edged Cape village of Hyannis,
which sprawls to encompass diners and ice cream shops, a dance
club in an old railroad roundhouse, a regional airport, and the
nearby bloat of the Cape Cod Mall, where hundreds of Nantucket boys have whiled away innumerable Friday afternoons
before game weekends. Hy-Line Cruises, once a harbor tour
company, purchased its first high-speed catamaran for one-
hour ferry travel in the mid-1990s, prompting the Steamship
Authority to add its own faster boats. For the budget-conscious
and those traveling with cars, the slow boat still runs several
times a day.

Only one daily ferry is scheduled between islands in the
summer months, and none at all in the off-season. When Nantucket's soccer, field hockey, or baseball teams commit to games
against the Vineyard, athletes and coaches must board a ferry to
Hyannis, take a meandering bus down Route 28 to Woods
Hole, then catch another ferry to the other island. The logistics
have given more than one athletic director conniptions.

Back when both islands were served out of Woods Hole, the
teams arranged for overnight accommodations for each other.
At first the players stayed with host families. Ron Borges stayed
with Dick Glidden's family. Tankard stayed with Joe Santos,
growing close with his parents. Dennis da Rosa stayed with the
Ferrantella family. Curfew on game night was at nine, but in
the fall of 1966, da Rosa's senior season at quarterback, some
of the Vineyard players went out to a party on Nantucket. The
curfew shirkers included two brawling linebackers, Joey Smith
and Bill Kingsbury.

"Man, they loved to fight," says da Rosa, sitting at his desk in the back room of da Rosa's Printing, the old-fashioned office supply shop he and his brother Tony run on Circuit Avenue. "If you looked at them the wrong way, they'd fight you—even if you were on their own team." Frustrated by a loss to Nantucket earlier in the season, the two Vineyard linebackers got into a war of words with some locals that quickly escalated into a melee. "They tore into those guys. Beat the hell out of them," recalls da Rosa, a handsome fellow with blown-dry silver hair, wearing a yellow oxford and a light utility vest. The police demanded that the two players ship out on the first available boat. Players on both sides would not stay in each other's homes from that day forward.

Tankard's mother, Audria, became smitten with the Vineyard during summer vacations when her children were young, and she eventually moved her family to the island year-round. She'd read about the beauty of Cape Cod in the *Amsterdam News*, the voice of Harlem. "Actually," says Tankard, who has a talk show on the island's community television station, "what sparked the coming was the Patti Page song—the sand dunes and the salty air and all that." His mother brought a few of his sisters—there were ten kids in the family—on a getaway to Plymouth, to see Plimoth Plantation. There they met a woman who told them about the island to the south: "If you think this is pretty," she said, "you should see Martha's Vineyard." Audria brought the girls over on the ferry, staying several nights. Back in Newark, she convinced her husband to rent a house in Oak Bluffs the following summer, 1959.

All seven of the children who were still school-age were there. The rental cost them five hundred bucks for the whole season. Two years later, the family bought a little home on Dukes County Road, across from Oak Bluffs's historic campgrounds, where Methodists had been congregating for more than a century. At first setting up for the summer in tents, the Methodists soon started building the iconic gingerbread houses that now surround the open-air Tabernacle, the huge house of worship on the commons that still hosts community gatherings today. The four youngest Tankard children finished their public school education while living in that house. Tankard and his twin sister arrived during their sophomore year, for the 1961–62 school year. Their younger sisters were headed into eighth and fifth grade, respectively.

The Vineyard was already a haven for African Americans. Oak Bluffs had been a summer resort for black families since the Great Depression, when servants and housemaids of early, well-to-do Vineyard families began buying and building homes in the town. One attraction was the fact that the island's public waterfront featured some of the only unsegregated beaches on the East Coast. Oak Bluffs has a stretch of beachfront still known as the Inkwell, where black families have swum, picnicked, and played in the sand for generations. Some residents today, having grown accustomed to the summer influx of prominent black Americans such as Spike Lee and Henry Louis Gates Jr., find the name hopelessly antiquated in its insensitivity. Others take it as a source of pride.

The Shearer Cottage, owned by Charles and Henrietta Shearer, was one home that welcomed visiting African Americans of distinction, including performers Ethel Waters and Paul Robeson and the Baptist preacher and future U.S. congressman Adam Clayton Powell Jr. He later bought his own home, known as the

Bunny Cottage, in Oak Bluffs. The Cottagers, a group of one hundred women formed in the 1950s to promote cultural pride and community service, are still a vital part of island life.

The black community on the Vineyard was largely college-educated, many working in the professions, wrote Jill Nelson in *Finding Martha's Vineyard: African Americans at Home on an Island*. "There was no need to be the exemplary Negro here, or to show white people that we were as good as or better than they were, to conduct ourselves as ambassadors for integration and racial harmony. For the months of summer the weight of being race representative—and all the political, emotional, and psychic burdens that come with demanding that an individual represent a nonexistent monolith—was lifted." The fact of the island itself, "where everyone and everything must be carried over water, either by boat or plane," was instrumental in building a racially tolerant community at a time when much of the rest of the country was failing at it, Nelson suggested. "Here, the intellectual understanding that we are all in the same boat becomes concrete and specific."

TODAY, THE YEAR-ROUND population of Martha's Vineyard is made up of three components. The largest group are "typical middle-class working people—policemen, firemen, plumbers, carpenters, nurses, school teachers," says school superintendent Dr. James Weiss. The island also has a "small but important" Portuguese-speaking community hailing primarily from Brazil, Cape Verde, and the Azores. This segment of the population is in constant flux, with friends and family members coming and going, not all of them legally. That fact, combined with the language barrier, presents an ongoing challenge to the school system.

There's also a small number of Wampanoag descendants, many of whom live on tribal grounds up-island, in Aquinnah.

"Add to that the people who come in the summer and decide to stay," says Weiss, who was entering his sixth year on the island at the beginning of the 2010 school year. In particular, there was an influx of affluent families after 9/11, when some Bostonians and New Yorkers sought the perceived safety of year-round living on an island. Although a growing number of well-to-do families now live on-island year-round, most put their children through the public school system. There is no private high school on the Vineyard; the nearest is Falmouth Academy, on the Cape. Weiss estimates that twenty or so students take the ferry each day during the school year to attend that school. Those children tend to go on to the classic New England prep schools— Deerfield Academy, Milton, Phillips Exeter, Northfield Mount Hermon.

The Vineyard has more than its share of interracial marriages. It also has a distinct back-to-the-land element, centered around the agrarian mid-island town of West Tisbury. Kate Taylor, known as "Sister Kate" to her folk-singing brothers James and Livingston—a third brother, Hugh, owns and operates an inn out by the Gay Head lighthouse—spent several summers during the 1970s raising her children in a tipi, as did several Vineyard families of the time. Strains of that kind of post-hippie lifestyle persist: "If you go up-island to West Tisbury," says Weiss, who was superintendent in a six-town region of coastal New Hampshire prior to leaving the mainland, "you sometimes wonder what year it is."

Like Nantucket, the Vineyard has a history of social issues, such as the high rates of alcohol and drug dependency, divorce, and what is now known as seasonal affective disorder documented in Milton Mazer's landmark 1976 study *People and Predicaments: Of Life and Distress on Martha's Vineyard.* "For the islander, the coming of the summer season is a time of both pleasure and pain," wrote Mazer. The vacationers confirm that his piece of land is desirable; "summer visitors think of it as another Eden," the author noted. But the crowded ferries also confirm the vastly different economic realities of the two groups. "What do you do here all winter?" the part-timers often ask, according to Mazer—"forgetting that once they leave the island, its real life, active and meaningful to its inhabitants, is taken up again."

The island's Youth Task Force has struggled to get the above-average incidence of early alcohol and drug use down to the state and national level. Weiss attributes the discrepancy to two factors—the islanders' natural sense of isolation, and the fact that for two or three months of the year the place is a summer playground. For some, the party mentality bleeds dangerously into the off-season.

Just days before double sessions began for the Vineyard football team in the summer of 2010, senior Michael Araujo was caught with beer on the beach, in the middle of the day. He picked the wrong place to catch a buzz: Coach Herman works in the summertime patroling Katama's South Beach, riding a four-wheel ATV in shorts and a T-shirt.

# AUGUST 2010

O N   T H E   W A R M, damp August afternoon when the football players straggled up to the equipment room in back of the high school to pick up their pads and uniforms, Herman held a brief meeting with his seniors in the weight room. It was a small facility in the back of an adjunct building between the school and the football field, the main tenant of which is the community television station. The program's numbers were down considerably: last year's squad had carried about seventy-five, seniors to freshmen. This year he hoped to draw fifty, though that looked perilous. Several seniors had chosen not to return. "They probably saw the writing on the wall" about their playing time, he said.

CHAMPS TRAIN, LOSERS COMPLAIN, said the actual writing on the wall in the weight room. Ten seniors filed into the weight room to listen to their coach, who was showing off his deep tan in a turquoise tank top, shorts, and flip-flops. They sprawled across weight-training benches; a few sat on the floor. Randall Jette, wearing a floppy rain hat and a sleeveless tie-dyed T-shirt, looked like he was trying to disguise his obvious status as the team's poster boy. Burly center James Bagnall, whose father,

Paul, was once a Vineyard player, wore headphones, an unruly dyed Mohawk, and a black concert T-shirt for the band Avenged Sevenfold. His Abe Lincoln beard would have to go; Herman, despite the dominating presence of his own thick black mustache, had long enforced a team rule against facial hair.

Michael Araujo's lapse in judgment would cost him, Herman told his seniors with a faint smirk. He'd violated sacred land: "Half the beach probably heard my reaction," said the coach. He handed the sheepish student a pair of scissors. "The practice field needs mowing," the coach said as the kid's teammates chuckled in disbelief. "Have fun, Mike!"

It was a good time to talk about the team's chemical health policy. Zero tolerance, the coach confirmed, as if the students weren't already aware. If they got caught, their season would be over. "I don't want to jinx you," he said, "but I've never had to do it to a senior." Playing football for the Vineyarders carried some responsibility: "People in the community know who you are, and it's not a very big community." Athletic stardom would not absolve them from paying consequences for their actions, if their actions were ill-advised. "I'll be the same prick to you that I'd be to anybody else," said the coach, who clearly relished the role.

Besides the mild pep talk about their expectations as team leaders, there were a few housekeeping items to attend to. The team's second game, against a new nonleague opponent from the South Shore's Sharon High School—a Division 2 team, a level above the Vineyard's Eastern Athletic Conference—had been moved to a Thursday evening start to accommodate the Rosh Hashanah holiday. There was an update, but no definitive answer, about whether an enormous player named Pete

Williamson—Herman called him "the Blind Side"—would return for the season. The student, who had experienced an irregular heartbeat the previous year, had been cleared by his cardiologist, but Herman was waiting to hear from his mother, whom he'd faxed while she was on vacation.

The coach was also trying to arrange a bye-week scrimmage against the Harlem Hellfighters, a club team made up of upper Manhattan students whose high schools did not field football teams of their own. Former NFL wide receiver Duke Fergerson, who played briefly for the Seattle Seahawks and the Buffalo Bills, later became a political organizer and attended Harvard Business School, despite debilitating dyslexia. Upon arriving in Harlem, the energetic Fergerson took it upon himself to remedy a situation in which boys from the thirteen high schools of Harlem had not played organized football in years. Three years after being granted permission to draw players from across the local school district, the Hellfighters played in a citywide championship game in 2007 against tradition-steeped John Adams from Ozone Park, Queens, losing 58–42. But the team has had trouble retaining its affiliations with sponsor schools in the years since, often relying on unofficial exhibition games to make up a schedule. The Vineyard was hoping to establish another tradition of sorts.

Finally, the Vineyarders would wear the number 21 on their helmets the week they played league rival Bishop Feehan. They'd be paying tribute to Larsan Korvili, a Feehan senior-to-be who'd drowned in the Atlantic Ocean over the summer while attending a religious retreat at the Craigville Conference Center in Barnstable with dozens of his classmates. Korvili had been an honor roll student from the fourth grade on, and he was a member of his school's Student Council. "That's a very sad situation," said Herman as he perched on an exercise ball, feet planted. "Somebody your own age." He looked down at the floor, and the room grew quiet for a moment.

Drowning was a sore subject for this island community. In 1999 a former Vineyard captain named Richie Madeiras drowned in a freak accident while scalloping off his boat near East Chop, one of two spits of land that bookend the Vineyard Haven harbor. Madeiras, a member of one of the oldest and most extensive Portuguese families on the island, died the same way he made his living: he was the longtime shellfish constable in Oak Bluffs.

Madeiras had been a captain for Jerry Gerolamo, the Vineyard coach from 1969 until 1977. He was a tough kid, a running back who also logged some time at quarterback, recalls Gerolamo. "All heart. Kind of like a Wes Welker sort." During his playing days Madeiras suffered a freak accident. It was an away game at Blue Hills Regional Technical School in Canton, at the foot of Great Blue Hill (the lookout point the natives called Massachusett), about fifteen miles outside of Boston. While making a tackle in the end zone Madeiras ended up on his back, and he was stepped on with the full force of the other player's weight. The impact crushed the Vineyarder's solar plexus, rupturing his liver. "By the time we got to the end zone from the bench, he was yellow," says Gerolamo. Rushed to the hospital, he eventually made a full recovery. He even played football the next season.

After Madeiras's death, the Vineyarders dedicated their next home game to the former player. His young sons served as honorary captains. Coincidentally, the game was against Blue Hills, the

same team against which Madeiras had been injured in high
school. The Vineyard routed Blue Hills that day, winning by a
margin that matched Madeiras's jersey number: 35–0.

WHEN THE MEETING broke up, most of the players headed for
their cars. Bagnall, the center with the Mohawk, grabbed his
saxophone case and walked across the dark parking lot to the
bench by the bus stop.

Coach wasn't a real easy guy to get to know, Bagnall admitted. "I just smile and do what he says," he said quietly.

James's older brother, named after their father—who was now
the island's shellfish constable—had been frustrated by his lack of
playing time for the team. Unlike some coaches, Herman isn't
always quick to give his bench players and JVs much playing time
when the Vineyard takes a sizable lead.

"Coach wants to score so many touchdowns," said the soft-
spoken young man.

# Chapter Three

## NEW ERA

JOHN ALOISI SAT at his desk in his basement classroom. After joining the school system as a roving substitute, he'd secured a permanent position for his second year back on Nantucket teaching social studies. The ground-level windows were streaked with the light rain that was falling outside. The students would not be back in class for another week; the young coach was preparing for his first day of practice for the new season.

Choosing wisely for his coaching staff was a priority, he said. "My major goal was to get six quality people, knowledge aside. Your reactions are what the kids see." With one year under the coaches' collective belt together—a year in which they'd surprised almost everyone who noticed by eking out a winning record—Aloisi was feeling good about the hires he'd made.

Whether he had the horses was another story. As Charles McGrath noted in his *New Yorker* article about the rivalry in 1984, old Nantucket was once known for producing larger-than-life figures, such as the six-foot-six-inch Revolution-era Navy man Reuben Chase, who, as local lore has it, unfolded his body like a carpenter's rule when he stood up. But besides Terrel and Mack McGrath, a senior lineman who took after his father—a mountain of a man with a wiffle haircut straight out of the basic training handbook—the 2010 edition of the Nantucket Whalers had almost no size to speak of.

"I remember the 1996 team had full-grown men," said Sean Dew, fetching a bottle of locally brewed beer (Whale's Tail Pale Ale) for a customer from behind the bar at Easy Street, a casual lunch-and-dinner joint within stumbling distance of the Steamship Authority ferry building. Dew, a good-sized kid in his mid-twenties, had somehow managed to elude Coach Capizzo's long arm during his high school years, when he played soccer and golf. During football games, he was known to roam the grounds around the field in a yellow rain slicker, carrying a harpoon—a self-appointed team mascot. "The size of Nantucketers has been shrinking, it seems like," he said.

Taylor Hughes, the quarterback, was a chiseled six-footer who took pride in his weight and endurance training. His father was Jimmy Hughes, one of the hardest-hitting defenders ever to play for Coach Capizzo. "As a family, we strive to do our best all the time," says Taylor's father, "and sports is one thing we're very good at."

On the day the team came to the field house to pick up their equipment, Taylor stayed on the field in a sleeveless T-shirt for the better part of an hour, setting his feet, bringing the football up to his ear with a precise swivel of his hips, and firing crisp 30-yard passes to any teammate who could be bothered to jog downfield. It wasn't hard to see that Taylor had been a very good pitcher in baseball for years already; with the football, he could repeat his delivery identically, every time.

"You're still throwing?" hollered Bill Manchester, the offensive coordinator, shaking his head. "It's like a disease with you!"

Running back Mike Molta, a team captain with a muss of hair, a Roman nose, and a confident smile, was another kid in great shape. But most of the team was average-sized, at best. Cocaptain Kevin McLean, a receiver and defensive back who was born in Jamaica, barely came up to the letters on Terrel's jersey. Senior Tim Marsh, maybe 175 on a good day, was going to play nose tackle, a position typically reserved for the kid who could put away two or three meatball subs before dinner. Alex Rezendes, a compact, conscientious junior who would be playing linebacker and offensive line, wasn't more than five foot eight. There was a bit of promising size on the JV; freshman Trekwan Wilson, for one, looked as though he'd be tough to move. But he also looked like an ongoing project for the coaches, moping a little when told he was needed on the line. He'd envisioned himself plowing into the end zone as a ball carrier.

Not all of the boys were going to be thrilled with the roles they were given, but it was imperative that they understood the team concept. Each player would have a responsibility, and if each one carried it out to the best of his ability, they might have a season to look forward to.

"If the last kid on the roster enjoys himself, then we've made progress," said Aloisi, sitting at his desk, where a little Hulk Hogan figurine was the only indication that it belonged to a new teacher preparing for the school year. "We focus on the intangible things," said the young coach. "I don't know what our record will be, but the intangible things are there."

For Aloisi and his staff, the 2009 season ended with a consolation prize. The Whalers closed out their year against league rival Cape Tech, the vocational school to which they'd already lost earlier in the season. Down 12–0 at halftime, Nantucket rallied to score two touchdowns in the third quarter. Hughes, who'd become the starting quarterback as a sophomore when senior Jamie Viera went down with a knee injury, connected with receivers for both scores. He completed one to Terrel Correia, then just a freshman, and the other to Viera, who was back on the field. Both extra-point kicks were good, and the team held on for a 14–12 win.

The victory sealed a winning season for Aloisi in his first year on the job. Mere months after the futility of the football program had sparked some debate about whether it should continue at all, Nantucket finished at 6–5. It was the team's first winning season in four years—a huge moral victory for the coaches, and the island. "In terms of perseverance we have come a long way this year, handling adversity and moving forward, and getting mentally tough," Aloisi told the local paper, the *Inquirer and Mirror*, known to all on the island as the *Inky*. "We have a lot of work to do, but I would like to think we are heading in the right direction."

As the 2010 season got under way, the coaches let themselves raise their expectations just a notch. They would have their hands full with West Bridgewater, a perennially solid program coached by twenty-five-year veteran Bill Panos. But the Mayflower Small, the Division 4A league Nantucket had recently joined, was not otherwise stacked with talent. Tri-County, the regional high school that won the league title in 2009, had lost several key players to graduation, and Holbrook and Old Colony weren't scaring anyone.

Opening day featured a fortuitous rematch with Cape Tech on

the team's home field in Harwich. Nantucket was hoping to make a statement with a win and the players were feeling confident, having ended the previous season on a high note. Cape Tech would be playing without the benefit of its sixteen-year partnership with Harwich High, which had been dissolved by the Massachusetts Interscholastic Athletic Association for the new season. But the young team from the island beat itself with penalties, tentative coverage, and an offense that couldn't get untracked. The defense had no answer for a blocky sophomore running back named Malik Lee, who ran for nearly as many yards as he carried pounds, and Nantucket absorbed a disappointing loss, 8–6.

Fortunately, the schedule was kind. For its first home game, Nantucket played Old Colony, a team that had gone winless the previous year. After Correia returned an opening kickoff to midfield, the Whalers' offense marched downfield with little trouble, keeping the ball on the ground. A draw play to Mike Molta put the team in the end zone for the first time that day. Just a minute and twenty-seven seconds had ticked off the clock.

It quickly became a rout. DuVaughn Beckford caught a screen pass and took the ball 40 yards for another score. Then he grabbed an interception, and Hughes crossed the plane on a QB sneak. After Old Colony fumbled on a bad snap, Molta caught a short pass for yet another touchdown. On the sidelines, holding their helmets by the face masks, Mack McGrath, Chris Bell, and a few other team leaders wore American flag bandannas on their heads and big grins on their faces. It was 34–0 midway through the second quarter, 41–8 at the half.

"Too many good things to mention," Aloisi told his team,

without smiling, at the break. "Our values are not circumstan-
tial. Whether we're down or up forty-eight to nothing, it doesn't
matter. We still play our tails off."

"Yes, sir," murmured a few of the boys.

Manchester, the assistant, pointed out that Old Colony was
playing a five-two on defense—five men on the line, two linebackers, four defensive backs. Nantucket hadn't anticipated that
at all and hadn't prepared for it. Not that it mattered. "Great
job," said the coach.

Moments after the teams took the field for the second half,
Hughes returned an interception to Old Colony's 15-yard line,
and Molta scored on the Whalers' first play from scrimmage. It
was time to empty the bench, get some playing time for the
younger guys. On fourth and 8, Trekwan Wilson, playing on
the defensive line, met the visitors' running back at the line of
scrimmage and slammed him to the ground.

Fellow freshman Bryan Depass, taking snaps at quarterback,
added to the total with an unimpeded 75-yard end run. The final
score was 55–14. Hughes, the classically athletic starting quarterback, accounted for five of the touchdowns—running for two,
throwing for two more, and returning a fumble for the fifth.
"Do not rest on this," Vaughan Machado, the special teams
coach, told the huddle on the field after the clock ran out. "West
Bridgewater is a good team, and they're coming."

Aloisi told his team that their third game would be a playoff-
level game. "I'm getting chills thinking about it," said the typically reserved coach. "It's exciting."

After the players gathered all the equipment and trudged off
to the locker room, assistant Tim Psaradelis took his young son

out onto the field, under the lights. His wife, more than seven months pregnant with another baby, watched as Psaradelis knelt down with a ball and set up a kickoff for his son. Gus wandered back at least 20 yards, then turned and began to toddle his way toward his father and the ball.

"Longest kickoff ever," Psaradelis joked, rolling his eyes, as he waited for his son to get close enough to boot the football.

It was a new era of sorts for the Vineyard, too. The year 2010 would be the team's second season in the Eastern Athletic Conference, which was in Division 3, a step up from the Mayflower Large. Between 1990 and 2003, the Mayflower champion was either Nantucket or the Vineyard, every year. Now Donald Herman was facing the prospect of finishing somewhere in the middle of the pack, even if he put a quality football team on the field.

Like Nantucket, the Vineyard would open against the same team it had ended the 2009 season against. For the Vineyard, this meant Brighton, a program of city kids from the annexed corner of Boston once known as "Little Cambridge," across the Charles River (and a world away) from Harvard Square. The Vineyarders had beaten the stout boys from the city handily, 41–8, to round out the 2009 season, and they jogged onto the field at White Stadium in Franklin Park—the site of two consecutive team Super Bowl triumphs in the early 1990s—fully expecting to cruise to another win.

Early on, it certainly looked like that would be the case. On the first play from scrimmage, Randall Jette turned the corner. After gaining first-down yardage, he was shoved out of bounds onto the asphalt track that ringed the field. He rolled on his shoulder and sprang to his cleats in one motion, clacking as he jogged back to the huddle. Brian Montambault took a handoff, hit a wall at the line—Brighton had several well-fed young men anchoring their defense—and kept his legs churning. By the time the whistle blew, what looked like no gain ended up with the ball 20 yards downfield. When Tyler Araujo rumbled for another big gain, the announcer butchered his surname, calling him "Ara-hoo." (The family name is pronounced "A-roo-zho.") Montambault converted on fourth down at the 5, and a few moments later Jette scored from the 1. With most of his teammates lined up to the right of the ball, Tyler's cousin, the big tight end named Delmont Araujo, caught an easy toss to the left side of the end zone for the two-point conversion. It was 8–0, Vineyard.

Few Vineyard families had made the long trip into Boston, and Brighton was playing far enough from its own home turf. The big concrete stadium, capable of seating ten thousand, was eerily quiet, save for the occasional sounds of grunting and the collisions of hard plastic shoulder pads. Vineyard assistant Bill Belcher sat in the stands, looking for mismatches and resting his bum knees. He hollered to fellow assistant Jason O'Donnell, who was on the sideline. "You don't need your headset," he joked. "I can hear you from here."

On Brighton's first play from scrimmage, Jette intercepted. The Vineyard offense had trouble advancing the ball, but Brighton fumbled a punt and the islanders recovered. When Brighton got the ball back, Montambault stepped up from his linebacker position and drilled their running back. In the stands, the smattering of Vineyard parents let out appreciative gasps. "He'll definitely think twice about that next time," said Tom Smith, an

Edgartown cop whose son, Conor, a junior, was another Vine-yard defensive leader.

"T, O, U-G-H, get tough," chanted the Vineyarders' sparse cheerleading squad. "Vineyard, get tough!" But the team couldn't get near the end zone. The two sides ran out the first half trad-ing broken plays, futile scrambles, and punts. "I'm sure Donald will have a few things to say to the team at halftime," said Ken Goldberg, the Vineyard's longtime play-by-play announcer, from his makeshift perch halfway up the stands.

When the clock ran out on the half, the beefy Bengals, clad in black and orange, disappeared down a ramp on the opposite side of the field, headed for the locker room beneath the stands. The Vineyarders, meanwhile, gathered on the field, kneeling or sitting on their helmets. As the sweating players handed around a bag of orange slices, Herman addressed his team. "There's no way in hell this should be an eight-nothing ball game right now," he fumed. Brighton's quarterback had no idea how to read de-fenses, he pointed out: "He's shittin' and gittin'. Let's see if you guys can think on your feet."

As the second half began, seventy degrees was beginning to feel like ninety to the players. Brighton fumbled on a fourth-down conversion try. On an end run, Jette was forced out of bounds, then popped well beyond the line. With Vineyard coaches and parents groaning and shouting about the late hit, a referee belatedly tossed his yellow penalty flag to the ground. "All right! Thank you," one Vineyard father called out sarcastically. A Brighton player went down in a heap amid the substitutes on the Vineyard sideline. Herman quickly determined the kid was cramping, and he grabbed the player's cleat and put pressure on the leg. Play was stopped a few minutes later so Montambault could get some medical attention of his own. "Oh, no, that's his knee," said David Montambault, the captain's father, sitting in the stands with his wife, Debbie. His wife caught her breath. But it was just another cramp, and both parents let out sighs of relief.

Carrying little depth on his roster, Brighton coach James Philip was forced to use his five starting linemen all day long, on both sides of the ball, and they were utterly exhausted by the fourth quarter. Jette, who spent much of the day zigging and zagging behind the line of scrimmage, still managed to gain 138 yards on the ground. But he was also sacked five times, and the final score was the same it had been at halftime: 8–0.

"We looked like a champion offense that first drive," Herman lamented after the game to a correspondent from the *Boston Globe*. Still, hey—a win is a win. "It is huge to get that first W," the coach said. "Now we know what a taste of victory feels like." For some of his younger players, it may have been a new sensation. But the coach was plenty familiar with the taste of victory. He was closing in on two hundred wins as a high school head coach.

This year, he was fortunate to have Jette on the roster, and he knew it. There were other Vineyard kids who could play: Montambault, for one, was taking a look at Fitchburg State and a few other schools that had expressed some interest in him. But the Vineyard had little exceptional talent outside of Randall, and the team's depth chart was a potentially serious issue. The only kid with overwhelming size was Max Moreis, and he was injured. Herman and his assistants were hoping to make a lineman out of sophomore Adaaro Blackhawk, a six-footer who had trimmed down considerably from the 270 pounds of his freshman year. Blackhawk was a mischievous kid with an unruly mat of longish black ringlets and an eye for the cheerleaders. Herman would spend an inordinate amount of time over the course of the season trying to get the boy to remember his assignments.

THERE ARE PLENTY of stories of hardship, transgression, and tragedy on both islands. Few, however, can rival the heartbreaking youth of sixteen-year-old Adaaro Blackhawk. The boy, along with his little brother, Xavier, was new to the school system. They'd been home-schooled by their grandmother after their mother died.

Julia Blackhawk was born to a German father; her mother was a member of the Winnebago tribe of Nebraska. The father was abusive to Julia, and the man who would father her kids turned out to be suffering from schizophrenia. Though Julia had a German surname, she chose the tribal name Blackhawk for her and her young sons. She gave the boys traditional Winnebago names that translated as "Thunder" and "Walking Thunder." They bounced from city to city, often living without a home, while Julia looked for work.

Always interested in her appearance, no matter how bad her circumstances became, Julia eventually earned a grant from the Winnebago tribe to study at the Aveda Institute, a beauty school in Minnesota. While she was enrolled in the year-long course she sent the boys to live with their paternal grandmother, Valerie Redanz, on Cape Cod. Julia called every day and sent presents, once shipping the boys iPods. She and Adaaro dreamed of traveling together to Tokyo—he'd always wanted to see the skyscrapers there.

One day in the summer of 2007, Adaaro realized he hadn't

heard from his mother in a few days. He'd heard something about a bridge collapse on the Mississippi River in Minneapolis, and he told his grandmother that he felt sure his mother had died in the accident.

His instincts were right. Julia was one of the thirteen casualties of the bridge failure. The firefighter who recovered Julia's body told her mother that when he'd arrived there was a bird standing over her body with its wings outstretched. A nearby light fixture should have fallen directly onto Julia's head, but it had not. The look on Julia's face was peaceful, the firefighter told her mother. When he'd arrived, the bird flew off, as if to pass along its guard duty.

That week Redanz and her grandsons had been compiling a slide show of beach pictures to send to Julia. Instead, she took the boys to the beach, where they staged their own primal scream ceremony. Their grandmother had no answers for the distraught boys. "There are people who have worse mothers," Adaaro told her. "Why would God take my mother when she was good to me?"

Redanz and her husband, Jesper, took in her grandsons and moved to Vineyard Haven, where school administrators said they would welcome the opportunity to help raise the boys. A chunky kid, Adaaro expressed some interest in joining the football team. In his first year at the high school he'd become something of a pet project for the coaching staff. He'd actually trimmed down some, losing forty pounds after attending a weight-reduction camp, and he'd begun dabbling with vegetarianism. He still had a long way to go, said his grandmother, both physically and emotionally.

"But when he's playing football, he does everything well,"

she said. "Maybe it's like sending a young man off to the military. The coach has given him a way of thinking, a way of getting things done, that makes him proud."

RANDALL JETTE WAS another kind of player altogether. He liked being a leader, took a little pride in his schoolwork, and tried hard not to make too much of his celebrity status on the island. He could bust a game wide open not only with his spectacular running skills but also with his outstanding playmaking ability on defense. In fact, an assistant coach from Boston College's Division I program was planning to make a midweek trip over to the Vineyard to take a close look at Jette. Given his lithe frame and his exceptional speed and quickness, the kid would likely become a full-time cornerback if he were to play at that level. Whether to attend an elite football school such as BC, where he might not be guaranteed playing time, or potentially star for a Division II or III school was proving to be a dilemma. For Jette, who had a gentle nature and a magnetic smile, football wasn't necessarily the whole future. He was actually looking forward to landing some kind of desk job, preferably with a Nerf hoop within reach.

"Depending on who you ask, Randall may not be the best athlete in his family," said the quarterback's stepfather, Albie Robinson, a former Vineyard star himself, one night during the season. Randall's older sister, Kristen, was away at college. His younger sister, Kendall, was playing on the Vineyard's JV field hockey team. The girls bickered with their brother, but they adored him, too. "His sisters are like his agents," said Grace, their mother.

Grace Jette had been a star athlete herself in high school,

playing soccer and basketball and competing on the track team. "I was such a boy. You wouldn't catch me running now," she said, sitting with her family around the kitchen table, which was covered in a tablecloth patterned with autumn corn. She and Albie had just returned from the high school, where they'd helped the Booster Club serve the team's customary Friday night dinner. After the meal—pasta and salad—most of the team moved into the library, where they watched an old copy of *Varsity Blues*. A few players stayed in the cafeteria, where they played board games with Bill Belcher and Phil Hughes, the JV coach.

Randall's biological father was James Campbell, the middle son of a Jamaican-born single mother who'd moved her sons to the Vineyard from Richmond, Virginia. Vamp, as James was known, was a little rough around the edges. Both he and his older brother, Jermaine, came out for the football team one year, but they didn't last more than a few weeks. At that age, discipline was not their thing.

Grace's brother, on the other hand, was a standout running back for Bob Tankard's teams in the mid-1980s. Albie, Grace's husband, was a split end and defensive back on Coach Herman's first successful teams in the early nineties. A favorite target of quarterback Jason Dyer, Robinson still holds team records for most receiving yards in a season and in a career. (Dyer served as Albie's best man in his wedding.) When he and Grace started dating, he made her sit down and watch the videocassette of his team's highlight film. Little Randall later erased the closing minutes of the Vineyard's thrilling come-from-behind Island Cup win in 1992—Albie caught the winning touchdown pass—when he accidentally hit record while watching an episode of *SpongeBob SquarePants*.

"My bad," he said with a sheepish grin, after listening to his stepdad tell the story for the umpteenth time.

Now running his own business, the calm, quiet Robinson still gets worked up when he's talking about football—specifically, the discipline and collaborative skills he believes the game gives its players like no other organized sport. It's like violent chess, he likes to say. He still has plenty of nagging injuries from his playing days—fingers, knees, ankles. Mothers of Randall's teammates often ask him whether he'd do it again if he knew the damage the game would inflict on his body. Every time, he answers: Of course.

As a boy, Randall was not exactly star-quality football material. "I used to suck!" he blurted out cheerfully. For one thing, he was small. "In sixth grade, you could see his ribs," recalled Grace. And he wasn't a big fan of diving on the grass and getting dirty. "I hated the bugs on the ground," said Randall, wearing a purple T-shirt from the trendy Boston designer known as Johnny Cupcakes, with an image swiped from the iconic *Jaws* poster. When the Vineyard's Pop Warner league disbanded, Albie helped start a flag football program so that Randall, still in middle school, could continue to sharpen his game.

Now that his senior year was under way, Jette and his parents were beginning to hear from plenty of recruiters. Bryant University, in Smithfield, Rhode Island, had already come in with a scholarship offer, and the family was hearing from the Universities of Massachusetts, New Hampshire, Maine, and others. Grace and Randall had just been invited down to Rutgers, where he'd taken part in a showcase workout and watched the Rutgers varsity play. At a reception, he stood alongside Devin McCourty, the Rutgers graduate who was on his way to a Pro

Bowl selection in his rookie season as a defensive back with the Patriots. Randall's overriding memory of the trip was that his butt was freezing during the game. Grace couldn't forget the size of the other players who were invited to the workout. One, who wore number 10, was probably six foot seven, with triceps so pronounced that "his arms wouldn't go flat against his sides," recalled Grace.

On the second play from scrimmage in the Vineyard's second game of the season, at Sharon High School, Randall intercepted a pass. The Sharon Eagles play in the ten-team Hockomock League in Division 2, a full tier above the Vineyard's Division 3 league. Though the Eagles would finish the season near the basement of their league, Herman expected a good test for his players.

The Vineyarders led by two touchdowns at the end of the first half, but they would not run away with the game. Several plays after converting a crucial fourth down by lugging four Sharon defenders on his back, Tyler Araujo had gone down with an ankle sprain. He knew right away it was bad enough to keep him out of action for at least a few games. Helped off the field, he sat alone on the bench behind his teammates, cursing. After Jette scored, the quarterback slapped a few hands and headed straight for the bench, where he threw an arm around his dejected teammate.

Following the half Montambault put the Vineyard up 21–0 with an 11-yard run. But Sharon scored on a 78-yard return on the ensuing kickoff, and suddenly the home team was energized. The Eagles scored the next two touchdowns, both on runs by senior halfback Jordan Aronson, who was returning to a leadership role after a broken collarbone had curtailed his previous season. When Aronson followed his second score with a two-point conversion, Sharon improbably took the lead, 22–21.

Just four plays later, Jette streaked into the end zone from the 22 for his third touchdown of the day, and the Vineyard reclaimed the lead, 27–22. The quarterback tacked on 2 more points with a short pass to Michael Araujo. "That was almost too quick," muttered Albie, watching from the sideline. Sharon, now down 7, had plenty of time to mount a scoring drive, and they promptly marched the ball deep into Vineyard territory. But skinny senior Ken Handy stripped a Sharon running back of the ball at the 11-yard line with less than a minute to go.

The Vineyarders ran three plays, burning Sharon's time-outs, but were unable to gain the first down that would have let them kill the clock. They were soon staring at a fourth and 4 inside their own 20. While Sharon's fans pleaded for a defensive stop, Herman talked to Jette during a time-out. If they couldn't convert the first down, Sharon would have the ball and one last golden opportunity to score. With no time to spare, assistant coach David Araujo sprinted to Herman's side and made a recommendation. When play resumed, Jette scrambled behind the line of scrimmage, allowing the Sharon defenders to chase him into his own end zone, where he was downed for a safety as the clock ran out.

After such a nerve-racking finish, the team and coaches were relieved to escape with the win. "We can thank Coach Dave for calling that safety play," Herman told his players. "That was a great call." Sharon had twenty-two returning varsity lettermen from the previous year's team, he pointed out. "You did beat a quality team today," said the coach. He took a moment to give his team an update on Tyler Araujo's ankle sprain—"It's not like he's fast anyway"—and another to complain about the officiating. The Vineyard had been robbed of an early score, the coach believed, when a referee called back a Sharon fumble that was returned for a touchdown. The whistle had not been blown before the Vineyarder emerged with the ball, said Herman. The final score, he said, "was justice."

Most important, the team had faced down its opponent's ferocious comeback attempt. "Every time they scored, we answered," Herman said, pacing amid the cluster of kneeling players. "That's the sign of a good team. We grew up a bit today. We've still got some babes out there."

WEST BRIDGEWATER COACH Bill Panos sat in the last row of aluminum seats on deck, aboard the Steamship Authority's high-speed catamaran. On his team's sole trip to Nantucket for the 2010 season, the day was growing seasonably chilly. The deliberate, white-haired coach sat rigid in his customary maroon sweatsuit, oblivious to the stiff, spitting sea breeze.

He'd always hated coming to Nantucket. And the Vineyard was no better. In more than two decades of coaching, his teams had probably played each island fifteen times. He could appreciate everything that Vito and Herman brought to their respective islands. That didn't mean he had to like them. In fact, one year in the late 1980s, he'd lobbied to get Nantucket tossed from the Mayflower League after his team and its supporters took a hailstorm of abuse following an on-island game.

This year he was hoping to exact some revenge. In Aloisi's first year at the helm, Nantucket's midseason win over West Bridgewater had cost the mainlanders the 2009 Mayflower Small championship. The Whalers had actually won in a breeze, 26–6, after scoring three times in the third quarter on runs by Mike

Molta and graduating senior Jamie Viera and an interception return by DuVaughn Beckford.

Back when the only ferry option to Nantucket was the two-hour-and-fifteen-minute slow boat, teams typically traveled there late Friday for a Saturday game. They stayed wherever they could make arrangements, often sleeping two boys per bed. At one point, the West Bridgewater team was sleeping on the floor of the high school gym, on mats. Panos and his coaches were used to the island's trademark sleep-deprivation hazing, with Nantucketers surrounding their hotel, blasting air horns. Eventually he began scheduling travel so the team could arrive on the morning of the game and make the return trip the next day.

"I got kids, sometimes it's their first time on a boat," said the coach. "Some of them, all they want to do is go sightseeing. The cheerleaders and their families are all on the boat. It all amounts to a huge distraction."

Though he is not given to demonstration, Panos rolled his eyes when asked about Vito. He's seen his team's name up on a cross by the graveyard. He's stood on the field at game time, wondering why the home team hasn't appeared. Without telling the visitors, they've changed the start time to quarter past the hour. He's seen Vito run his eleventh man onto the field after the ball has been snapped. And on the rare occasion when his team has won on the island, he's seen all kinds of projectiles—rocks, eggs—coming toward the West Bridgewater bus as it pulls out of the parking lot. Lots of guys mooning the cheerleaders, too.

"Some of the kids just want to go home," Panos said. "I used to tell them, 'Maybe we lost, but we're lucky—we get to get off this damn island.'"

The pressure to win was much the same on the other island. Panos recalled getting beaten on the Vineyard, 53–0: "They should be embarrassed," he said. "They always conveniently didn't have any JV players available."

THE WEATHERMEN HAD predicted an eighty-degree day for the West Bridgewater game, but the fog and mist remained at game time. The visitors came out rumbling. A few plays after Taylor Hughes made a hard tackle at the 1-yard line, saving a touchdown, West Bridgewater got into the end zone anyway, only to have the score called back on a holding call. Nantucket cocaptain Kevin McLean, the defensive back from Jamaica, broke up a fourth-down pass attempt, and the home team took over on downs.

Nantucket worked its way to midfield, where Hughes never saw a defender coming as he tried to throw across the middle. Interception.

"Right in his hands! Sheesh," groaned Jeannie Dooley from the stands. The wife of Jack Dooley, an Island football standout back in the 1940s, she was sitting with her sisters, Jane Hardy and Joan Fisher. The Jaeckle sisters, as they were known growing up, still go to every Whaler home game together. Today they wore their matching blue windbreakers. They became devoted football fans through their father, Matt, a die-hard New York Giants fan, as were many New Englanders before the Patriots' inaugural 1960 season in the old American Football League. Though they loved their father, the Jaeckle sisters are now sickened by the mere mention of the Giants, who beat their beloved, previously undefeated Patriots in the Super Bowl to end the 2007 season.

The sisters, now in their seventies, have been attending Patriots home games for half a century, since the team was formed. They still have season tickets to Gillette Stadium, where they were named co-recipients of the team's Fan of the Year award in 2005. They have become such an attraction that they were recently asked to appear in a television commercial for the NFL. Their portion was filmed on the ferry.

As she watched the West Bridgewater game, Jeannie Dooley complained that her granddaughter had planned her wedding for the following Sunday, without first consulting her grandmother. Now she had to sell her Patriots tickets. Jeannie, who was contending with the side effects of Lyme disease, habitually shielded the side of her face where the muscles had palsied.

On the field, Nantucket junior Andrew Benson nearly made a fine catch, but he was drilled in midair. As he went down, the ball popped up and was intercepted.

"He better be OK," said Jane, looking worried. "He's tough."

Panos's no-nonsense offense eventually ground down the Nantucket defense. D. J. Jamieson, a senior, ran for over 100 yards and scored all three of the visitors' touchdowns. The final score was 20–7. Addressing their players on the field after the game, the losing coaches took different approaches. Aloisi was disappointed. "That was Physical Football 101," he said, peeved. "They stuck it right up our tails. We need to be the more physical team, and I don't think there should be much disagreement that was the difference tonight."

Bill Manchester, the assistant, tried tempering Aloisi's assessment with some positive reinforcement. "That was a great high school football game," he said, wondering aloud whether the team had gotten tired or simply lost faith as the clock wore down.

Machado, the designated old-schooler among a staff young enough to be his sons, remarked that the team had turned into "pixie dust" during the game.

"Are we gonna go halfway," he wanted to know, "or are we gonna man up?"

As the players began wandering toward the locker room, Aloisi remained on the field under the lights, submitting to a brief on-camera interview with Ian Dooley—Jeannie Dooley's grandson. He was a former Nantucket soccer player who was hoping to break into big-time TV sports reporting. Were there any positives to take away from tonight's game? he asked the coach.

Aloisi set his jaw and let a long pause hang in the night air before he answered. "Yeah," he finally said, fixing his gaze on the middle distance. "I'm sure there are some positives."

*Chapter Four*

# TOO PROUD TO GO
# OUT OF BOUNDS

FOR NANTUCKETERS, WHO have resisted the encroach-
ment of the outside world for dozens of generations, Starbucks may never mean the green-branded coffee franchise with
free Wi-Fi. On the island, the Starbucks will always be the real-
life whaling family that inspired the first mate of the same name
in a certain great American novel.

Nantucket's heroic whaling industry once made the island
the envy of adventurers and capitalists across the globe. The resident of this tiny island, as Melville wrote in *Moby-Dick*, could
lay claim to two-thirds of the planet Earth: "For the sea is his; he
owns it, as Emperors own empires." But by the time Melville's
wordy tale of the great white whale was published, in 1851, Nantucket's improbable stature was already eroding.

Whale oil, once the dominant source of lamp fuel and candle
wax, was being superseded by the more cost-effective alterna-
tives of kerosene and petroleum. As if fanned by the onrushing
economic collapse, the fast-spreading Great Fire of 1846 devas-
tated the wharf district of the town of Nantucket. More than
three hundred buildings, covering at least thirty acres, were lost.
On top of that, the California Gold Rush of 1849 proved a

powerful attraction to locals who were losing their livelihood on the ocean. Fourteen ships bound for San Francisco, carrying hundreds of able-bodied men, sailed from the tiny island of Nantucket in the year 1849 alone, according to William Francis Macy in *The Story of Old Nantucket*. Many more of the old-time whalers who hoped to stay in the business departed for New Bedford, where deeper port waters and overland connections to the marketplace conspired to lure away what was left of the whaling industry. And from the dwindling pool of Nantucket men, the American Civil War drew several hundred more of them into service with the Northern army and the United States Navy, earning the island the distinction as "the banner town of the Commonwealth" in terms of per capita military enlistment.

The *Oak*, the last whaling ship to leave Nantucket, set sail in 1869. According to the historian Macy, the population of the island—just under nine thousand in 1850—dropped precipitously, by a thousand or so every five years for the next two decades. Houses now sold for a fraction of their former value. Many owners took to dismantling their homes and shipping them across the sound to Cape Cod to be rebuilt on the mainland. Young men with no prospects for employment began leaving the island for the shoe factories of Brockton and similar production jobs in farther-flung cities. "It was a bad state of affairs all round," Macy wrote, "and if it had not happened that just about that time the American people began to acquire the vacation habit, the probabilities are that our old town would soon have been almost entirely depopulated."

When summer visitors began arriving on the temperate island near the end of the nineteenth century, they were "gayer and more noisy" than the stoic townsfolk, Macy recalled. Local boys found themselves making good money by selling the eager intruders pond lilies two for a penny and sugared flag root at 5¢ a bunch. The transformation of the island from an internationally recognized hub of the maritime industry to a tony vacation destination was suddenly under way.

Just a few years after the islanders had presumed there would be no more building in their faltering outpost, foundations for new hotels were quickly being struck. President Ulysses S. Grant visited the island in the summer of 1874, confirming its remarkable reversal of fortune. "The fame of the island as a summer resort is spreading constantly," noted Macy, writing in 1915, "and thousands of people from all over the country, representing every state in the Union, now seek out 'the little purple island' every summer." Modern Nantucketers, conditioned to stiffen at the site of a purple football uniform, still bristle at the dead author's unfortunate description of his native land.

THE ISLAND, THEN as now, grew quiet and reflective when summer ended. The children and families who stayed year-round were fairly desperate for activity. Organized football came to Nantucket in the fall of 1937, when the island high school produced its first squad.

The coach was Harry Cleverly, who had just graduated from Boston University. That team ran the table, losing all four of its games, two of them to Provincetown and one apiece to Falmouth and Hyannis.

The football program was launched at the suggestion of a Congregational minister, who felt it would do the island boys some good to learn a team sport for fall. John Toner, an island native who went on to become a head football coach and athletic director at the University of Connecticut, played in the first high school football game on Nantucket as a freshman. At UConn, Toner would serve three years during the 1980s as NCAA president, and he was responsible for the hiring of the university's two championship-caliber basketball coachs, Jim Calhoun and Geno Auriemma. As he recalled, the gridiron game was utterly unfamiliar to most island locals in 1937. "People were asking whether the ball was blown up or stuffed," Toner once told the *National*, the defunct sports daily. "The local paper sent down a reporter, and he kept asking what inning it was."

Three years later, the islanders had learned enough football to ensure the program's first undefeated season—five wins.

But after back-to-back winless seasons in 1941 and 1942, football was suspended on the island for the duration of the war years. Cleverly, who left to join the military, later became the head hockey coach at his alma mater, where he took three teams to the national championships and was named Coach of the Year and president of the American College Hockey Coaches Association.

When the football program was revived after the war, the team had a regular visitor at its practices. Dick Coffin had been visiting the island every summer for years with his family. After his mother died, he and his sister decided to move there permanently. Coffin was working as a fisherman, but he loved football. After graduating from Massachusetts Agricultural College (the precursor to UMass), he'd played some semipro ball.

The Nantucket players were quick to recognize the level of passion and expertise this Coffin fellow brought to the field. One player, Bob Mooney, was soon chosen as a spokesman for his teammates. Son of the town's longtime police chief, Mooney was the great-grandson of "Shipwreck" Mooney, a literal wash-ashore who had settled on the island with his wife under trying circumstances. Making the crossing from Dublin to New York in 1851 aboard an old sailing ship called the *British Queen*, the Mooneys were rescued after the ship ran aground at Tuckernuck Shoal. The elder Mooney swore off water travel for the rest of his days and became an island farmer.

Almost a century after Shipwreck's arrival, young Bob Mooney was lobbying the school administration on behalf of Dick Coffin. The coach at the time, athletic director Howard Laundry, carried around in his pocket a small book called *How to Play Winning Football*. Having his hands full managing other teams, he was quick to concede that Coffin might make a better coach.

BILL MEDEIROS PLAYED football and basketball for Nantucket in the mid-1950s. The son of a landscaper who immigrated from the Azores, the former running back, now in his seventies, re-members pleading with his mother each year to sign the release papers so he could play. His father was a diligent worker who couldn't fathom his son's infatuation with these American games. *"Tudo o que você quer fazer é jogar enovelar!"* William would shout. "All you want to do is play ball!"

But Medeiros was good. He was the only boy in his class to make the varsity as a freshman, and he was a two-way starter, at linebacker and running back, by his sophomore year. "He was a short, stubby guy, hard to bring down," says Bruce King, who played a few years later. He would not have been fun to face in practice, King figures: "I'm glad I was in elementary school when he played." In 1957 Medeiros set a Nantucket record that would stand for thirty-five years, rushing for five touchdowns in a game against Medfield. When his record was finally broken, he was listening to the Whalers game on the radio. Longtime friends with Coach Capizzo, Medeiros found himself yelling at the coach from the comfort of his armchair at home: "For Christ's sake, take him out!" he hollered when the kid scored his fourth touchdown of the game.

Medeiros grew up across the street from Jimmy Duarte, a Nantucket native whose father was Cape Verdean. Duarte's mother, Minnie, was a Correia. As teenagers, Medeiros and his friends marveled at Jimmy's natural inclination for music. "We'd get a quart of beer and go out to Surfside, and Jimmy would bring his guitar," Medeiros recalls. It was the early years of rock and roll. Duarte eventually started forming his own groups. One was called the Islanders. Another, Jimmy D and the Acres, took their name from 30 Acres, the island's original R&B joint. Duarte became something of a guitar god to the younger musicians on the island, including Vaughan Machado and David Perry. "He was like a song stylist with a Cape Verdean flavor that was unique to himself," said Nick Ferrantella, a drummer who went on to become a tour manager for bands such as Mountain and Foreigner, when Duarte died of complications from Lyme disease in 2007. "And he always had that handsome Muhammad Ali smile."

In Medeiros and Duarte's day, the Nantucketers played teams from Cape Cod and southeastern Massachusetts—Tabor Academy, Dracut, Falmouth, Barnstable, P-Town. "I never left the island until I played football," says Medeiros, who followed his father into the landscaping business and spent thirty years as a commercial scalloper.

Nantucket played the Vineyard twice in the early 1950s, facing off in 1953 and 1954 against an informally organized all-island team from the three Vineyard high schools. Nantucket won the first meeting at home, 33–20, wearing down a Vineyard team depleted by injuries with three unanswered touchdowns in the second half. The second time they played, it was Medeiros's freshman year. The teams battled to a scoreless tie.

The Vineyard all-island team was the brainchild of Jack Kelley, who was a twenty-five-year-old first-year phys ed teacher in Tisbury in 1953. Kelley had grown up in Medford, Massachusetts, just outside Boston, where the high school has been playing archrival Malden each season since 1889, making it one of the oldest public school rivalries in the country. "For most of the kids on the team," Kelley once said of his island all-star team, "the first football game they ever saw was the first one they played in."

On his first day of practice he handed Leigh Carroll, who would become his star running back, a football. "Do you think you can pass one of these?" the coach asked.

The rookie had a wit that could turn on a dime. "I don't even think I can swallow one," he replied with a grin.

The faculty and administrators who helped organize the Vineyard team immediately agreed that Nantucket would be a natural rival. "It was a trial balloon," said Kelley. "But right from the start, people were thinking of Nantucket. The rivalry was obvious, and it helped us solve our biggest problem, which was how to get these Vineyard boys, who were fierce rivals, to play as one." They chartered two planes for players and family to make the first trip. The Vineyarders' respectable showing in that first Nantucket victory confirmed Kelley's hunch that the island would take to football. The Vineyard might even have won if the refs weren't such flagrant homers, he complained years after leaving the island.

Kelley left in 1955 to take a job coaching hockey at Colby College before moving on to coach his alma mater, Boston University, to consecutive national championships in 1971 and 1972. A former head coach of the old New England Whalers, he is a member of the U.S. Hockey Hall of Fame. (He is also the father of the television writer David E. Kelley.)

Nantucket teams in the 1950s typically hovered around the .500 mark. They were competitive but not dominant. The boys who played were hard-nosed. Jack McGrady, who went on to become a state police officer, was one of the few boys with any size. His brother, Bobby, was the team quarterback—a good athlete, says teammate Phil Marks, though Marks, a 140-pound linebacker, "used to practically knock him out in every practice. Bobby had a weak stomach," he says, still needling his old teammate. George Duce, a couple of years younger, was Russian, Medeiros points out. "He was a tough son of a bitch. He played basketball, too, and he'd go up for the ball and his arms would be swinging. You'd have to yell at him—'Hey, I'm on your team!'"

Though it's been accepted as part of the Capizzo legend, it was Dick Coffin who first organized games against the enlisted men from the old Navy base. The scrimmages sometimes grew personal: The young Navy men often sought companionship with the girls from the high school, so the boys played like they were defending the girls' honor. "The Nantucket girls would get taken with those southern accents—some cracker from Alabama," says Vaughan Machado.

There were so few kids on the Nantucket roster, Coach Coffin was in the habit of suiting up himself and scrimmaging with the teenagers. He kicked the habit after taking a vicious pop along the sideline, courtesy of Phil Marks. "He was too proud to go out of bounds, and I nailed him," says Marks, now retired from his supervisory post with the power company. "I felt bad."

Marks played right guard on offense and was the long snapper on punts. By the time he graduated, alongside Medeiros in 1958, he'd filled out to 150 pounds. "I was a little shit," he says. "I used to love the contact." Though he was offered a scholarship to play at Dean Junior College, he turned it down, electing to stay on the island. At the time, he didn't trust himself to do the schoolwork.

In such a small community, the Nantucket program was perennially challenged for players. Duarte, who worked for the police department and then as a foreman for the Department of Public Works, would dedicate much of his adult life to the development of young football players at the Boys Club. His son, Nick, coaches there today.

Medeiros recalls one trip with just nineteen varsity players to Somerset—the same high school that would beat up on the Vineyard more than fifty years later, during the 2010 season, and rank in the state's top twenty. In the early days, school athletics in the state didn't have five divisions, as the MIAA does today. They were simply pooled into Class A or Class B, depending on the size of the student population. Nantucket epitomized Class B. Somerset was Class A. When the islanders pulled in on their bus, recalls Medeiros, it looked like the home team had fifteen platoons ready to play.

He never knew it while he was playing, but Medeiros's father— the same man who questioned his son's work ethic every time he headed off for practice—made a point to watch every game from a safe distance. William Medeiros, "strong as a bull," died of a ruptured appendix at age forty-seven. His son, who served in

Korea after graduating from high school, learned at the funeral
that William had seen all of Bill's games.

"Never said a word to me," Medeiros says.

THERE WAS LITTLE fanfare over the 1960 football game between Nantucket and the new Martha's Vineyard Regional
High School. Nantucket, which was on its way to a 6–1 season, won easily, scoring four touchdowns and holding the
other side scoreless.

Dick Coffin left the Nantucket school system, where he'd
served as athletic director and gym teacher, after the 1960–61
school year. The school principal, Mary P. Walker—known on
the island as "Mary P."—had decided that any students with P's
on their report cards (for poor performance) should be declared
ineligible for all extracurricular activity. The move caused an
uproar among the faculty. Had they known, maybe they wouldn't
have graded so hard.

Coach Coffin was deeply disappointed. "It decimated the
team," recalls the coach's son, Bernie, who was a junior captain
and halfback during his father's last season. For his senior year,
his parents sent him to boarding school at Worcester Academy,
where he joined a team that would win a New England prep
school championship.

Dick Coffin was approached by a friend who owned a large
parcel of land out at Miacomet, a beachfront along the island's
south shore that also features a freshwater pond. Ralph Marble
wanted to build a golf course, and he enlisted the outgoing
coach to help. Marble, a Michigan native, had purchased a four-
hundred-acre dairy farm in 1956, but he'd had a tough go of it.
The two men began designing the golf course on a nonexistent

budget, borrowing landscaping equipment from any islander who owned it. When the original clubhouse burned down, they built a temporary replacement in a Quonset hut. Coffin, who died in 2003, spent his later years in real estate on the island. "Oh, he was a man with great ideas," says his widow, Grace, a Nantucket native who met her husband when she was serving as secretary to the Nantucket school superintendent in the 1940s.

After Coffin departed, Nantucket football struggled to find its footing. For the 1961 season the school administration brought in a recent Boston University graduate. Any coach would have had his work cut out for him; the players liked Coach Coffin and hated to see him leave. "He wasn't ready to retire," says Machado, who played as a freshman during Coffin's last season. "He was an old-school guy, but he had a soft side when he needed it." The new guy was something else. On his first day, he brought his new players and their parents to the old location of the Boys and Girls Club and showed them film of his college team. The first few minutes were intriguing, but the reel went on and on. The coach rented a house in town, where some of the players were known to hang out, drinking beer. Between that and the rumors about the young coach's eye for the female students, he wasn't long for the island. "He was kind of a hotshot," says Bruce King, who played linebacker as a "ninety-eight-pound" freshman that year.

Nantucket won both inter-island games that year, in two low-scoring contests. Vineyarder Tom Bennett remembers Whaler Bruce Watts, who later became the island's fire chief, dropping a Vineyard ball carrier "like you would an armful of wood. Everyone on the field just stopped in their tracks in awe."

For the game on the Vineyard, Bruce King stayed with the

da Rosas, whose son, Tony, was on the varsity squad, with younger brother Dennis on the way up. After the game, the Sunday ferry call wasn't until later in the morning. Over breakfast, the skinny Nantucket freshman could sense that his host family was uncomfortable. Finally the da Rosas told him they were getting ready to go to church. Would he care to join them? The da Rosas were Catholic, and they knew their houseguest had been raised Episcopalian. King said sure.

King didn't play football the following year. As a freshman, he'd made a tackle in a game against Tabor Academy, meeting a punishing ball carrier head-on. They took him to the hospital. "My mother freaked out," he says. "I thought I had a broken back. My tackling technique wasn't very good." For his sophomore year, he got involved with the school band, playing trumpet.

The island had another new football coach, Dave Otto, the former Dayton basketball star, who would only stay two seasons. The program was being trusted to a bunch of gypsies, King thought. That year the Vineyard eked out its first-ever victory against Nantucket: 2–0. Machado, by then the Nantucket quarterback, lost a fumble in his own end zone when he tried to pitch a desperate lateral. The Vineyard won the rematch that year a lot more convincingly, 24–0.

Nantucket didn't fare much better when King returned to the gridiron for his junior year. The Vineyard continued its sudden dominance, shutting out the other island twice more. Still, the Whalers played other opponents tough, including the sons of the fishermen in Provincetown, then their natural nemeses. King was impressed by Otto's enthusiasm, despite the coach's obvious allegiance to basketball. "He had quite a bit of passion for what he did," he says. "We didn't win a lot of games, but it was an enjoyable year." Those games were "just this shy of street fighting, man," says Machado. Some kid would put a fist or an elbow in your face, above your face guard. Then you'd go stay at his house overnight.

Though the Whalers were trying to settle their coaching issues and the Vineyarders were integrating kids from different towns, the inter-island games were already taking on an unmatched intensity. "I never hit people so hard in my life," says Bob Tankard, who was a safety, halfback, and split end in his playing days. Tankard was athletic enough to be scouted by the Pittsburgh Pirates as a baseball prospect. "It was blood and guts," he says. "Both teams walked off, and we felt pain and agony for two weeks after." In an otherwise undefeated season, the Vineyard's lone tie that year came against Apponequet, which played in Class A at the time. To the islanders, that team seemed huge. The Vineyard kept the bigger team from scoring, stuffing them at the 1-yard line to preserve the 0–0 tie.

"We were suffering by the time we played the Nantucket game," says Tankard. "Some of us were still limping."

THE ARRIVAL OF twenty-four-year-old Vito Capizzo for the 1964 season marked the fourth new Nantucket coach in five years. After playing for Otto and the playboy from BU, the players were taken aback by the hotheaded newcomer. The goddamned guy carried around a two-by-four at practice!

Today, he'd be in the state prison in Walpole for that, says King. "It was like a culture shock." The students knew the new coach had played for Bear Bryant at Alabama, but he didn't brag about it. He certainly knew how to run a practice. "Vito had a lot of energy in those days," says King. "He got everybody wound up."

Capizzo's first assistant was George Vollans, who knew nothing about football. "I just did what he told me," says Vollans, who came to the island that year as a recent college graduate, taking a job as a science teacher. A graduate of Bates College in Maine, he learned about the opening because Mary P. Walker, the Nantucket principal, was also a Bates alum. On his interview he brought a classmate, Kevin Gallagher, who was hired, too, and soon signed on as the football team's trainer.

Vollans took home a $4,800 salary that year, and he got an extra $400 for coaching. It didn't quite cover the time commitment. An away game on the Cape meant a three-hour ride on a 6:30 a.m. ferry to Woods Hole, followed by a long bus ride. After the game, they reversed the whole process, finally stumbling into their houses late at night. "Another three hours with bored teenaged kids on a boat. Oh, my word!" recalls Vollans, who left the island the following year to earn his master's degree at Wesleyan. He soon returned to the island, but not the football program.

The first island meeting of the year went much the same as the previous four—28–0, Vineyard. Capizzo's exhortations aside, the Whalers had little reason to think the rematch would be any different. A few days before the game, Nantucket sent the Vineyard its roster. The list included a player named Lawrence Lema, the team's starting fullback. The Vineyard put up a stink. Hadn't this kid stayed back a couple of years? Wasn't he at least nineteen? Lema was declared ineligible, and King, the cocaptain, was pressed into service as the new starting fullback.

Two days before the game, he was sitting at Capizzo's kitchen table, going over the team's playbook while Barbara fixed dinner. When the game began, King surprised himself by breaking off a big 50-yard dash, though he was hauled down just shy of the end zone, at the 1-yard line. As it turned out, neither team could put the ball in the end zone. For King and his teammates, who'd gone into the game with little hope for a win, it felt like a victory. It was the second scoreless deadlock in the budding series between the two offshore rivals.

BOTH SIDES WANTED to win, of course, but scoreless ties seemed somehow appropriate. Whether they recognized it or not, the children of the islands had everything in common. To the boys from both islands, there were two kinds of people—islanders and off-islanders. "We had a lot of resentment toward summer people," says one island native. "Their second homes were sometimes bigger than our only homes. We enjoyed the idea of leaving the island and whipping somebody's ass."

But if more and more well-off summer residents were arriving, neither island yet had a reputation as a place of privilege. It would be years before the two communities would be recognized as the sort of place where former defense secretary Robert McNamara, for instance, could sell his summer home to *Saturday Night Live*'s John Belushi, or Tommy Hilfiger's daughter could bring a camera crew to shoot a reality show for MTV.

When they ventured onto the mainland—into America—"we were freaks," says Ralston Jackson. How do you live on an island? other kids would ask. How do you get to school? Where do you get your food? "We could tell them anything," Jackson says, "that we swam to school, that we lived in three-sided houses."

"We felt as though nobody cared about us out here," says

Jackson's old buddy Bob Tankard. "Nantucket was like our best friend. And we were not gonna let our best friend stand over us. The rivalry became our identity. It was a rite of passage.

"It's like your brother," he says. "You'll punch each other in the eye, and when it's all over, you'll say, 'Let's go have an ice pop.'"

*Chapter Five*

# THERE WERE SHELLS
# ON THE FIELD

RALSTON JACKSON WAS the youngest kid on the Vineyard's first team at the new regional high school in 1960. The games, he doesn't remember. What he does recall are the practices. Each day after the closing bell, the team left the new high school and jogged a mile or so in the direction of Vineyard Haven. Practice was held on an unmarked field.

"I remember tackling Manny Jardin in practice," says the former Vineyarder, now a lawyer in Pittsburgh. His office looks out on the Monongahela River, which flows into the Ohio, which meets the Mississippi, which spills out into the Gulf, which sends weather patterns up the eastern seaboard. "I'm still connected to the Vineyard," he jokes. "I can spit on it."

Jardin, he says, "was probably nineteen at the time, and I was thirteen. He was the strongest guy on the team. You learned to tackle very low."

Though that first season might not have been particularly memorable, the 1960 Vineyard team was steeped in island history. There was one Mayhew in the backfield—halfback Lloyd, known as "Butch," who also returned punts—and another, Jeanne, on the cheerleading squad. Joe Araujo was one of eighteen children and the first of many from his clan to play football. When he attended a dinner commemorating his team's fiftieth anniversary, the husky former cop in the guayabera was introduced as the "fullback and Way-Back." Mike McCarthy, Coach Dan McCarthy's first son and a future team leader, was the water boy.

Charlie Davis was the first person to walk through the front door of the new regional high school in Oak Bluffs in 1960. Davis had been hired as the new principal. The World War II Navy veteran and his young family had been living in Maine, where he'd taught math and coached track and field, attended grad school, and become a school principal for the first time. As an undergrad, he'd been a center at New England College.

Getting the boys from across the island to play nice with each other was easily the biggest challenge of the new prinicipal's transition to life on the Vineyard. The old basketball games between Oak Bluffs and Edgartown, or Vineyard Haven, were like lion's dens, says Chuck Davis, Charlie's firstborn son. Chuck—Charles A. Davis Jr.—was ready for kindergarten when his family arrived on-island.

In the beginning there was no football field at the new high school. The team played its games in Vineyard Haven, on a field behind the old grocery store, where the town post office and a Cumberland Farms convenience store now stand. The field, located on landfill, had no permanent football markings; a groundskeeper laid out the gridiron with lime. Falling players often landed on strewn seashells. Occasionally a piece of metal would surface from an old, buried jalopy. There was no grandstand. Fans stood on the sideline.

"I still remember the smell of fresh-cut grass, and the lime," says Davis. Even in those days, with the island's football program just beginning to take shape, the parents were enthusiastic supporters. Davis can remember Timmy Downs's mother—the prim, church-lady-ish wife of superintendent Charlie Downs, who'd played on the 1953 all-island team—mustering a frightening roar: *Go get 'em, boys!*

Swimming was for the summer kids. Boys who grew up on the Vineyard went to the water with a purpose: they were clamming, looking for quahogs. Tom Bennett's family frequented the beachfront at the end of Fuller Street in Edgartown, where he grew up, for big cookouts.

For Bennett, the rivalries weren't so much between townies, or between the Irish kids and the Portuguese. They were between the islanders and everyone else.

"In the summertime, we all felt our identity was to be an island guy," says Bennett, a Vietnam-era Air Force veteran who has worked for forty years for Martha's Vineyard Community Services, counseling fellow veterans. Off-island kids would come over in the summer months to take swimming and sailing lessons. "A lot of island people don't swim," he says.

When Bennett was a sophomore, in 1961, he befriended a newcomer, a black kid from Newark named Bobby Tankard. At first Tankard was shy, a little daunted by his new surroundings. It didn't take long, as he grew more comfortable on the island, before his natural amiability took over.

Bennett was born into an atypical family. His mother, Edith, was a lifelong islander whose father had moved to the Vineyard from Stoughton to take a job at Pimpneymouse Farm, the last working farm on Chappaquiddick. Edith was one of nine children. She had a son by a first marriage who suffered from mental

health issues: Dexter Mello, Bennett's half brother, died in a
car accident on the island in 2006. His disability, combined with
Bennett's wartime experiences, helped lead the young veteran
into his community service work.

After his mother's first marriage ended in divorce, Bennett
was born out of wedlock. His biological father was a wartime
Navy man. Unbeknownst to many of Bennett's friends, the boy
was born off-island, after his pregnant mother went into hiding
at her great-aunt's house outside of Boston. Though he has lived
on Martha's Vineyard for all of his sixty-five years, the fact that
he was born in a hospital on the mainland technically qualifies
him as what the islanders disparagingly refer to as a "wash-ashore."
As a boy, Bennett wasn't quick to offer up that bit of information.
He prefers to think of himself as a "love child"—after considering giving the baby up for adoption, his mother brought him
back to the Vineyard, he says, out of love.

Edith later remarried and had two more sons. Then she took
in Bennett's cousin, Roy, when her sister died. "Basically, she
brought up five boys," says Bennett, who still sees his ninety-
year-old mother every Tuesday night for dinner.

Bennett took his last name from his mother's second husband,
the stepfather who provided for the family. "I had all the respect
in the world for him," says Bennett. "He made it possible for me
to be housed and sheltered. He was there as my male role model."
Still, he acknowledges, he struggled with being a stepson.

Like plenty of his classmates, Bennett found an emotional
outlet on the new high school football team. Bringing together
the townies from the three down-island communities for the
first time created an instant atmosphere of competition, he says.
"We wanted to respect each other. We were very competitive

during our scrimmages. That first team had a lot to do with bringing that spirit, from being separate townies to the regional high school team."

Coach McCarthy had been a Little All-American as an undersized guard at Boston University. "He was a tough egg," says Bennett, who was a starting linebacker as a freshman on the 1960 team. Wearing a tie and a trench coat, McCarthy taught the fledgling football team the fundamentals of the game—how to drive off a three-point stance, how to cradle the football on a handoff. That first team played just four games—a home-and-away series against Provincetown, an away game at Apponequet, and the inaugural Nantucket rivalry matchup on the Vineyard's home field. They won the opener against Provincetown, 14–8; the game ball still rests in the display case at MVRHS. The Vineyarders lost the other three games, including the shutout thumping at the hands of the other island.

McCarthy, a crusty Irishman who smoked and could put away his share of booze, somehow knew that Bennett's biological father was a fellow Irishman. The coach liked to play head games with the freshman, who was being groomed to take over the fullback position from Joe Araujo, who was graduating. After practice, McCarthy would chide his youngest player, purposely noting the solid effort of some other player who could conceivably take Bennett's starting spot. "I'd get pissed and try harder," Bennett remembers. "He knew how to get the most out of me. It was like a game between us. I don't even know if other people were aware, but I appreciated it," he says. "It kind of brought out the Irish in me."

The team started to move in the right direction during McCarthy's second and third years as coach. By Bennett's junior

year, 1962, some good football players had signed on, including
Lenny Donaroma, cocaptain John Bunker, and two of the big
DePriest boys, Ashley and Don. As a sophomore, Tony da Rosa
was a starting end on both sides of the ball. The halfbacks were
both excellent athletes, Manny Nunes and Bill "Boo" Bassett.
"We were not huge, but we were strong island kids," says
Bennett. "We grew up shellfishing, helping our fathers. I was
working from age ten. We were really physical. We'd go play
other teams, and it was obvious to them, and to us."

The Vineyard boys felt especially close to Francis Pachico,
the football assistant and head basketball coach, a fatherly figure
whom everyone knew as "Sancy." After a student graduated
from the high school, if he ran into any trouble at work or with
the cops, he'd be upset if Sancy heard about it. "You wouldn't
want to disappoint him," says Bennett.

A painful slipped disc in his back convinced Dan McCarthy
to step down as football coach before the 1963 season. The
school hired Maury Dore, a strapping, no-nonsense Down Eas-
ter who had been an All-State end and basketball cocaptain
while attending the University of Maine. "To me, he might
as well have been playing at Notre Dame," recalls Ron Borges,
who played center for Dore until 1966.

But Dore was uninterested in reliving the glory of his collegiate years. When Borges's older brother, who had played on Jack
Kelley's Vineyard all-star team, went off to UMass, he found a
football program from an old game against Maine and brought
it back for Ronnie. Borges proudly took it to show Dore, he
says, "and he looked at me like I was nuts."

Dore pushed his starters relentlessly. During sprints, he ran
behind his players, stepping on their heels, and sometimes tram-

pling them, to get them to run faster. "He never subbed anybody, unless you had a bone sticking out of your skin," recalls Dennis da Rosa, who played behind Ral Jackson as a quarterback in his freshman year. After Jackson graduated, da Rosa became the starter for the next three years. During one game he took a shot to the nose inside his face guard. Borges, his best friend, took a look at the blood gushing from his nose. Laughing, he ordered his dazed friend to the sideline for the next play. "Maury had the trainer wash my face," says da Rosa, "and I went back out."

Borges's family came to the island like a lot of families have—illegally. His grandfather left the Azores on a fishing boat, which connected him to a larger vessel out in the middle of the Atlantic. Speaking no English, he thought he was headed to Canada, but he ended up in Providence, Rhode Island. From there, he made his way to the South Shore fishing city of New Bedford, and then on to the Vineyard. Borges came to football with a family reputation. His mother, who grew up on a farm in Chilmark, was well known as a tiny but scrappy basketball player. In the days when the island towns played one another, she once fired a basketball right into the gut of a much taller girl from Oak Bluffs who was guarding her.

"We hated Oak Bluffs," says Borges, who grew up in Vineyard Haven.

Coach McCarthy laid a strong foundation, and then Dore helped each player realize his potential. "He was a new face, and he seemed to be an expert at football," says Bennett. "In my mind, he was a real leader. As island kids, we were looking for that kind of attention, that approval. It was almost like Marine boot camp with Maury. He wanted to win, and man, we responded to him."

Dore's first team, in fact, went undefeated. When the 1964 season ended, there were just two blemishes on the schedule. There was the scoreless tie with Apponequet. And at Provincetown, the Vineyard gave up its only touchdown of the season.

"That was such a disappointment to us all," says Bennett, who was an outside linebacker. When the season ended, the Vineyarders had outscored their opponents 92–6. The combined total of their two games against Nantucket was 44–0.

The new Nantucket coach was a pipe-smoking, stick-wielding newcomer named Vito Capizzo.

IN HINDSIGHT, THE island rivalry clearly grew more acrimonious when the boys stopped staying at each other's houses. You couldn't really despise your opponent when he was sleeping next to you, says Borges.

The animosity ascended to a new level after the infamous brawl that took place on Nantucket in the fall of 1966, when the home team was on its way to its own undefeated season, including two wins over the Vineyard. The guys who took the brunt of it weren't football players but servicemen stationed on the island. According to the Vineyarders, it was the older men who started the fight by talking trash at a party. "Billy and Joey were two bad dudes," says Borges of the two Vineyard teammates who took particular exception to the taunting. "They beat the hell out of quite a few folks. That was typical of our team—we'd rather win the fight and lose the game. And we were pretty adept at winning the fight."

Borges, who'd been battling a knee injury, arrived at the high school earlier than his teammates the next morning so Dore could help him wrap his leg in elastic bandages. The coach grilled him about what had happened the night before. "I denied all knowledge," Borges says.

The Nantucket game on their island that year was the only time Borges's parents saw him play football. They were working people who didn't have time for games. Borges's mother cheered almost as much for Dickie Glidden, who'd stayed in her house, as she did for her own son.

As the center, Borges had to line up against Karsten Reinemo, the huge Whalers nose tackle. Reinemo got the best of his counterpart on the Vineyard's first play from scrimmage. In the huddle da Rosa upbraided his buddy about it, and Borges responded on the next play by grappling with Reinemo until well after the whistle blew. That got the big guy's attention. "I played over my head the whole game," recalls Borges. Afterward, as he left the field on crutches, his father beamed with pride for his tough kid. His mother, on the other hand, scolded him for pulling on another player's jersey.

Unlike their rivals, the 1966 Vineyarders were serious underachievers. Though they were stocked with talented players, they went winless on the season. "That was the weirdest team I was ever associated with," says Borges.

By then Dore, who was about to get divorced, had effectively checked out. He quit after the following season, after beating the Whalers by a touchdown on the final inter-island game of his career.

# Chapter Six

## WHALER PRIDE

BARBARA CAPIZZO WAS used to the weather back home in Georgia, where it starts warming up in February. The coach's wife wasn't thrilled about the long, lonely winters on Nantucket.

Vito wasn't too smitten with the place, either. We'll give it three years, he told his wife when they arrived. If it doesn't work out, we'll get the hell out of here.

He didn't have much to show for his first two seasons, an ugly combined 2–9–3 record. But the coach knew that his program was starting to come together. Interest was growing. The players were getting tougher, in large part due to their weekly scrimmages with the Navy guys. Vito suddenly had size—one lineman, Karsten Reinemo, was six-five, 250-ish; another, Mike Kalman, was a tough 200-pounder. The coach had some skill players, too. Glenn Santos, whose brother, Joe, had been a basketball star for Dave Otto, was the team's best all-around athlete. Glen Menard was a tall, lanky receiver and quarterback—a bit of a punk, as his teammates recall, which gave him an extra edge on the field. And Frankie Psaradelis was a Tasmanian devil on defense.

The quarterback for Vito's first two seasons was Dickie Glidden. Though not big or especially gifted as an athlete, he was a natural field general. In a game against the Vineyard during Glidden's sophomore season, his first on the varsity, Capizzo's rookie team salvaged a 16–16 tie when a sure touchdown pass sailed through the hands of a Vineyard receiver. Glidden, playing defensive back, had been beaten on the play and could only watch helplessly as his man strode under the ball. It would have been the winning score. The coach eventually made Glidden take an eye exam. "He couldn't see worth a damn," says Capizzo.

The coach brought a new team concept to the high school. Learning the game at the Boys Club, they'd simply lurched after the ball, wherever it was. The new coach taught them that every position on the field has an assignment—a zone, a block, a fake. If each player carried out his role, the play would be successful.

Alan Costa came to the varsity as an end on both sides of the line. He'd grown up catching the ball against his body, which led to an inordinate number of dropped passes. Every day after lunch, Capizzo put Costa against the wall in the gym. On a two-count, the player spun around. The football would already be in the air, spiraling toward his nose. The drill taught Costa to catch with his hands.

"We had bad ingrained habits," recalls Costa. "It took a while to sink in."

Some of the coach's methods might get him fired, or at least reprimanded, today. He swung a broom handle at the heads of his linemen, to teach them to get down and play in a crouch. One day the same kid who'd wet his jockstrap against the Navy guys decided he'd had enough. He announced he was quitting and began walking off the field. Capizzo chased him down with the broom handle, tackled him, and roughed him up. "Nobody quits on us!" he thundered. Later, the boy's father showed up at practice with a local cop everyone knew as Billy Bigfoot. After a private conversation, the boy said he wanted to rejoin the team. Capizzo let his team take a vote, and the player was reinstated. The player went on to serve in the honor guard in the Marines; Capizzo says he introduced him to the recruiter.

It was a different era. Capizzo certainly wasn't the only one using his hands to discipline. Steve Lamb once told the coach he had to miss practice for a fictitious dentist appointment. When the boy's father found his son shirking the team, he punched him in the mouth and brought him down to the practice field, blood streaming from his lip and gums. "He didn't miss another practice," recalls the coach.

"You're not out here to impress the girls," Capizzo told his team repeatedly. "You're here to win football games. Forget the skirts." It was an order he seemed to take seriously himself. When Mary P., the principal, assigned Capizzo extra duties beyond gym class, the coach found himself teaching sex education. Explaining the female reproductive system, he mispronounced *womb* as "womp." When Alan Costa corrected his coach, Capizzo shot back, "All right, brain surgeon!"

Such comic episodes endeared the coach to his players, who began to see that his shouting and whip-cracking were just one side of his demeanor. The Whalers started to click as a team toward the end of the 1965 season, Capizzo's second. After getting pummeled by Nashoba Regional—a school that had a pool of twelve hundred students, compared to Nantucket's two hundred—the team found its footing. They beat Apponequet, then a powerhouse, and they played the Vineyard to that scoreless tie in their second meeting of the season. Though the team finished with just two wins against five losses and the tie, it was undoubtedly moving in the right direction.

The Mayflower League had not yet been created. As an independent, Nantucket had its traditional rivalries with Provincetown, Apponequet, and now the Vineyard. It was difficult then (as it remains now) for both island teams to round out their schedules. Early on, Capizzo fostered an alliance with the Catholic Central League, arranging games with St. Clement, Christopher Columbus, and St. Mary's of Lynn, which was then celebrating the rise of its star athlete, Tony Conigliaro, to the major leagues, where he had just broken in with the Red Sox as a nineteen-year-old, home-run-bashing rookie.

When St. Mary's showed up on the island in the middle of the 1966 season, the home team had yet to lose a game. These, however, were some very big boys. "They really looked like a football team," says Glidden. The Whalers fell behind early; it was one of the few times all season they had to contend with a deficit. Menard, playing quarterback, tossed a short screen pass to Glidden, who was lined up as a wingback. "Go!" Glidden yelled. Reinemo, his childhood buddy, was supposed to be his blocker. Instead, he turned to watch Glidden catch the pass, just as a St. Mary's defender popped the receiver in the back, causing a fumble. But Santos, who had a nose for the end zone, picked up the football and motored 40 yards for an unlikely touchdown. It proved to be the difference in the game.

Each time the Nantucketers climbed off their bus for away games that year, big Karsten Reinemo was the first player to step through the door. In his coach's words, the big fella, who'd only joined the team in his junior year, was a gorilla. Playing nose

tackle, Reinemo was such an impressive athlete that Glidden says
he probably should have been quarterback. "He played the big,
dumb goof," says Glidden, "but he was dumb like a fox." On offense, he and Kalman and the rest of the line created huge holes
for Santos, whose game intensified the closer he got to the end
zone. "He tended to take a little time off between the twenties,"
says Glidden. "But if he knew he could get his name in the paper, that boy was tough." Santos did, in fact, see his name in the
papers plenty that season—he led all scorers in the division with
more than 120 points.

And the team continued to roll. It beat Provincetown twice.
It beat the Vineyard twice. It beat Apponequet. On the last
weekend of the season, the Whalers traveled all the way to the
western part of the state—"out by Amherst someplace, at the end
of the earth," says Glidden—to play Pioneer Valley, a regional
school that had beaten the islanders handily the previous year.
"They'd killed us, beaten us up," says Glidden. He remembers
hitting a runner at midfield, trying to strip the ball, and hanging
on like a baby koala while the guy rumbled 20 more yards.

In the rematch out west, the home team took a 6–0 lead into
the locker room at halftime. Worse, Glidden, who'd returned
to his old quarterback position after Menard sprained an ankle a
week before, had been knocked out of the game. His own ankle
was swelling like a balloon. Manny Perry, who took snaps as
the emergency third-string quarterback, played the end of the
half, but he was clearly uncomfortable in the role. In the locker
room, Capizzo looked at Menard, who was wearing his street
clothes. I can go, the tall kid told the coach. Capizzo ordered
Glidden, his perfectly average-sized quarterback, to give the

six-foot-five Menard his uniform. Somehow they got everything to fit, except for the cleats. Menard wore sneakers.

In the second half, the gimpy replacement passed for a pair of touchdowns. Playing defense, he capped the scoring with another touchdown on an interception return. "It was the fastest number twelve had ever run," says Glidden. "I was slower than death." The Whalers won going away, clinching an undefeated season. They returned home to an exhilarating reception. "My God, we had the fire trucks, the police escort, the whole nine yards," Capizzo recalls. "It was like coming home from Vietnam."

As *Sports Illustrated* would note thirty years later, that 1966 team kept the coach on the island: "The dynasty and the legend had begun."

AFTER ITS UNDEFEATED season in 1966, Capizzo's Nantucket team waded through an understandable letdown. Glidden, Reinemo, and other core players from that season graduated the following spring. A 12–0 victory over the Vineyard was one of just three wins for the 1967 team; the Vineyard's 18–12 revenge later in the season was one of four losses the Whalers took that year. A galling home loss to Provincetown (whose coach, Steve Goveia, shared a mutual distaste with Capizzo) featured a Whalers offense shut down so thoroughly that it recorded negative yardage for the game.

In ten years as Provincetown's head coach, Goveia would post just one losing season. He and Capizzo often conducted shouting matches from across the turf during games. On the Monday after the loss, a fuming Capizzo led a two-and-a-half-hour practice that consisted entirely of grueling Oklahoma tackling drills. When the sun went down, the coach ordered his players to move their cars alongside the practice field, where their headlights let him extend the workout after hours. Chris Maury, the future athletic director, was a freshman that year. He shakes his head when he thinks of the longtime coach's archaic methods. "The stories of him swinging a two-by-four over our heads as we ran through tire drills are absolutely true," he says.

By then, though, Capizzo had created a mystique around his football program. His tenure on the island was no longer in doubt. For away games, the entire school took part in a new ritual: with each student assigned to a vehicle, the community organized a massive car parade to make the short trip from the high school campus to the Steamship Authority ferry landing in town. There the town sent the team off with a pep rally on the dock.

If the year after the undefeated season was a disappointment, the bounce-back was quick. As a sophomore linebacker, Maury was named the team's outstanding defensive player, leading a stingy squad to a 6–2 record. For his third high school season—1969 was the inaugural year of the new Mayflower League—Maury was moved to quarterback. To keep him healthy, he was forbidden to play defense, where he played best.

"That's some of the wisdom of Coach Capizzo," says Maury with a chuckle. "There's a logic in there somewhere."

For his senior year Maury was restored to his rightful place as a defensive leader, playing linebacker and, when Nantucket had the ball, tailback. He was a cocaptain that year, along with fellow linebacker Dennis Egan and Joe Viera, the sizable athlete who was also a force on the basketball team. That year's seniors had to take their SATs on the Vineyard on the morning of their inter-island game. It wasn't much of a distraction. Nantucket, then in the middle of an eight-game winning streak against the other island, won by shutout that day. "They were really hurting at that point," says Maury. "They could play a decent game, but they never had any kind of real success against us." Nantucket finished the season 5–2–1, winning its first of many Mayflower League titles.

After graduation, Maury went to Clemson, where he participated in some "scrub team" scrimmaging for the Tigers (who would become national champions in 1981) before taking up rugby. He and his fiancée were married the summer after Maury's junior year, and they had their first of three children, future Whaler Chris junior, the following year while he attended summer school to complete his education. The young family soon moved back to the rock, where Maury started the construction business he would run for the next thirty years. As his kids got older, he coached junior varsity baseball, then became the high school's head softball coach when his daughter, Elizabeth—"our only three-sport athlete," he says proudly—started playing.

COACH CAPIZZO BEGAN to expand his coaching staff in the early 1970s. Boston University graduate Dick Herman, who was raised in Cambridge, came to the island near the end of the sixties to take a job as a middle school math teacher. Though he'd spent summer weekends during his childhood in Falmouth Heights on Cape Cod, he was another import who knew nothing about Nantucket before he moved there. With his future wife teaching in Boston, he got in the habit of leaving the island every weekend to return home. Capizzo found out and asked his young teaching colleague if he would mind doing some scouting on his trips to the mainland. On his first assignment Herman told Maureen they'd be spending their Saturday afternoon together watching student football at Our Lady's High School in Newton. She was none too pleased, recalls Herman, a tall, white-haired man with big hands and a wry sense of humor.

After their marriage, the Hermans settled on Nantucket together, buying an acre and a half for the princely sum of $6,500 in 1968. It was roughly the same amount as their teachers' salaries. No longer making his weekly off-island trips, Herman became an assistant coach. He eventually saw both of his sons, Peter and Rick, become Whaler cocaptains—Peter in 1992, Rick four years later.

In 1972 Capizzo hired another assistant, Swampscott native Dennis Caron. Caron had been intrigued by island life since he was a boy, when a friend of his mother's moved to Nantucket. When he got married, he and his wife arranged to have their honeymoon on the island. Before accepting a teaching job in the Nantucket school system, Caron had been a junior high school football coach for five years in Gardner, an old furniture-producing community in the central part of Massachusetts. With enrollment numbers growing for Capizzo's football program, the newcomer took over the coach's new junior varsity, which would work in tandem with the Boys Club to feed the varsity a constant supply of fundamentally sound young football players.

"He was great to work for in a lot of ways," says Caron. "Vito trusted me to run the subvarsity program, as long as I didn't do anything too radical." On a Sunday morning in October, he got up to let his two old dogs in from the backyard. Barefoot, he wore a pair of shorts and a Whaler Pride T-shirt from the 2008 season, his last as an assistant. His hair was matted from a long night's sleep. Caron lives alone now. His wife, Janice, a beloved guidance counselor at Nantucket's Cyrus Pierce Middle School, died a few years ago from breast cancer. A charcoal drawing done by their younger son, Rob, a Marine stationed in Afghanistan, hung on the wall in the kitchen.

Rob followed in the footsteps of his big brother, Dennis junior, becoming the quarterback for the Whalers teams of the early 2000s. Rob, who went on to play as a backup at Hobart College—Dennis junior had been a backup quarterback at Tufts—learned a lot about grace under pressure from football, says his father. "He was not a great player, but he was able to manage a huddle. I think that translates into being a combat officer, not that I advocate that for anyone."

Caron's career as Capizzo's right-hand man would last twenty-five years, until the year his wife died. Once you're on the island, he says, "it's hard to leave."

*Chapter Seven*

THE DOTTED LINE

M AURY DORE'S VINEYARD replacement, Sherman
Hoar, assumed his sole season at the helm in 1968. Recently retired from the CIA, for which he'd served in Asia,
Africa, and South America, Hoar hailed from an impressive
family of lawyers and congressmen. One of his ancestors was a
signer of the Declaration of Independence. A history and political science teacher who spent his boyhood summers in his family's two-hundred-year-old house on Chappy, Hoar specialized
in Vineyard lore, and he once asked his seniors to devise an is-
landwide system of government.

As a football coach, Sherman Hoar was an educator. He wanted
his players to truly understand the game. Yet like most coaches
of the era, he also subscribed to Vince Lombardi's philosophy
of hard work and aggression. Lombardi's legacy was confirmed
when he appeared on the cover of *Time* magazine in late 1962,
representing "The Sport of the '60s," three years after assuming
his head coaching position with the Green Bay Packers.

Hoar brought in Pop Warner's old single-wing formation.
Mike McCarthy, the oldest son of the former coach, was a junior that year. Playing fullback, he blocked for tailback Bobby

Hagerty, a cocaptain, alongside Mike Donaroma. McCarthy had been taught to hit the previous season by Coach Dore, who pushed the kid, then all of five foot four and 130 pounds, into two-on-one drills against two of the team's biggest linemen. After the former water boy got leveled on his first try, Dore made him get down in his stance. Then he shoved him into contact with the bottom of his shoe on the player's backside. McCarthy learned to take the action to the bigger man, rather than hanging back and catching his block. During Hoar's tenure McCarthy touched the ball only rarely, running an occasional counterplay. It wasn't until the following season, 1969, that he would run up some significant yardage.

Though Hoar was an interim coach, he put the effort in. "We were losing, but it didn't matter," says McCarthy. "He had a good soul about him. I think he was a little frustrated we weren't very talented."

"We did windsprints till you drop," recalls Chuck Davis, who was also on Hoar's team. With his deep, rumbling voice, the coach treated his boys like men. "No butts, no booze, no broads," he demanded. Davis was a freshman that year, one of only two on the squad, with Louis Larsen. He was barely old enough to daydream about a chaste kiss from a classmate, let alone bagging himself a "broad."

As the son of the principal, Chuckie Davis sometimes felt like a target of subtle hazing. "If a kid had an issue with my dad, he'd take it out on me," he recalls. For a time the principal considered sending his son to Tabor Academy, the exclusive prep school on the mainland, on Buzzards Bay. But Chuck, who grew up to become an underwater photographer, loved the island, and he opted to stay.

As a kid, Davis was transfixed by *The Undersea World of Jacques Cousteau*, the television program hosted by the French inventor and explorer. Sure to be in, on, or near the water every chance he got, Davis dreamed about someday working for Cousteau. He studied French in high school. One day, when he was complaining about his homework, his mother looked up from her ironing and scolded him. "When you work for Jacques Cousteau," she said, "you're going to have to know French." The teenager decided then that he'd better tighten up his study habits.

Chuckie had an art teacher who set up a darkroom in the chemistry lab. As a sophomore, the student had an opportunity to use his budding interest in photography on the football field when he suffered a season-ending injury. At Blue Hills, just as a teammate stood up the ball carrier at the line of scrimmage, Davis, a defensive lineman, drove low. Just before contact he felt his knee give out. Another teammate had accidentally clipped him. "Back then we wore long spikes," he says. "My foot didn't move, and my knee became a universal joint."

Jerry Gerolamo, the coach who replaced Hoar, screamed at his injured player to crawl off the field so the Vineyard wouldn't have to stop the clock. Initially diagnosed with ligament damage, Davis was called back when doctors spotted a hairline fracture of his femur, just above the knee.

Wearing a cast from hip to toe, he had plenty of time to mess around with his camera. It was his first underwater camera, a Nikonos, designed in part by Cousteau, that could also focus on land. Davis took plenty of photos of his teammates and coaches while he recuperated.

He returned to play his junior and senior years, earning a berth on a divisional all-state team as a center in his final season. Davis remembers having epic battles on the line with a heavyweight Nantucket kid named Joe Viera. For one game Viera wore a knee brace, so the 190-pound principal's son tried to beat him with quickness. But they also squared off with helmet-to-pad pile drivers. "I hit him so hard one time, not that he went anywhere," says Davis. When he got up, he was seeing stars: "Remember those old Warner Bros. cartoons, where there's a ring of canaries flying around?" He was so dazed, he couldn't figure out which huddle to return to, the purple or the blue.

After graduation Davis went to UMass, where he studied fisheries biology and played football his freshman year. Not destined for much playing time at that level of competition, he was a cornerback on the "look" team for the varsity during game weeks. Mike McCarthy, the former Vineyard star who had gone on to play cornerback at UConn, spent the summer helping the younger Davis prepare for the position change.

The head coach at UMass was Dick MacPherson, a future College Football Hall of Famer and short-lived head coach of the Patriots (1991–92) who was then coming off a stint as an assistant with the Denver Broncos. The Minutemen won the Yankee Conference that season with several players who would go on to the NFL, including Paul Metallo, drafted as a defensive back by the Kansas City Chiefs, and Yogi Berra's son Tim Berra, who had a brief career as a wide receiver for the Baltimore Colts.

Davis quit playing during his sophomore year. "I wasn't going to the NFL," he says. Still, on the Vineyard and then at UMass, he developed a love for the game that he finds useful even now. Documenting the natural world can take heroic levels of patience and endurance, and Davis often finds himself drawing on his football training. "The weather might be crappy, and the wildlife's not showing," he says. "But you always have more inside than you think."

After graduating from UMass, Davis drove out to Santa Barbara to enroll at the Brooks Insitute of Photography. He worked for several years as a commercial diver, inspecting oil rigs in the Gulf of Mexico and supertankers off the California coast. Hoping to break into underwater filmmaking, he began to volunteer for the Cousteau Society around 1980 and, after a thirteen-month stint based in the Middle East, came back to the West Coast with a full-time job awaiting him aboard Cousteau's new ship, the *Alcyone*. Later, he was transferred to the *Calypso*, Cousteau's classic exploring vessel.

By then married and soon to be a father of two—a son, Cole (actually Charles A. Davis III), and a daughter, Martha—he traveled to both poles and around the globe with his hero. Like Cousteau's closest friends, Davis called his mentor "JYC"—pronounced "jique"—after his initials. It was, quite literally, a dream come true. "I used to have dreams on the Vineyard where I'd be on the deck of the *Calypso*," he says.

JERRY GEROLAMO ARRIVED on the island in 1969, hired to teach history by Charlie Downs, the superintendent who went to Holy Cross. Gerolamo interviewed for open coaching positions with the baseball and football programs, and he was given the keys to both. A standout performer on a Belmont High School football team that won a state championship in the mid-1960s, Gerolamo recalls crowds of ten thousand at the Marauders' annual Thanksgiving clash against archrival Watertown. The two teams have been playing each other since 1921. (The greater Boston area hosts some of the oldest traditional high school football rivalries in the nation, including Wellesley-Needham, which dates to 1882; Boston Latin–Boston English, since 1887; Medford-Malden, 1889; and two series that began two years later, Beverly-Salem and Amesbury-Newburyport.)

Upon graduation Gerolamo went away to college in South Dakota, where he was named team captain in his senior year at the small, Christian-affiliated Yankton College. Lyle Alzado, the future NFL star who once boxed Muhammad Ali in an exhibition, was Gerolamo's teammate at Yankton. Alzado, one of the first professional athletes to admit to steroid use, died of brain cancer in 1992 at the age of forty-three. In a *Sports Illustrated* article that ran not long before his death, the defensive lineman recounted his continual use of performance-enhancing drugs from 1969 on. Known for his feral, unruly behavior, Alzado was like that long before he started taking PEDs, recalls Gerolamo: "He was absolutely out of his mind."

Like Vito Capizzo, who thought he was going to Nantasket, Gerolamo had no idea that the Oak Bluffs school district to which he'd applied was located on an island. "I looked it up on a map," he says. "I saw a dotted line across the water, and I realized I had to take a boat there."

Not until he arrived on the island did he become aware that the Vineyard's football team was struggling badly. "The program was pretty much in shambles," says Gerolamo. One player had been seriously injured the previous season, and parents were becoming less inclined to let their boys play football. The team had little success under Hoar, and there was no feeder program in place—no Pop Warner or Boys Club team—to encourage younger kids to take up the game.

On top of all that, it was the late 1960s, when high schoolers were dressing in fringe and patched jeans, experimenting with psychedelics, and rebelling against anyone with a military haircut or a disciplinarian's attitude. Gerolamo's first team had only eighteen or so boys on the roster, top to bottom—no junior varsity or freshman teams—and, as he recalls, nine or ten of the players were set to graduate at the end of the school year. Opposing teams typically had forty players on their sideline. When he asked one boy to take a shot at playing center, the kid lined up sideways to snap the ball, like he was playing flag football.

The team won only two games that season, but the new coaches did all they could with the kids they had. Both Nantucket games were close. One of the team's wins, a surprising 28–0 blowout of a very good Provincetown team, occurred early on. It sparked some unprecedented support from the islanders, whose attendance numbers grew enough to require several buses delivering people to the games for the first time.

Gerolamo, brimming with youthful energy, loved to laugh with his players. And he knew how to rally his troops. "It was scary in the locker room sometimes," recalls Mike McCarthy. "You'd leave there so pumped up, you'd want to run through a wall for the guy."

In time Gerolamo and the assistant he'd chosen, a fellow teacher named John Bacheller, would rebuild the football program. Their youth was a big factor, Gerolamo says. "We were pretty much fresh out of college. Kids related to us. Other coaches were much older. Talk about a generation gap—this was the 1960s. Trying to create discipline in that time period was not easy. You could either be Woody Hayes, or you could try to get them to come along with you."

For the 1970 season, the coach hired two new assistants, Vineyard graduate Ron Borges and Connecticut native Andy Coe, a Yalie who had been a second-team All-Ivy linebacker. When they traveled to Nantucket that year, Capizzo took the opposing coaches out for dinner. As Gerolamo went around the table making introductions, he mentioned that Borges was the only Vineyard coach who'd played in the island rivalry.

"I know him," said Vito, his eyes narrowing.

Coe, too, knew something about rivalries. He'd played in the infamous Harvard-Yale game of 1968 that ended in an improbable 29–29 tie, and the Harvard comeback still gnawed at him. Upon graduation he'd moved into his grandmother's house out on East Chop. Despite his football experience, Coe was growing interested in radical politics. The following year he left the island to drive out to California in a Volkswagen Beetle, where he worked as a union organizer for Cesar Chavez's United Farm Workers union for $5 a week.

By then, the countercultural spirit had undoubtedly arrived on the islands. The Vineyard in particular—always a little scruffier than its counterpart, where the upper crust was creating its own preppy style with the distinctive salmon-colored khakis known as "Nantucket reds"—began to earn a reputation as a haven for hippie kids. Hitchhiking had always been a neighborly courtesy on the island, so it was easy to get around. Though there was a clear-cut generation gap emerging, the island community's ingrained sense of mutual support meant that the Vineyard was more predisposed than many communities to sympathize with the Vietnam generation.

"The overall theme was feeling for these people," says Tom

Bennett. "Some kids were going astray, and the question was, how can we help them?"

Danny Bettencourt, from Edgartown, was the first Vineyard boy to be killed in the war. Bennett, home on leave during the summer of 1967, bumped into his old friend and teammate William Hagerty on South Beach. Bennett, serving in the Air Force, had just gotten orders to ship out to Turkey. Hagerty had orders for 'Nam. "I remember shaking hands on the beach and wishing him good luck," says Bennett. "That was the last time I ever saw him."

When Bennett first went into the service, he was shocked to witness the realities of the Jim Crow South. In Montgomery, Alabama, where he attended basic training for the Medical Corps, Bennett saw the Confederate flag flying higher on the capitol than the American flag. He went into a cafeteria "for coloreds only" and was refused service. "It was the first time I realized there were things wrong in this country," he once told a writer from the *Martha's Vineyard Times*. Before going to Turkey the young man was stationed at Andrews Air Force Base, where he was a litter bearer, hauling wounded soldiers off planes. It was 1965; the war in Vietnam had just begun escalating with the battle in Ia Drang. "I was nineteen years old," recalled Bennett, "and I was just opening my eyes to the fact that there was a war going on."

In Turkey, Bennett opened the *Stars and Stripes*, the armed forces newspaper, to read about a major drug bust halfway around the world—on his little home island. "They were all guys I'd grown up with," he says. "Some of them played football." When he finished his service and returned to the island, his first job was as a coordinator of volunteers for a drop-in center called Summer Project.

Though Gerolamo and Bacheller were committed to football, they faced some stiff opposition. They spent many evenings during their first few years together attending island school board meetings, where board members and parents were debating whether to drop the program. The injury on the field during the 1968 season helped convince some to call for the abolition of the game. After successfully arguing his case to preserve football on the island, Gerolamo eventually started a booster organization called the Touchdown Club. Revived by Donald Herman, the Touchdown Club funnels thousands of dollars annually into Vineyard football through various fund-raisers. Sales of $10 Purple Pride cards, which provide discounts to island businesses, typically net about $20,000 in a single night.

It was Gerolamo and Bacheller who began the tradition of chartering Air New England (later, Cape Air) jets to take the players to the opposing island for the rivalry games. Flying meant the teams would no longer need to stay overnight. They instituted the practice the year after their team was kept awake by rowdy Nantucketers camped outside their hotel, the historic brick Jared Coffin House on Broad Street. "Our argument was that it was too much responsibility to have the kids over there, managing them overnight," says Gerolamo. "The cheerleaders, and their adrenaline wired . . ."

After four years of futility, fighting to keep the program alive and restore interest in it, Gerolamo finally started earning some rewards. The 1973 season ended just before Thanksgiving with the Vineyard's first homecoming weekend. Eight hundred people—the largest crowd for a game on the island to date, crowed the *Vineyard Gazette* in its front-page coverage—turned out to see the Vineyarders handle the Whalers, 33–6. State Representatives Arthur L. Desrocher of Nantucket and Terrence P. McCarthy of Oak Bluffs (who would soon find himself in the middle of an island controversy) wagered a twenty-pound turkey on the game, with the big bird going to the winning island's hospital.

Early on, the game was tied at six. But a hawkish Vineyard defensive group caused a series of turnovers before the half, setting up three quick touchdowns. Linemen Paul Bagnall and David Look each threw the Whalers for losses, and Peter Moreis fell on a blocked punt at the 26-yard line. Peter's brother Anthony, known to all as "Wills," caught a pass from quarterback Ron Brown for the score.

With its win over Nantucket, the 1973 Vineyard team clinched a tie for the Mayflower League title with Apponequet, who were 50–15 winners over West Bridgewater on that final weekend. The cochampions finished with identical records of 7–2, each 6–1 in the league. When the Nantucket game ended, Vineyard fans streamed onto the field "as balloons supplied by Raul Medeiros floated gaily overhead," the newspaper reported. The opponents then met at Chez Pierre, where they ate pizza together.

THE 1973 VINEYARDERS had survived an early-season incident that threatened to undermine the year before it got under way. Two of the team's better players had argued with Coach Gerolamo during week three, and they walked off the practice field. Later, when they repented, the team took a vote and decided not to let them rejoin.

"I was one of the ones who said, 'Let's don't take them back. We don't want quitters,'" says Ron Brown, who was then in the junior year of one of the Vineyard's most impressive careers. Gerolamo earned the respect of his remaining players when he said, "'If you're not supposed to be on this bus, then get off at the next stop.' He said, 'This is an express, not a local,'" recalls Brown, who has been an assistant coach for the perennial contenders at the University of Nebraska for twenty years, over two stints. In the mid-2000s he took a few years off to serve as the Nebraska state director of the Fellowship of Christian Athletes.

Brown's story is indicative of the middle-class, diversified realities of the year-round populations of both islands. Born out of wedlock to an African American mother from Tennessee and an Indian father then studying in New York, the baby was placed in the New York Foundling. A wealthy New York woman who summered on the island and happened to be involved with the Foundling learned that her groundskeeper, Arthur Brown, and his wife, Pearl, were having trouble conceiving, so she directed them to the orphanage. Arthur and Pearl brought Ron home to the Vineyard with them as a foster child, then officially adopted him two years later. Soon after that, they went back to New York to bring him a sister.

Pearl Brown's parents were originally from Cape Verde. Arthur's mother was a Moreis, making their adopted son an instant member of the island's extended football family. In their Vineyard Haven neighborhood, the Browns were surrounded by four blocks of Araujos and Moreises.

Brown, a gifted athlete, started on the Vineyard varsity for Gerolamo as a freshman, in 1971. During his sophomore year, having moved from tight end to running back, he scored twice in the Vineyarders' only game against Nantucket—beginning that year, the teams would play each other once annually—a 20-point victory that marked the first time in nine matchups, dating back to 1967, when the Vineyard had bested a Capizzo team. One of Brown's runs, for 92 yards, stood for years on the island as a record run from scrimmage. By then, the Vineyarders had become a "dangerous" football team, Brown says, threatening a breakout season.

In Brown's junior year, Gerolamo switched to a wishbone offense, hoping to find ways to maximize production from the talented pool of athletes he suddenly had on his roster. Among them were running backs Mark Landers and Jon Fragosa, blocking tight end Jeffrey Clements, and Wills Moreis, whom Brown believes could have had a solid college career had he chosen one. As quarterback, Brown threw the ball sparingly, sometimes as few as a half dozen times in a game. In a third-and-short situation against Nantucket, in a game that would result in a rare Vineyard blowout, he stepped out of the huddle and noticed that the defensive line was leaving a lot of space in the A-gaps. Brown tapped his center, Tom Welch, on the back of his thigh, signaling their secret cue to switch the play to a quarterback sneak. Fooling everyone, including his own teammates, Brown raced through a hole as wide as a barn door and galloped 40 yards for a touchdown. The final score was 33–6. "We whooped on them pretty good," says Brown.

The previous week, the Vineyard had played Apponequet at home. Led by almost 100 yards rushing from Brown, they took a lead into halftime. But the quarterback threw two sloppy interceptions in the second half, which helped hand the visitor the come-from-behind win that would seal the team's share of the league title. "I got careless and lost my confidence," says Brown, still disappointed almost forty years later. "We lost our poise. I blame myself."

By Brown's senior year, most of his supporting cast had graduated. The team's new starting linebackers included three freshmen whom the players and coaches took to calling the "Peach Fuzz Brigade." Though Brown still holds the record for most points scored for the Vineyard varsity basketball team, taking the team to the state tournament at the old Boston Garden, his football records have been eclipsed by more recent island stars. Yet he chose football over basketball, accepting a scholarship to play at Brown University. Playing defensive back, Ron Brown was chosen twice for the All-Ivy first team, and he was named to the school's Sports Hall of Fame and its All-Century team.

Brown came perhaps closest of any Vineyarder to making the pros, starring for the semipro New Jersey Rams and attending training camps for several coaches in the defunct U.S. Football League in the early 1980s. After a knee injury finally forced him to give up his dream of becoming a pro, he accepted a job as the freshman coach at his alma mater.

Gerolamo never babied him, Brown says, and the former star still appreciates it. He winces as he recalls one game in which he'd played well, only to find himself berated by the coach in the locker room afterward. Gerolamo ticked off the facets of the game on which Brown would have to improve if he hoped to play college football.

"It was embarrassing," the Nebraska coach says. "He took the pedestals away. He was a big stickler for mental toughness." And his coach's lessons have carried over into Brown's own coaching career. Several of Brown's players at Nebraska have gone on to pro careers, including Tyrone Hughes, a Pro Bowl kick returner for the New Orleans Saints, and Johnny Mitchell, a first-round pick in 1992 for the New York Jets. "Even now," Brown says, "I drive my guys hard because I came out of an environment that didn't baby me."

THE 2010 VINEYARD team had a bye week after the Sharon game, so Coach Herman made arrangements to bring his players to a Bridgewater State game off-island. The university, a little over an hour's drive from the Hyannis ferry terminal, had been a prime destination for college-bound Vineyard kids for years. Pam Herman earned her teaching degree there, though she never got around to catching a football game. It was, of course, a running joke in the Herman household, where Bill Belcher, the coach's longtime assistant, was considered Donald's significant other during football season.

The game had local implications for the islanders. Mike McCarthy, the namesake of the former Vineyard running back and AD, had just transferred to Bridgewater State after a year as a redshirt freshman at Merrimack College. He was rooming with Josh Paulson, a fellow islander who'd also played well for Herman. (Also on the Bears' roster was a former Whaler, cornerback Josh Holdgate.)

The Bears were playing Plymouth State, where Mikey's older brother, Eric, happened to be a linebacker coach. "It's a civil war," joked their father a half hour before kickoff. He was standing outside the stadium, scanning the parking lot for the arrival of the two Vineyard school buses. He hoped they weren't lost; the game would take place on the high school field across town from campus, where Bridgewater State's stadium was surrounded by temporary fencing in preparation for a major overhaul.

When the Vineyard players arrived, they were each given a blood-red Bridgewater State T-shirt. The public-address announcer extended a welcome after they took seats under the warm sun on the aluminum grandstand. "It's a good day to get off the rock," he said over the loudspeaker.

Herman and a few of his coaches sat down several rows above the cluster of matching red shirts. Belcher lowered himself gingerly onto the bench, wearing his customary oversized khaki shorts. The scar on one knee was from his recent surgery; he'd be getting the other one cleaned out the day after the season ended. He should have stopped coaching way back in 1995, after his son Greg graduated, he said. "But I like it too much. Plus," he joked, "I've got nothing else to do."

Nearby, line coach Neil Estrella got off his cell phone after checking in at home. His six-year-old daughter had just that week broken two forearm bones in a gymnastics mishap.

The oldest McCarthy boy, Ryan, sat with his father and the coaches, wearing a pair of Chuck Taylors and a revolutionary military cap. After living in Arizona for six years, he'd recently taken a job teaching special-needs students in Connecticut. He made the trip that morning to see his younger brothers face off on opposing sidelines.

The Vineyard players were on their best behavior, fully aware that their coaches were looking over their shoulders. Only

Adaaro Blackhawk, the heavyset sophomore, strayed. He sat on a bench over near the stadium gate, chatting up a high school cheerleader. Dhonathan Lemos, the stocky Brazilian kid who was emerging as a defensive standout, sat with his teammates, beaming. When he'd switched from soccer to football a couple of years earlier, he'd felt out of place. Now he was thoroughly enjoying himself.

With his thick right leg, Lemos made five of his six extra-point attempts the following weekend. James Jette was on hand to see his nephew, Randall, score five touchdowns, one for 90 yards, in a 41–32 shootout victory over league opponent Coyle and Cassidy on their home field. The spectacular young Jette ran for nearly 200 yards, completed three passes for 47 more, and led his team with six tackles. Fullback Tyler Araujo was still out with an ankle sprain. In his absence Brian Montambault, the solid, well-conditioned athlete whom Herman had considered as a lineman, gained over 100 yards of his own, scoring the team's sole touchdown not attributed to Jette.

Still, the coach was not thrilled. Coyle was on its way to a winless season, locked in the basement of the Eastern Athletic Conference. It was good to get a win, but it stung the coach to give an inept team so many scoring opportunities. Coyle had actually led as late as the third quarter, and they kept the game close on a successful flea-flicker. After the game, Herman told the *Cape Cod Times* that his team needed to work on creating more offensive versatility. "We've got to get our slots and receivers involved because we need more than a one-two punch," he said. "Our bread-and-butter play is the option. We feel we have one of the best athletes around in control of that. But he still makes mistakes."

There was work to be done on the defensive side, too. "Where the hell are my linebackers?" the coach thundered the following Friday, as a steady drizzle dripped outside the big shed behind the Dan McCarthy Memorial Athletic Field. It was halftime, with the Vineyard holding a precarious two-score lead against South Shore Vocational Technical School. Herman had made good on his promise to diversify the offense; in the second quarter Jette connected with his best friend, receiver T. J. Vangervan, for a 19-yard touchdown passs. But now the players sat submissively on wooden benches, staring at the ground beneath their cleats, as their coach outlined all of the ways they were failing to secure a sure win. The smell of orange slices mingled with that of soggy, sweat-drenched, grass-stained polyester as Herman paced. "You could've put them away, but you didn't," he grumbled.

The second half began with comic flair, as Lemos's line-drive kickoff drilled a South Shore player in the shoulder and rocketed straight up into the raindrops falling into view under the lights. Jeremy Maciel caught the ball cleanly for a Vineyard fumble recovery. Both teams struggled to make progress until a costly 15-yard face-masking penalty helped the visiting Vikings mount a 37-yard, eleven-play scoring drive.

The fourth quarter was sloppy and frantic. South Shore, wearing the green-and-gold color scheme of the Green Bay Packers, committed a critical turnover, fumbling away a Vineyard punt. Jette was shaken up after a pell-mell scramble that netted just 4 yards, and he needed a moment on the bench. His twiggy backup, a sophomore, fumbled away his first snap. With a little over four minutes left, a South Shore ball carrier converted on fourth down with an end run. One play later, however, linemen Harry

West and Delmont Araujo collapsed the pocket, sacking the Viking quarterback for a big loss. Finally, on fourth and 15, South Shore tried another end-around, but lineman Ramon Espino made the tackle behind the line of scrimmage.

And still it wasn't over. Hoping to chew the clock with his running game, Herman called Montambault's number. The fullback ground out 9 yards on the first play of the series, only to fumble as he was hit. The ball bounced straight back up into his hands. As he was tackled, he banged up his knee.

Players on both sides were letting their frustrations show. "Donald!" Belcher barked into his headset from up in the press booth. "Tell Adaaro to relax!" After Jette willed his team to the 3-yard line, Chris Costello slashed into the end zone for the clincher. At the end of the play, a Vineyarder drew an unsportsmanlike-conduct call, but the score stood. Off in the drizzle, the cannon boomed.

"I expected a lull, but we've had two pretty emotional games," the coach said afterward. His team was 4–0. "We're off to a better start than I thought we'd have," he said. The big test would come the following week, against Somerset.

*Chapter Eight*

# ROLL—CUT—PRINT

F OR YEAR-ROUND ISLANDERS in these two places, "America" is almost a dirty word. Over the years the two islands have shared the perception that they are slighted and forgotten by the American mainland. In 1977 Nantucket and Martha's Vineyard took their collective grievances to an extreme.

At issue was a proposed redistricting for the Massachusetts state legislature. In the late 1960s, state representative John Toomey of Cambridge filed a bill calling for a statewide legislative overhaul, which would have reduced the number of representatives from 240 to 180. In a commonwealth where each elected official represented an average of ten thousand constituents, some of the most egregious examples of unreformed districting occurred on the islands: approximately four thousand Dukes County voters (including Martha's Vineyard and the sparsely populated Elizabeth Islands) had their own representative, while Nantucket County, with just two thousand registered voters at the time, still had its own seat in the State House. The *Boston Globe* argued in favor of the redistricting. The legislature was unconstitutional, the paper proposed, because "it is grossly malapportioned and in flagrant violation of the 'one man, one vote' precept laid down by the U.S. Supreme Court."

Though the Supreme Judicial Court ruled that the islands could keep their representatives for the time being, redistricting remained an open debate nearly a decade later. A week after the New Year's holiday at the beginning of 1977, the Legislative Committee on Redistricting took islanders by surprise when it proposed merging the island counties with the residents of five outer Cape towns, from Chatham to Truro. The plan would lump together the interests of twelve thousand or so islanders with about twice as many Cape Cod residents.

A month later the redistricting committee held a hearing on the Vineyard. Chilmark selectman Everett Poole, a lobsterman whose ancestors had been whalers, argued that the islands had been assured of separate representation in the original state constitution. In fact, Martha's Vineyard was an independent colony for three decades after Thomas Mayhew purchased the islands in 1641. From the days of its earliest European settlement, as historian Ann Coleman Allen told *Martha's Vineyard Magazine*, the island already harbored "a sense of having been separated from the mainstream." Mayhew had been appointed "governor for life" when the state of New York annexed the region in 1671. When meddling Massachusetts assumed jurisdiction over the islands twenty years later—a development that did not please many of the independent-minded islanders—Martha's Vineyard lobbied successfully for its own representation in the state. Nantucket followed suit in 1696.

Now the selectman fumed. "If they want to take that away from us, then the hell with them," Poole warned. "We'll set up another state." Fellow Chilmark selectman Lewis G. King took the proposal more personally still. "We are given short shrift almost all the time," he complained to the committee. "No matter how hard you try to understand, no matter how compassionate you are, you cannot understand how lonely we are."

This feeling of dire isolation was well documented in *People and Predicaments*, the book-length case study of the Vineyard's social troubles that had just been published by Harvard University Press. The author, Milton Mazer, was the psychiatrist who had hired and mentored a young Tom Bennett at the island's Mental Health Center. Mazer's book noted the island's uncommonly high rates of depression, alcoholism, and suicide. The stresses of living year-round in a remote, waterlocked community "cannot be prevented," the author wrote, "but are compensated for to some degree by its inhabitants' awareness of a common destiny."

Four days after the hearing, selectmen from across the island voted to secede from the Commonwealth of Massachusetts if redistricting was approved. Martha's Vineyard would become the fifty-first state in the Union, and the residents of Nantucket were welcome to join. The cause quickly drew widespread attention. One islander wrote a Vineyard "national anthem," and a supporter from the mainland designed a new state flag. When the secession proposal was put to a public referendum, voters on both islands approved it overwhelmingly.

Vineyard representative Terrence P. McCarthy filed a bill mapping the secession movement if redistricting were to pass. When Massachusetts governor Michael Dukakis vowed to veto the bill, the enthusiastic revolutionaries just dug in deeper. They began fielding offers—some half serious, some less so—to join the legislatures of other New England states. Everett Poole received a half gallon of maple syrup from Vermont's governor, who claimed that his state would be thrilled to annex its own coastline. The selectman sent back four pints of quahog chowder. In Maine, the governor's office pointed out that his state had itself separated from Massachusetts in 1820 over "feelings of remoteness," and that it had a representative-to-constituents ratio of 1:2,000.

A few of the most eager secessionists went so far as to suggest that the islands should break completely with the United States and form their own offshore nation. In the end, the secession threat was little more than a publicity ploy. Still, the islanders' voices had been heard. When redistricting passed, the new Cape and islands representative's office created special ambassador positions for the Vineyard and Nantucket. And after nearly a year of amused national news coverage, tourism and real estate—already well established as the bedrock of the islands' long-transforming economies—began their steady rise to the astronomical heights they would reach at the end of the century.

BEFORE THE SECESSION attempt, the hottest topics of conversation on the Vineyard were two things pulled from the water. The first was a 1967 Oldsmobile.

On the morning of July 19, 1969, the car was towed from the water at the edge of a ferry landing called Dike Bridge on Chappaquiddick, the small island, separated from Edgartown by a narrow channel, that makes up the easternmost portion of Martha's Vineyard.

The submerged car belonged to Senator Ted Kennedy, who had accidentally driven into the water late the previous night while escorting a young woman named Mary Jo Kopechne from a nearby party. The gathering was a reunion of the so-called boiler-room girls, six campaign aides from the 1968 presidential bid of the senator's late brother Robert F. Kennedy. Senator Kennedy would later claim that he made repeated attempts to rescue his companion by diving into the water. He then swam five hundred yards across the channel, walked to his hotel room, and collapsed in bed. Kopechne's body was discovered in the morning inside the car, which had flipped upside down into the water. Kennedy's nationally televised appearance a week after the incident would haunt the rest of the senator's life and career. The name of Chappaquiddick Island, meanwhile, would become synonymous with the senator and the death of Mary Jo Kopechne.

Ralston Jackson, the freshman on the 1960 team, remembers how his homeland's name recognition seemed to explode overnight. "When we were playing football, few outside of Massachusetts had heard of Martha's Vineyard," he says. In 1969 he hitchhiked out to California and back: "Whenever I was asked where I was from I had to explain that it was an island. No one had heard of it. When I did a similar trip two years later, all I had to say was 'Martha's Vineyard.' No matter where I was, people knew about it because of Dike Bridge."

A few years later, in the summer of 1974, something else entirely was dragged from the water: a monstrous great white shark. "Roll—Cut—Print!" read the headline on a large spread of sketches that appeared in the *Vineyard Gazette* at the end of the season. The drawings showed the outdoor film set for an upcoming movie named *Jaws*, a new kind of horror film by the young director Steven Spielberg, in which a man-eating shark terrorizes a beachside resort. For filming, Martha's Vineyard was chosen as a stand-in for the fictional Amity, Long Island, as described in Peter Benchley's original novel. The "shark" in the papers, of course, was actually a mechanical model, which the crew took to calling "Bruce," named after Spielberg's lawyer. The film crew paid island natives, many of them children, $5 a day to serve as extras in beach scenes, cavorting in the water and running to dry land, shrieking, each time the shark's dorsal fin surfaced.

When it debuted across the country the following summer, *Jaws* famously set the standard for the movie industry's subsequent summer blockbuster seasons. The first truly successful film to demonstrate the efficacy of a major national ad campaign and a wide-release strategy, *Jaws* has drawn an inordinate amount of attention to the Vineyard over the years. In 2005, an estimated four thousand people attended JAWSfest, a three-day celebration of the film's thirtieth anniversary.

*Jaws* owed an obvious debt to the literary classic that epitomizes Nantucket. The character of Quint, the irascible, mustachioed shark hunter played by veteran actor Robert Shaw, was evidently inspired by *Moby-Dick*'s Captain Ahab. Both men meet their gruesome deaths after becoming obsessed with their prey.

Like Melville's novel, Nantucket remains rooted in the cobblestone streets and horsehead hitching posts of its central town, which looks much the same as it did at the tail end of the whaling industry. There is a certain anachronistic formality that still permeates the island's lifestyle. When Nantucket town is trimmed and illuminated for the island's annual Christmas Stroll, the nineteenth century positively comes to life.

With the exception of the Federal-style captain's houses of

Edgartown, Martha's Vineyard feels like the product of a more recent past. Though Circuit Avenue in Oak Bluffs is now home to upscale clothing stores and cafés, the town's main drag still has traces of its boardwalk heyday of the mid-twentieth century, with old cinema buildings and arcades. In their sweatshirts, waders, and bushy mustaches, many men who live on the Vineyard still look like they just walked off the local crew hired for Spielberg's 1970s production.

As the film crew was making its way off-island after an arduous 159-day shoot (more than 100 days over schedule), Vineyard football coach Jerry Gerolamo was still grappling with sports funding in the school system. At the time, the estimated annual cost of scholastic sports was $35,000, out of a total school budget of $1.4 million. Some were calling for sports to be cut. "We want to insure that the programs we support are life-enhancing," explained a member of the school committee.

Football was then undergoing a period of intense scrutiny on a national level. ABC-TV had just broadcast a special report labeling the game "the danger sport." "We're not trying to justify football on a national level," Gerolamo told a local reporter. "We're trying to look at it in the context of this particular school." Recent graduate Ron Brown testified that the game had given him an Ivy League opportunity he might not otherwise have had. High school junior Patty Leighton told the *Gazette*, "It's a way of sharing. We all share football."

But there wouldn't be much to celebrate on the Vineyard field for a few more years. While the islanders basked in the blockbuster success of "their" movie, the 1975 Vineyarders finished with a disheartening record of 1–7. Though they were never truly blown out, they didn't find ways to win, either. One season-ending wrap-up in the *Gazette* concluded with the most encouraging words the writer could summon: "Basketball practice has started."

One of the few highlights of the following season came when the Vineyard beat Provincetown by 10 on the last weekend of the season, leaving their longtime rivals in sole possession of last place in the league. Quarterback Kenny Davey, who had been injured most of the season, returned to carry his team, running for over 100 yards and passing for 63 more.

Around that time Vito Capizzo arranged for Chuck Fairbanks, then the coach of the Patriots, to make an appearance on the Vineyard. Capizzo knew how much the island rivalry meant to his own program, and he was not about to let those idiots on the Vineyard fold their football team.

Provincetown, once Nantucket's true archrival, had trashed its own football program that season. Though dwindling enrollment and the rising costs of team travel were taking a toll, the death blow came much more abruptly. The Fishermen had a short-tempered coach, a successor to Steve Goveia, Capizzo's old nemesis. In a thumping on their home field at the hands of the Whalers, the coach grew increasingly agitated with the referees. At the beginning of the fourth quarter a Provincetown player ran back a Nantucket kickoff for a touchdown, only to have the play called back on a penalty. The coach snapped. Screaming like a banshee, he ordered his team to stop playing, effectively forfeiting the game. In the confusion, the refs told the Nantucket coaches to keep their players on the field until the clock ran out. Those eight minutes "seemed like an eternity," says Dick Herman. Provincetown never again played a high school football game.

After losing one league rival, Capizzo was determined to reinforce the Whalers' annual meetings with the Vineyard. "We saved their program that year," he told the *New York Times*.

WHEN GEROLAMO STEPPED down after the 1976 season, John Bacheller, who'd been the coach's assistant through 1973, was lured back. "I'm putting my name in only because I don't want to see the program disappear," Bacheller said.

He did better than that. In his first year, the team got off to an 0–4 start before Bacheller shook up his roster. When he moved several players to new positions, the wins started coming. He made hefty center Matt Ferro the new fullback, and he moved Mike Gibson, previously an end, to quarterback. The Vineyarders rattled off five straight wins and wound up with a winning record, culminating in an exhilarating 14–12 win over Nantucket. Gibson scored one touchdown and Ferro, "the big lug," ran for 82 yards and the other Vineyard score. "They were just sky-high for this game," Bacheller said after it was over.

So were the fans. Apathy toward the football program was suddenly becoming a thing of the past. New athletic director Mike McCarthy was making plans to start a booster club with $1 memberships, and the hundreds who turned out to see the island face-off made their presence known. "Multi-colored confetti burst through the cold fall air whenever the Vineyard gained or Nantucket slipped," wrote the *Gazette*'s reporter. "Orange plastic horns delivered toots of approval at touchdown and penalty calls . . . All signs at the Saturday afternoon battle with Nantucket said this was a football island."

There was a simple explanation, said Sancy Pachico, by then the assistant superintendent of schools.

"Nantucket draws," he said.

Bacheller grew up in Danvers, a suburban town north of Boston, where two neighboring cities, Beverly and Salem, shared an award that went to the winner of their annual Thanksgiving matchup. It was the coach's father who first suggested some sort of trophy for the offshore rivalry.

Plenty of other traditional rivalries featured spoils, such as the Little Brown Jug, the five-gallon earthenware vessel that came to symbolize Michigan's Big Ten rivalry with Minnesota. "Do the islands have anything like that?" asked Bacheller's dad.

They did not. Bacheller contacted Capizzo and asked whether he'd be interested. He'd go to the trophy shop in Falmouth to pick it out, the Vineyarder offered. He and Tankard chose a two-foot-tall silver chalice with a Heisman-like athlete in motion on the lid and spread-wing eagles guarding the corners of the base.

The Nantucket coach was welcome to go see it and decide if he approved, Bacheller said. "Nobody seems to know whether he did or not," said the former coach one afternoon during the 2010 season. Now retired from his final post as an assistant principal, he was sitting on a couch on the four-season porch of his tidy Vineyard Haven home, wearing an L. L. Bean chamois shirt and a pair of chukka boots. His wife leaned into the room to say hello. She was wearing a purple sweater. It was, after all, a Friday in autumn.

Contrary to the claims of many Vineyarders, Vito did contribute toward the Island Cup—fifty bucks, Bacheller thinks. Somewhere in the house he still has a copy of the check from his Dukes County Savings Bank account, made out for $102.40 to the Falmouth Trophy Shop.

The first official Island Cup game did not go well for the Vineyard. On the Whalers' home field, the Nantucketers trounced their visitors, 36–0, carried by the fleet feet of a sophomore running back named Beau Almodobar. It was over by halftime, with the compact back scoring three touchdowns before the break. Capizzo's defense held the opponent to less than 100 total yards rushing. "All traditional football rivalries are supposed to be close," complained the writer for the *Cape Cod Times*. He would have to wait.

Football was still facing plenty of scrutiny. The plight of Patriots wide receiver Darryl Stingley was in the news after he was paralyzed from the neck down on a tackle by the Oakland Raiders' self-proclaimed "assassin," Jack Tatum, during a preseason game that August. Meanwhile, *Newsweek*'s public affairs manager wrote a widely syndicated opinion piece for the *New York Times* in which he lamented his lifelong injuries from the sport and his coaches' disregard for player safety. "Football coaches tell you only the Good Truth—that playing college football will be exciting, prestigious, and a challenge," he wrote. "When it is all over you will have nothing to show for it except permanent injuries and, if you are lucky, a bowl game wristwatch and a monogram sweater."

On the islands the coaches had their hands full keeping their athletes out of trouble. "We had to really stay on the kids to keep them clean," says Tankard, who took over as head coach on the Vineyard in 1980 after Bacheller stepped down from the program for the second time.

One player who could discipline himself was David Araujo, Tankard's nephew, who was also a nephew of Joe Araujo, the fullback for the 1960 team. On the Vineyard, the Araujo family name is recognized as the name on the purple Port-O-Lets behind the football field. Members of the family co-own an island-wide septic system service. The Araujos are also known for their legacy on the field.

David was the first of a new generation of Araujo boys who would dominate the Vineyard rosters into the 1990s. His 1,200 rushing yards playing tailback in his senior year, 1984, would stand as the team record for more than a decade. Araujo's younger brother, Jason, played, as did cousins Woody, Derek, and Aaron. Another cousin, Todd, would become a Vineyard leader in several categories over the course of his own career. Some said Woody had the most natural ability of the bunch; Aaron, who later played some semipro football for the Cape Cod Bears, was the one who might have had the best shot at playing in the pros. "Aaron was solid as a rock," says Tankard.

Though he was an uncle to all the Araujos who played for him, Tankard was often harder on them than he was on the rest of his players. In fact, David Araujo went home after practice one day and told his mother he was going to quit. "So turn in your uniform," she said. The next day he practiced.

Araujo's parents had separated when he was twelve, and he'd looked up to his uncle as a role model ever since. His mother came to every one of his games, but his father, he recalls, showed up only sporadically. "I was looking for my dad's approval," just like so many boys from broken homes, says the counselor.

If Tankard was a father figure, he seldom let up on the eldest of his football-playing nephews, whose talent level was so much higher than his peers' that he had a tendency at times to coast. David's uncle felt he had to push him to play consistently exceptional football. In his high school years, the game wasn't always

David's first love. Though he was scouted seriously by schools including BC and Army, he eventually accepted a scholarship to run track for the University of Connecticut.

Upon graduation David spent almost a decade in the Jamaica Plain neighborhood of Boston, working on contracts for the Department of Public Health. When he first moved back to the Vineyard, he got a job in a liquor store. Now he's a licensed therapist for Martha's Vineyard Community Services. He's also one of Donald Herman's assistants.

"I wanted to help people in my own community, not people I didn't know," he said, sitting in his cramped office in the rambling complex opposite the high school, behind the skate park. A box of Legos sat on the floor; a tiny orange Wiffle bat for his young son, Ryan, jutted out of his leather briefcase in the corner. On the bookshelf, titles included *Honor Your Anger* and Irvin Yalom's *Theory and Practice of Group Psychology*.

The thoughtful, bespectacled Araujo was not always thrilled with the way his uncle challenged him on the playing field. His teammates noticed, too. Peter Duart was a cocaptain for Tankard who blocked alongside big Eric Blake, the future Oak Bluffs police chief. Between the two of them, they carried about 500 pounds. The team, unsurprisingly, ran many of its plays right behind them. One day in practice Duart asked his coach why he was tougher on the Araujos than the rest of the team. Tankard was stunned by the comment. He hadn't realized he was overcompensating against the possibility that he appeared to be partial toward his nephews.

The coach had a particular affection for players who made up for their lack of size with an abundance of effort. Scotty Dario, who runs a bus company with his father, Jack, a former athletic director at the high school, was a bantamweight whom Tankard made into a running back and linebacker on his teams of the mid-1980s. "He was a little thing, but he'd hit you with all his hundred and twenty-five pounds," recalls the coach. When he carried the ball, it often took two or three tacklers to drag him down. Scotty's older brother, Jimmy, who graduated in 1982, was another standout, representing the island in the Mayflower League all-star game.

Spike Smith, who was an inch or two taller and a couple of ticks heavier than Scotty Dario, was another courageous tackler, a defensive back who threw his body around like a bag of bricks. Concussions had not yet become a topic of debate, but Tankard is convinced Smith must have suffered several of them. "He got his bell rung all the time," he says. "Back in those days, we just thought it was a 'Welcome to high school football' thing."

If Tankard's Vineyarders had enough talent to be a force, says James Jette, they never quite put it all together. Jette, known in those days as Jimmy, took over as the team's primary running back in 1984, when Woody Araujo went down with an ankle injury against Blue Hills. Jette's performance that day (as he remembers it, two touchdowns and a two-point conversion) earned him Player of the Game honors. The following year—the year that the Vineyard finally beat Nantucket after a seven-year drought—he was the team's MVP, and he was named to the Mayflower's All-League team.

Jette moved to the island with his younger brother, Bernard, a year before he was due to start high school. The four Jette siblings, including sisters Christine and Grace, were raised in the Jamaica Plain neighborhood of Boston. Personal issues in the family, combined with the lingering effects of the city's infamous school busing problems of the 1970s, spurred a decision to have the siblings move to the Vineyard. Their great-aunt, Mary Holman, then in her seventies, had recently retired to her summer home in Oak Bluffs. Christine and Grace went first, and the two boys followed two years later.

The Jettes were already familiar with the island from summertime vacations at their great-aunt's place. The school year was another story. If there were tens of thousands of people on the island in the warm weather, the number dwindled in those days to six thousand or so for the off-season. Classrooms in Brighton, where Jette had been bused, were packed with as many as thirty-five students. In Oak Bluffs, there were sometimes as few as eight to a teacher. Jette's high school graduating class would include just ninety students. And the island could be a lonely, painfully quiet place in the off-season.

"I'd never had the winter experience there before," says Jette, now principal of Pierce Middle School in Milton, just south of Boston. "That was shocking to me." Fortunately, his great-aunt lived in a neighborhood with several athletic boys who were James's age. Mike Joyce, Mike deBettencourt, Jason Harris, and Jette became fast friends, and they were also becoming a basketball powerhouse. Playing together in middle school in Oak Bluffs, they demolished their competition. They played in the same summer leagues and then on the Vineyard varsity together. In their senior year, all four were named to the Cape and Islands team. They reached the state championships, where they lost to Dorchester's Jeremiah Burke High School. They also ran track together; the four friends went to the states in the sprint relay in their senior year.

Tankard, a well-groomed man with a trim mustache and a

fondness for fitness clothing, could do his share of shouting on the football field. Not that he had a foul mouth. "Gee whiz, man!" he'd holler when a player jumped offsides or blew an assignment. Off the field, he had a chummy word for everyone, and he parlayed his gregarious nature into the principal's job at West Tisbury Middle School. Years later, Tankard started his own local interview show, *Tank Talk*, on Martha's Vineyard Community Television, hosting discussions of island issues and conversations with high-profile visitors such as former UN ambassador Andrew Young and *Jaws* star Richard Dreyfuss.

For James Jette, as with David Araujo, Tankard was a father figure. The coach was a confidant and a mentor, says Jette, and not just for him, but for plenty of his teammates as well. "He helped me more than he even realized," says Jette. With two daughters at home, Tankard got as much out of his relationship with his players as they did from him.

Mike Joyce, who would later become another of the Vineyard's athletic directors, was one of the better quarterbacks the island ever produced, leading the successful 1985 football team. With Joyce and Jette in the backfield that year was Glenn Gonsalves, another undersized overachiever who went on to play some college football at Bridgewater State. As a boy, Gonsalves hung around the gym at Tisbury Elementary in Vineyard Haven, where Tankard, then Bacheller's assistant, was the phys ed teacher. Even then, everyone called him Coach T.

The Gonsalves were yet another family intertwined with the Araujos and Moreises; Ron Brown's adoptive mother, Pearl, was Glenn's aunt. At age ten, Glenn Gonsalves was the water boy for the Vineyarders. He remembers watching a pretty good player named David Grain, who played wide receiver for Bacheller and Tankard in the late 1970s before moving on to study at Holy Cross. Grain was a big-time achiever, the youngest child in a large family that moved to the island when he was thirteen, when the patriarch, Walter, retired from the trucking business. Walter Grain put all seven of his children through college and most of them through graduate school; David's older siblings included a neurosurgeon, an architect, and a computer scientist. David Grain went on to become a highly regarded businessperson—a Wall Street millionaire, a senior vice president at AT&T, and the CEO and founder of his own wireless communications company. He raised hundreds of thousands of dollars for Barack Obama, who would soon become a summertime Vineyard regular, during the president's 2008 election campaign.

A few years after handing water bottles to players like David Grain, Glennie Gonsalves was wearing the purple himself. By his own admission just five-seven and 160 pounds in high school, he blew out his knee in the first half of the Nantucket game during his senior year. He got back from the hospital just in time to see Eric Blake make the play of the game, an interception that he ran back for the clinching touchdown.

Injuries would curtail Gonsalves's college career, too: When he was a junior at Bridgewater State, a nagging hamstring injury kept him off the field for most of a season in which the Bears went undefeated before losing in the ECAC Division III North finals. He got a measure of consolation a year later. Playing slot back for the school, where he would eventually become an assistant AD, he was summoned to replace his roommate, the team's starting quarterback, after an injury at Stonehill College. With the Bears losing at halftime, Gonsalves ran the team's option offense to perfection in the second half, running for 205 yards and scoring three touchdowns to seal a thrilling come-from-behind win.

But none of his memories are quite as vivid as his very first play on the Vineyard varsity, when he ran back a kickoff to begin the second half of a game against West Bridgewater. Glenn's two older brothers, Wayne and Brian, both of whom had been Vineyard players in Grain's era, were at the game, and they ran the length of the sideline alongside their kid brother, shouting joyously all the way into the end zone. On the radio, Ken Goldberg had to re-create the play a few moments later, without any crowd noise. The station's commercial break had run long.

*Chapter Nine*

## LIKE "CHOPSTICKS" FOR MONK

B Y  T H E  T I M E  the *New Yorker* sent writer Charles McGrath to chronicle the island rivalry in a lengthy, elegiac feature story that ran during the last week of 1984, the Island Cup game had reached near-mythical proportions. McGrath estimated that a thousand spectators attended the game he saw that fall on Nantucket. When the Vineyard hosted, the crowds had grown as big as three thousand or more. Considering the scrawny full-time populations of both islands, the numbers were considerable. "Collectively, the spectators formed a kind of diorama of contemporary New England," McGrath observed: "kids in snowsuits; old gents in felt hats and tweed overcoats and flannel shirts; bearded young fishermen, with ponytails coming out from beneath their knitted watch caps; small boys in stocking caps piggybacked on top of bareheaded fathers; babies in crocheted bonnets; preppies in down vests and Bean shoes; grandmothers in print kerchiefs; middle-aged women with frosted hair, wearing leg warmers and fur coats; girls in short, wide-shouldered jackets and tight jeans; men in corduroy car coats and tweed caps; even a couple of women wrapped in blankets—all stamping their feet and beating their arms, eager for football."

BEAU ALMODOBAR WAS always eager for football. He came from a large family of boys, including his twin, Dino, twenty-five minutes older; their younger brother, Daniel, whom everyone called Dan-boy, born a year to the day after the twins; and a half brother, Manuel Martin, who was seven years younger than Dan-boy. Beau was named Darian; as a toddler, already shot through with energy, he amused his grandfather with his crazy-legged dance steps whenever someone put the music on. "Go, Bojangles, go!" his grandfather would hoot, and it stuck. Nicknames were a family trait. The boys' mother, Verna, called Manuel "Mano," after a character on the television Western *The High Chaparral*, which was popular at the time of his birth.

Mike Almodobar, the boys' biological father, was a wild one, a young schemer who left his wife and children in San Francisco and embarked on a long career as the leader of a bank-robbing ring before he was finally caught and imprisoned. The brothers recently traveled to Arizona, where their father had been living, to meet him for the first time as adults.

After her husband left, Verna met a merchant marine named John Martin in a Cape Verdean bar in San Francisco, and they fell in love. Martin was a Nantucket native, and the new couple eventually moved with Verna's three sons to the island of Martin's birth. It was the first time she had been to the East Coast.

Beau Almodobar, his wife, Liz, and their two children still live in the Atlantic Avenue cottage where he grew up, just a block from both the public school complex and the island's Boys and

Girls Club. John Martin's mother owned two adjacent homes on the first block of Atlantic, renting one out. When Martin brought his family back from San Francisco, they took over the rental property.

From the time Beau and Dino were seven, when they could start taking advantage of the resources the Boys Club had to offer, they were at the big old building constantly. When the weather was bad, they'd be in the gym, playing touch football. The club was practically in their backyard, a two-minute walk around the corner. Football at the Nantucket Boys Club was a well-developed program, with several levels of competition from midgets on up. The Almodobars played for several former Whalers, including Jimmy Duarte, the rock-and-roll bandleader, and Bruce Watts, the fire chief. One alum from Capizzo's first undefeated team, Manny "Bubba" Perry, was a particular inspiration for Beau. He was the club's athletic director, an older cousin to Joe Perry, who would become Beau's high school teammate, and Joe's younger brother, Richard. A cocaptain of the 1966 team, Bubba was an exceptional athlete. More than that, however, he was a mentor. He refereed the Boys Club games, patiently explaining his penalty calls. "In my mind, he was a guy you could look up to," says Almodobar. "He ran that program very strict. You knew the rules. Everyone respected Bubba. If he raised his voice, you knew you were in trouble."

Not that Perry had to raise his voice very often. He never lifted his hand to anyone or berated the kids. It was a marked contrast to Vito's temperamental style. Almodobar has a theory about his high school coach: with his Sicilian accent, Capizzo stood out like a neon sign in the salty old New England culture of the island. "People here knew he was different," says the former running back, "so he had to have that tough-guy persona. He was going to get the best out of his players no matter what, and he pushed their buttons." In those days, Almodobar notes, parents as often as not sided with coaches, not their sons. If a boy came home complaining that the coach had cursed him, his father was likely to assume that the boy must have deserved it.

By his own admission, Almodobar was not especially fast or quick. At just five-nine, maybe 175 pounds, he certainly wasn't big enough to run over tacklers. But he had moves—an abundance of infuriating, quicksilver moves. By the time he got to high school, he also had the luxury of a bumper crop of blockers his age who had size and agility. Bucking the odds for a group drawn from a tiny student population such as Nantucket's, his linemen were a hefty bunch. Center Stephen Marks was 210. David Diamond, whose father was the school principal, was 220. Greg Moore, the right guard, was 210 or so. Bobby Ramos was the biggest of them all—six-three, 230. "I had some big guys," recalls Almodobar. "And they were tough. They weren't just taking up space."

Blessed with a bright personality and a can-do spirit, Beau knew as a teenager that he wanted to try to play the game professionally. He'd lie on his bed and gaze at the posters on his wall, posters that came with his subscription to *Sports Illustrated*, featuring the best running backs in the game at the time: Walter Payton, the silky Chicago Bear known as "Sweetness"; Terry Metcalf, the St. Louis Cardinal who set an NFL record in 1975 for most combined yards in a season; and Tony Dorset, the Dallas Cowboy and former Heisman Trophy winner who was the aspiring Whaler's favorite player. "I wanted to play pro football," Almodobar says. "That's all I ever wanted to do, my whole life."

By his junior year, touchdowns came as easily for him as "Chopsticks" came to Thelonious Monk. Almodobar had an uncanny nose for the end zone, scoring "twenty-five or twenty-six" touchdowns, as he recalls. That season he tied for the state lead in points scored—a whopping 204—with one of the all-time great running backs in the state, Joe Fuller, who played for Greater Lowell. (Fuller scored precisely the same number of points during the 1978 season, too.)

The Whalers lost their first game of that 1979 season to Norwell in disappointing fashion, on a blocked punt. It would be the team's last taste of losing for a good long stretch. Vito's boys reeled off twenty-three straight victories after the Norwell loss, extending through the following autumn, which would see the Whalers' second undefeated season under Coach Capizzo. "I always thought the '79 team was more talented than the '80 team," says Dick Herman. "They just hadn't caught on to winning yet."

Over the next several seasons, it would all come together for Nantucket football. The team went 56–7 between 1979 and 1984, including the undefeated year and three more seasons with just one loss. Thirty-one of the victories would come by shutout. "We just rolled over people," says Herman.

In addition to running the ball, Almodobar threw a lot of halfback passes, many of them to Dan-boy, just to keep the opposing defenses honest. Despite Beau's star status, his brothers never felt as though they were playing in his shadow. "They always kept me in my place," he says, "which was a good thing." The 1979 Whalers had Jay Anderson at quarterback, who ran the option flawlessly in an easy win against the Vineyard; Jimmy Hughes, Taylor's linebacker father; and Bobby Hickman, a kid who had been Capizzo's water boy and then a babysitter for the coach's young son, Scott. (Vito would later serve as best man at Hickman's wedding.)

The 1979 team might have had more depth, says Almodobar, but his own class of 1980 was more talented. That team also had the kind of camaraderie that makes certain teams special. Before double sessions began that August, Almodobar's teammates— Joe Perry, Steve Ciarmataro, and Scott Herrick, who took over for Anderson at quarterback—started talking about going to a state Super Bowl.

After steaming through its first nine games, Nantucket put its eighteen-game win streak, its undefeated record, and a Mayflower League title on the line against another mediocre Vineyard team. It was no contest. An interception immediately after the opening kickoff set up Almodobar for a 5-yard touchdown run; Perry's two-point conversion made it 8–0 one minute into the game. It was 31–0 by halftime, 31–12 at the end. The Whalers held the purple to an embarrassing −15 yards on the day. "This team is a powerhouse," Vineyard coach Bob Tankard said afterward, stating the obvious. He and his players would support them as they headed off to the championship game: "They're representing the islands as well as Nantucket."

In early December the Whalers traveled off-island and north on I-495 to Battis Field in the town of Middleborough, where they played the Super Bowl game. Their opponent was Christopher Columbus, a Boston-based Catholic high school (now defunct). The team was led by running back Jim Costigan, a state rushing leader who was named Division 5 player of the year. Almodobar twisted his ankle in practice the day before the game. Game day was cold, and as he iced it down in the Middleborough locker room, he was worried.

Nantucket High graduate Billy Santos sat in the stands with a couple of his buddies from college. He'd come to see his cousin Bobby Ramos play. Santos's father, Isky, was a former selectman who was often called the "Mayor of 'Sconset." "I remember that big running back," says Santos, who owns a rubbish-removal company under the family name. "They stymied him."

In the early going the teams battled back and forth, breaking for halftime with the score knotted at 20. By then, however, Nantucket's biggest offensive weapon had forgotten all about his injury. After the half he took the opening kickoff at his own 10-yard line, bobbled it, then retrieved it at the 5. Then he bolted upfield, all the way into the end zone, for an improbable 95-yard touchdown. Nantucket never let up after that, coasting to a 44–20 Super Bowl victory.

"I think we just wore them down," says Almodobar, who remembers running the ball nearly every play that day. Near the finish, after carrying the ball more than ten plays in a row, he lay on the sideline, utterly exhausted.

As the accolades piled up, Beau began to believe he might really make football his career. The letters started pouring in, from Yale, Boston College, and elsewhere. Eventually he settled on Norwich, the military academy in midstate Vermont, which had been the first school to send a recruitment letter. When he visited the campus, he found, much to his surprise, that he was impressed with the military focus of the place. "Something clicked," he says. "I went with my gut instinct."

But just after his mother and stepfather dropped him off to move in as a freshman, he learned that he wasn't guaranteed an opportunity to play. There was a good-sized guy who'd be the starting tailback, one of the coaches told the newcomer. We know you're a team player. Would you be willing to try playing flanker?

Though the school motto is "I Will Try," Almodobar was not especially inclined. At the team's first classroom meeting, players were seated according to the depth chart at their positions. To his horror, the rookie was placed in the fifth row of wide receivers. "Fifth string!" he recalls, still smarting. "I called my dad and said, 'This isn't for me.' And he said, 'If you come home, I'm going to kick your fucking ass.'"

A freak series of injuries to the receiving corps soon gave the discouraged freshman his chance. First the starter hurt his ankle. Then, in the preseason opener, the second-stringer broke his collarbone. When the next guy went down with a strained hamstring in the team's first game, the flanker ahead of Almodobar promptly dropped the first passes thrown in his direction. At halftime, the coach looked at the Nantucket kid. "You ready?" he asked. Almodobar caught a few passes in the second half, including one for a touchdown, and his college career was under way.

For the 1984 season, his senior year playing for the Division III Cadets, Almodobar was named an All-American on both the Kodak and Pizza Hut teams. The Cadets finished 9–2, the best record a Norwich squad has ever compiled. After graduation Almodobar picked up with a semipro football team, the Connecticut Giants. The team program noted that practice visitors Jim Kelly and Doug Flutie especially liked throwing to the sure-handed receiver. The Giants won league championships in both of Almodobar's seasons with them. He has the rings.

But the pay wasn't much, and he found work as a carpenter

to make ends meet. It was far from glamorous, and it seemed as though it was time to give up the dream and decide on an alternative career path. In the fall of 1987, however, the NFL Players Association organized a walkout to protest a labor dispute. The players went on strike two games into the season. Week three was cancelled, and each NFL team went about the sticky business of assembling replacement teams. After trying out alongside two hundred hopefuls (about twenty from the Connecticut team), Almodobar was one of forty or so players who caught on with the New York Giants—the defending Super Bowl champions. His new head coach was Bill Parcells; the defensive coordinator was a prodigy named Bill Belichick. Almodobar signed a contract for the players' minimum. "I looked at that contract for an hour," he remembers. "It was more money than I'd ever had." When he first sat down in the locker room at the old Giants Stadium in East Rutherford, New Jersey, he was overwhelmed. I can't believe it's me, he thought.

He played receiver and returned punts and kickoffs in the Giants' three games over the duration of the strike. He played alongside Lawrence Taylor and quarterback Jeff Hostetler, two of the veterans who crossed the picket line. Still, it was not the best of circumstances. The replacements lost all three games, effectively ruining any chance the team had to repeat as champions. When the strike ended and the holdouts returned, Parcells called the Nantucketer into his office. The memory is still vivid. "You're a good football player," he told Almodobar, "but we're going to have to let you go."

On the bus home out of New Jersey, Almodobar thought long and hard about what he'd just been through and what he would do next. Getting a taste of pro football, even during a strike, was an amazing stroke of good fortune, he finally decided. At least you got to play.

He went back to school, to Springfield College, where he soon earned his master's degree. After serving there briefly as an assistant football coach, he took a job as AD and phys ed teacher at Thayer High School in Winchester, New Hampshire, where he remained for five years. While back at home on the island for Christmas one year in the mid-1990s, he bumped into Earl Girroir, the executive director of Beau's beloved Boys and Girls Club, in a Cumberland Farms convenience store. "Ever think about coming back to work here?" asked Girroir, a former boxer and baseball prospect. Girroir's was the only Boys Club in the state that ran a football program. He funded a $100,000 annual budget with donations and memberships, which were just $2 or $3 apiece. When Girroir first arrived on the island, the Boys Club football team had twenty-two jerseys, twenty-two helmets, and one football. Each time the coaches (among them Dick Coffin, the onetime high school coach, and Dick Glidden, the former quarterback, who often roamed the sidelines in the suits he wore to his law office) made substitutions, their players had to change shirts on the field. "We treasured what we had," said Girroir.

Almodobar took the bait: he moved back and became the AD. He spent one year as Girroir's successor as executive director before moving into the public school system. When his old coach, Capizzo, retired as the middle school gym teacher, he encouraged his former star running back to apply.

HOURS BEFORE NANTUCKET'S 1981 home opener, the year after the team's Super Bowl victory, workers were hustling to finish the roofing on the new field house. After the old one burned to the ground, local builders Dick Kalman and Ron Da Silva, both former players, offered crews to build the new two-story facility, which was quickly dubbed "Capizzo's Castle."

The king was feeling a bit dyspeptic, or at least that's the way another former player, Nick Ferrantella, saw things in his coverage of the first game for the *Inky*. Madison Park, the visiting team against which the Whalers would open their next four seasons, was a nonleague opponent, a city team from Roxbury, and the coach was unsure what to expect. He'd already figured that his squad would have some offensive difficulties, given the number of leaders from the championship team who'd graduated.

With "a stomach full of butterflies and a pocket full of Rolaids," as Ferrantella imagined, Capizzo watched as one of his exchange students, a Chilean kid named Yuri Vega, used his soccer-style kicking to put up the first 3 points of the season. The ball banged the crossbar before flipping end over end through the uprights. Winning 17–12, the team was led by junior John Bartlett's fantastic defensive performance. The farm boy, who preceded his twin brothers (Dan, a future cop, and David, who would injure his hand in a thresher accident) as Capizzo favorites, logged eight sacks and many more unassisted tackles, and the *Globe* named him Division 5 Player of the Week.

The following weekend's shutout win over the regional technical school at Bristol-Plymouth ran the team's unbeaten string to twenty-two, prompting the local paper to note that Concord High School had set the state record with fifty-six straight victories beginning in the late 1940s. If Capizzo was thinking about it, he didn't let on. "It's nice to be on a streak," he said, "but we don't play it up."

That was the right answer. The streak screeched to a halt the following week, in a shocking 12–6 loss to West Bridgewater. Was the coach relieved? asked a reporter. "No," he replied angrily. Though he wasn't inclined to be more forthcoming than that, he finally gave his interrogator a few more words. His Whalers had beaten themselves, Capizzo said. He'd be shaking things up in the coming week's practice, that was for sure. "I don't like to lose," said the coach, "and I don't plan to anymore this season, I'll tell you that."

He was angrier still the next week, when Nantucket dropped another game, this time to Apponequet, by a single point. The team had "no killer instinct," Capizzo complained. They'd been inside the 10-yard line nine times in the two losses, with just two touchdowns to show for it.

They couldn't get into the end zone the next week, either. At the end of regulation play, the Whalers were locked in a scoreless tie with Manchester, a powerful team from the North Shore. State rules called for both teams to get the ball for one series of downs in overtime, each starting at their opponent's 10-yard line. After Joe Perry gained 7 on the first play, Bartlett stormed into the end zone on a halfback draw. The defense sandwiched Manchester on its set of downs, and the Whalers won, 6–0. "We regained our pride this week," said Capizzo. Not only that, but they got some unlikely help: the Vineyard upset Apponequet, keeping alive Nantucket's hopes for another league title, at least for the time being.

The rest of the season featured the sudden rise of freshman Tim Ostebo, who was given the opportunity to jump-start the sputtering Whaler offense. A classic golden-boy quarterback with a tousle of sandy hair and a ski-slope nose, Ostebo would be described in the *New Yorker* article three years later, after the completion of his senior year, as having "the quiet, almost royal bearing of the one boy in every high school class who everyone knows is special." In his varsity debut as a starter Ostebo, wearing number 9, threw touchdown passes to Perry, Rocky Fox, and Dana Howard, leading the team to a 41–0 laugher over a hapless squad from Southeastern.

Going into the Island Cup game, the Whalers knew they were out of the running. At 6–3 they were tied with Blue Hills for second place; the league title would go to either Manchester or Norton, both of which were 8–1. Though the Vineyarders came in with shaved heads—reminiscent of the 1977 season finale, when they'd stunned their rivals with that 14–12 upset—they proved to be no threat, bowing 25–0.

Despite falling short of a postseason berth, Capizzo and his staff could take solace in the fact that they were playing in what was perhaps the best Division 5 league in the state. Theirs was still the smallest high school in Massachusetts, with only a little over two hundred students. When they whitewashed Old Colony 40–0 in the second game of the 1982 season, the players carried their coach off the field: it was his one hundredth win. Twenty Old Colony players had quit the previous week, after an even more brutal drubbing in their season opener. Still, the score counted. Vito's only son, Scott, was then in middle school, awaiting his turn to play for his old man, by now an island legend. "In another forty years you might break Bear Bryant's record," Scott told his father.

Over the next few weeks it became apparent that the Whalers had regrouped from the relative disappointment of their 1981

Captains meet at midfield, 1969. (Photo © Chuck Davis/tidalflatsphoto.com)

A whale of a game. (Photo © Chuck Davis/tidalflatsphoto.com)

Former Martha's Vineyard coach Jerry Gerolamo, 1969.
(Photo © Chuck Davis/tidalflatsphoto.com)

Nantucket coach Vito Capizzo with star running back Beau Almodobar. (Courtesy of Beau Almodobar)

Nantucket's Donick Cary, who went on to become a television writer.
(Courtesy of Donick Cary)

Future Nantucket coach John Aloisi celebrates an Island Cup
victory with friend Josh Kane. (Courtesy of Matt Aloisi)

Coach Donald Herman. (Courtesy of Diane Caponigro)

"The Kick," 2004. (Photo by Ralph Stewart, reprinted with permission from the *Martha's Vineyard Times*, 2004)

Archrivals share a laugh. (Photo by Ralph Stewart)

Under Donald Herman, the Vineyard program flourished. (Photo by Ralph Stewart)

First two island inductees to the Great American Rivalry Series Hall of Fame: Vito Capizzo and Jason Dyer. (Photo by Ralph Stewart, reprinted with permission from the *Martha's Vineyard Times*, 2010)

The Vineyard's Randall Jette outraces Nantucket's Terrel Correia.
(Photo by Ralph Stewart, reprinted with permission from the *Martha's Vineyard Times*, 2010)

Nantucket assistant coach Beau Almodobar watches from the tower as the 2010 Island Cup game gets under way on Martha's Vineyard. (Courtesy of Diane Caponigro)

Touchdown, Nantucket. (Courtesy of Diane Caponigro)

season. Capizzo's defenses were always stingy; now his offense was dominating again, too. After a 26–0 shutout over Apponequet, the team narrowly defeated Blue Hills, its chief competition in the Mayflower League that year, in nasty weather conditions that became monsoon-like in the second half. Sophomore Richard Perry, Joe's younger brother, was emerging as an elite running back; it was his 79-yard first-half gallop that sealed the win. Glidden remembered the younger Perry from the touch football games in the Boys Club gym, when the kid was in seventh grade. No one could touch him.

Nantucket earned its fourth shutout of the season against previously undefeated Norton, which had one of the three wins against Capizzo's team the year before. "We weren't going to underestimate them two years in a row," said Dick Herman after the game. It was starting to look as though the season-ending Vineyard game might have some real consequences: the purple had just one loss on the season, to Norton. "They've been talking about it since September seventeenth," Capizzo groused.

The Whalers gave up 13 points over their next three games, breaking the scoreless streak at five games. The fact that the seniors had to take their SATs on the morning of the game against Bristol-Plymouth contributed to "a lot of mental mistakes" in the first quarter, Capizzo complained. He was grasping at straws: the island won, 47–7.

True to expectations, the Vineyard played them tough—just not tough enough. Despite injuries to Perry and Steve Visco, his fellow running back, the Nantucket offense put 12 points on the board, and the defense kept a zero on the other side.

Though Capizzo knew his team had clinched another Super Bowl berth the week before the Island Cup, he would not accept a letdown.

"Nothing's official until you beat the Vineyard," he told his players.

OCTOBER 2010

AFTER THE TOUGH West Bridgewater game, the schedule grew a little softer for the 2010 Whalers. The team ran
off a string of wins beginning at Tri-County, a regional vocational school in southeastern Massachusetts. Nantucket took
an early lead after running back Mike Molta connected with
DuVaughn Beckford on a halfback pass, which brought the ball
down to the 2-yard line. Hughes then dove in for the score.
Tri-County's quarterback fumbled on a sack, setting up another
Nantucket touchdown. Trekwan Wilson, the lumbering freshman, came up with the fumble.

At halftime, the Whalers grouped on the grass on the edge of
the field while their coaches huddled off to the side. The players
grumbled that their opponents were taking cheap shots.

"Good. Let 'em play dirty," said cocaptain Molta, an upstand-
ing kid who had his teammates' full respect. "We gotta come
with the same intensity." When Aloisi strode over to address
his team, he too focused on the quality of play. He wasn't happy
that his defensive line seemed to be getting drawn into the
antagonism.

"Don't play dirty," he said. "You're gonna let them back in the game. Tell the refs."

On the sidelines stood a man in a Navy baseball cap. Sam Aloisi had driven over from his home in Plymouth to watch his son's team. Divorced from the mother of his children, he took every opportunity to see them on the mainland.

Growing up in Harrison, New York, Aloisi was a center on Harrison High's phenomenally successful football team, which won thirty-three games in a row, lost once, then plowed through an identical thirty-three-game win streak. The coach was Big Ralph Friedgen, who'd played alongside Vince Lombardi at Fordham. Aloisi was stationed on the old Nevers Navy base in the 1960s—he was one of the servicemen who suited up against the high schoolers—when he met Dick Glidden's sister, Joanne. Their marriage produced four kids, including John's older brothers, Sam and Matt, and their sister, Kristen. The first Aloisi son, Sam's namesake, was born a healthy eight and a half pounds. The new father told Capizzo, "Hey, Vito, Joanne and I just had a halfback for you."

While raising his family, Aloisi served for several years as one of Capizzo's assistants. When Vito and Barbara adopted a son, they asked Sam to be the godfather. Vito, in turn, was godfather to the Aloisis' firstborn.

When Nantucket's offense stalled in the second half against Tri-County, the coach's father shook his head and recalled his high school coach's no-frills philosophy: "Move the ball ten feet every play, no penalties, and you win every game." With Tri-County attempting to mount a comeback bid, junior Sam Earle, a long stick figure in pads, kicked a 35-yard field goal.

Two defensive stops on conversion tries after Tri-County touchdowns helped secure the 22–12 win.

"I've got about thirty-seven new gray hairs," Coach Aloisi told Peter Martin, the young sports reporter for the *Inky*. "That game was closer than it should have been."

The next week, his team let him rest a little easier. Nantucket thoroughly dominated Bishop Connolly on the mainland, in Fall River. Under a beautiful blue sky on a sixty-degree fall day, a schnauzer barked from the other side of a fence as the players lined up to stretch. Aloisi walked among the evenly spaced players, clasping hands and slapping helmets; Almodobar whispered a few words in the earholes of their helmets and slipped each player a breath mint, as if he were bestowing the sacrament. The Whalers cheerleaders emerged from a shaded area where they'd been practicing and lined up for their traditional pre-game cheer: *Kevin . . . McLean . . . he's our man! If he can't do it, Molta can! Mike . . . Molta . . . he's our man! . . .*

Playing opposite a sign for the Cardinal Medeiros Old Age Home for Retired Priests, the Whalers got the scoring started on their second possession. Molta bolted for 10 yards, Beckford picked up another first down on a catch in the flat, and McLean burst for a 35-yard gain, leaping over one falling defender. After Molta recovered a fumble in the backfield, McLean caught a wide-open pass from Hughes right up the middle for the first touchdown.

When the Cougars went three and out, Beckford caught a short punt and raced all the way down to the Connolly 38. On a quarterback keeper, Hughes ran hard, refusing to go down until he was inside the 20. Molta and Beckford connected on another

halfback pass, and the Whalers led by two scores before the end
of the first quarter.

Bishop Connolly's small quarterback, just a sophomore,
gamely tried to push his team back into the game, but he had
little help. Forced to scramble out of the pocket for much of
the day, he threw three interceptions. It turned out to be Molta's
day: after passing for one touchdown, he ran for two and caught
a Hughes pass for one more. Molta's 133 all-purpose yards were
almost half his team's total.

Late in the game, Aloisi substituted several of his reserves
and JVs. Dylan O'Connor, a feisty, flyweight defensive back,
grabbed a late pick, and Bryan Depass, an athletic freshman,
absolutely demolished a Connolly kickoff returner, speeding
around the end to put a clean, uncontested, NFL-quality hit
on the boy, who fumbled. After the play was whistled dead, the
player got up, staggered, and fell. While he lay motionless, tended
by trainers and coaches, Depass jogged back to the Nantucket
bench, moaning loudly, his left arm dangling by his side. He'd
separated his shoulder.

A hush fell over the sparse crowd, and the Connolly player's
parents looked stricken as they were summoned onto the field. As
both teams kneeled, the Cougar player remained on the ground
for at least fifteen minutes. An ambulance eventually arrived,
and he was taken to the hospital. Though the teams later learned
that the injured player would be fine, the incident put a damper
on Nantucket's convincing victory. Depass—quite possibly Nantucket's quarterback-in-waiting—was lost for the season.

THE YOUNGER PLAYERS ate up plenty of varsity minutes in
the following week's game as well, an off-island rematch with

week-two opponent Old Colony. Nantucket arrived at the high school in the woods of Rochester, Massachusetts, to find a locker room with no power. During warm-ups, students used a generator to blast a hip-hop medley. Deb McGrath, Mack's mother, walked along the sideline with the family dog, a tiny Yorkie named Jake, who was wearing a blue-and-white doggie jacket that Deb had altered to read "Whaler Pride." Pinned to Deb's long down coat was an oversized button featuring a photo of her son.

Codie Perry's grandmother carried a copy of the school paper, the *Veritas*, proudly showing friends her grandson's new column, printed under the heading "Codie's Corner." His subject this week was Whaler pride.

Despite a bumpy ferry ride to the mainland, the Whalers picked right up where they'd left off the week before. They recovered an Old Colony fumble on the opening kickoff, setting up a broken play that quarterback Hughes turned into a 25-yard touchdown gallop. A long Molta run and another fumble recovery on the ensuing kickoff led to a 20–0 lead before most folks had so much as unwrapped a hot dog. The school never did get the scoreboard working, which, for Old Colony's sake, was probably just as well.

At halftime, the two cheerleading squads performed mostly for each other. "We are the Whalers from the isle of Nantucket," chanted the visitors, limerick-style. "What you have seen is a drop in the bucket!" Up in the media booth, a spare, unheated room on the second floor of an oversized shed behind the home team's grandstand, longtime Nantucket announcers Sandy Beach and Bill Abramson discussed the team's dominance and took turns reading their commercial sponsors' advertising copy.

"For the freshest and finest meat on Nantucket, it's Cow-boys," said Beach. He was a large man in a pink polo shirt and a colorful Bill Cosby–style sweater. Beach, whose real name is Larry DeHaan, took his on-air name during the heyday of ra-dio personalities named Dusty Rhodes and and Rocky Shores. He was an oldies DJ for Nantucket's WNTX, which he came to own for a time. (The former station is now a member of the lucrative network operated by Boston sports-talk radio giant WEEI.) As play-by-play announcers, DeHaan and Abramson have been partners since the 1960s, when Abramson was the sports information director at the former Bentley College and DeHaan, fresh out of Boston College, was the school's sports correspondent. DeHaan has been doing Nantucket games since 1990, and Abramson joined him a decade later.

"We know each other's moves," said Abramson with a grin.

With the rout on, Aloisi once again began shuttling in his JVs. "A lot of white jerseys out there for Nantucket," Abramson, a big pair of binoculars hanging from his neck, told listeners at the start of the second half.

Abramson had worked at the old *Herald-Traveler* in Boston before becoming sports editor at the *Brockton Enterprise*, where he covered Super Bowls, NBA finals, the Stanley Cup, and the 1986 World Series. But his passion has always been high school sports. He's best known in the state for designing the point system that created the season-ending divisional Super Bowls. A onetime math teacher, he approached the old Massachusetts Secondary Schools Principals Association, predecessor to the MIAA, and asked the group why football was the lone team sport that had no postseason play at the high school level. At the time, football champions were determined by an archaic point system. Teams in Class A were awarded ten points for a win; teams in Class B, eight points, and so on down to Class D. If a team in a lower class defeated a team a division above, the winner was awarded an additional two points.

In Abramson's twist, teams would be awarded ten points per win, plus two points for each win the opponent had logged to date. A victory over an 0–10 team would be worth ten points, but a victory over a 7–3 team would net twenty-four. The new system, which the state's coaches and athletic directors quickly adopted, ensured that schools would no longer jockey to schedule weaker opponents from higher divisions. Beginning in 1972, the teams with the top two point totals in each division played each other in a Super Bowl game. Abramson secured agreements from several colleges that had artificial turf fields, such as BC and BU, in case the December weather refused to cooperate.

Until Abramson's proposal, schools had been loath to consider a playoff system that might jeopardize their traditional Thanksgiving rivalries, which all but guaranteed each school's athletic department a significant biennial windfall. Perennially strong programs such as Brockton and Everett had been in the habit of accepting year-end invitations to play standout southern schools at major venues like the Orange Bowl. The new Super Bowls helped keep such teams, and their fans, in their home state.

In an effort to bring more teams into the playoffs, Abramson's point system was eventually abolished when the divisions were split into two levels. Every Massachusetts league champion now goes to the postseason, and some teams play their Super Bowl games at Gillette Stadium, the Patriots' home field. All these changes have benefited both island teams. Incredibly, the Mayflower League was represented in an EMass Super Bowl game by either Nantucket or Martha's Vineyard throughout the entire decade of the 1990s.

For Nantucket's 2010 homecoming weekend, Chris Maury scheduled a "Vineyard Day" with the other island's fall sports teams—field hockey, golf, boys' and girls' soccer. The football team would play Holbrook to cap the afternoon. This was a big day for the athletic director, who had argued the previous year that the rivalry should be enjoyed by all student athletes from both high schools, not just the football teams.

A few hours before the five o'clock start against Holbrook, Maury made the rounds of the fields behind Nantucket High in a golf cart, monitoring the progress of the various Whalers-Vineyarders games. Several trucks decorated in blue and white streamers and balloons sat overlooking the football field, awaiting the kickoff. SOPHOMORES ARE ROCKIN' OUT WITH WHALER PRIDE, read the lettering on a big cardboard *W* propped on a Ford F350, which was covered with colorful pieces of construction paper, strings of silver CDs, and printouts of classic album covers. SINK THOSE GRAPES, read the banner on another truck, a small Mitsubishi flatbed featuring a shipwreck setting, like something out of a school play, with a captain's wheel, some netting, and a couple of creepy, half-dressed pirate skeletons.

A brand-new wind turbine towered over the fields, motionless. The state of Massachusetts was then in the midst of a heated debate over Cape Wind, an offshore wind farm proposed for Nantucket Sound. The issue pitted alternative-energy advocates against locals who believed the wind farm would ruin the natural beauty of the region. Debate-weary islanders had heard endless arguments from both sides about the perceived benefits of the new turbine, which was expected to generate up to 20 percent of the power used by the high school. Though a majority wanted to erect the turbine on the outer reaches of the grounds, in the fields back by the old cemetery, the Historic District Commission—the committee that requires Nantucket home-owners to adhere to the island's unmistakable gray-shingled tradition—disallowed it. So the turbine stretched a few hundred feet above the Boosters Club volunteer who sat in a folding chair at the gateway to the football field, just behind the school, sell-ing tickets to the games. Hunching his shoulders against the cool breeze, he wore a large windbreaker, a coin apron, and a classic fisherman's beard.

The field hockey team played the Vineyard to a scoreless draw on the dry, patchy field a few hundred yards from the foot-ball stands. Afterward Maury watched the parents filter toward their cars as he talked about the strength of the school's fall sports programs. On the football field, the boys' soccer team was on its way to a convincing 5–1 thrashing of the Vineyard, in a chippy game that featured several yellow cards. Both the boys' and girls' Whalers soccer teams were undefeated in their leagues and headed to tournament play. The field hockey and golf teams, too, were going to tournaments. Basking in those success stories, the AD used them to tease his second-year foot-ball coach.

"I told John, 'No pressure, but you're the only one left to go to the postseason,' " Maury said.

Over on Cape Cod, the Vineyard's football team was already cruising to an easy victory over Cape Tech, the team that had beaten a frustrated Whalers group in the opening game of the

season. "I'd like to see us play Tech again," said Maury, who
was encouraged by the progress of Aloisi's coaching team. He
thought it wouldn't be close: though undersized, this season's
Whalers had skill players "up the wazoo." He was looking forward to the upcoming rematch with West Bridgewater—a
good team, he said, but nothing fancy.

Just across Sparks Avenue from the high school fields, the
Boys Club's seventh-and-eighth-grade team was pitted in a
high-scoring battle against a visiting team from the Blackstone
Valley region of Rhode Island. Travis Lombardi, the high
school's junior varsity coach, was getting a long look at this Boys
Club team for the first time, and he couldn't help but grin. Nantucket's stocky running back, wearing number 44, executed a
deft spin move to elude tacklers on his way into the end zone.

"Back off, Trav," joked Codie Perry's father, Joe, himself a
former Whaler. His youngest son was playing in the game.

On defense, Nantucket's Boys Club team had a truly enormous lineman, dwarfing his competition like an eighteen-wheel
big rig crowding out two teams of Smart cars. After watching
the big boy create havoc in the middle of the field for a few
plays, Lombardi strode off to look for his wife, a teacher in the
middle school. They call him Big Mike, she told her husband,
and he's only in the seventh grade. The coach's face lit up as he
considered the prospect of adding Big Mike to his own roster
in two years.

Inside the high school later that afternoon, the football
coaches were making last-minute preparations. Cocaptain Kevin
McLean shuttled in and out, assisting the coaches with various
tasks. He wouldn't be playing today; he'd been suspended from
school after getting into a scuffle in the hallway with a classmate

who'd been gunning for the football player for weeks. Though the coaches were disappointed in their cocaptain, they were satisfied that he'd done everything he could to avoid the altercation. They joked that the players should call their teammate "Coach McLean" for the week.

Another player complained that he hadn't figured it would be this chilly by game time. Did anyone have an Under Armour shirt he could borrow?

"Hey, we're not your parents," said Almodobar with a smile. "We love you, but we can't help you."

Coach Aloisi had been telling his assistants about *Season of Life*, Pulitzer Prize–winning journalist Jeffrey Marx's book about former pro player Joe Ehrmann. As a coach at Baltimore's all-boys Gilman School, Ehrmann helped build a remarkable program that rejected the "false masculinity" of football culture. The Gilman coaches routinely told their players that they loved them. In the book Marx describes Ehrmann and Gilman head coach Biff Poggi evaluating their program not by wins and losses but by the number of good men it turns out. When Poggi is asked how his team is doing, he likes to reply, "We won't really know for twenty years."

Coach Lombardi got up and walked out of the room. He was going to give the chilly player his own Under Armour, Bill Manchester reported.

Aloisi was expecting a lot of desperation passing from the talent-challenged Holbrook offense. He suggested going with a nickel defense—five deep backs in pass coverage. When the Whalers had the ball, he wanted Tim Psaradelis watching the Holbrook staff for an indication of the defense they'd be using. "Tim, be looking for four or five fingers from the other coach," he said. Vaughan Machado sat quietly in one of the classroom-style tablet arm chairs, chewing gum, looking through half-glasses at his playbook.

A half hour later, the Whalers took the field. Several players from the Boys Club lined the field behind the short fence to watch them stretch. The kids all wore their team jerseys and had their faces painted half blue, half white. They could barely hear each other over the warm-up music. *I got a feeling tonight's gonna be a good night,* went the refrain leaking out of the loudspeaker at top volume.

"Oh, I love this!" said one of the boys to no one in particular.

On the field, the offense walked through its sets. Taylor Hughes threw a pretty rainbow pass to Terrel Correia, his towering tight end, who was loping toward the corner of the end zone. With his back to his quarterback, the tall sophomore reached up with his right hand and plucked the ball effortlessly out of the air, tucking it against his hip just before he tiptoed out of bounds. The team had clearly gained some confidence on its modest winning streak.

The homecoming crowd streamed steadily into the stands. After parents and guardians were called out on the field to accompany their boys for Senior Recognition, a couple of students ran across midfield waving the black Jolly Roger and the blue-and-white Whaler Pride flag. On the far sideline, below the windows of the field house where Dick Herman and his crew were going over the starting lineups for the Plum TV cable-access audience, the Holbrook players looked small and uneasy in their purple uniforms. A few dozen of their family members stood along the fence near the bench.

When the game finally got under way, Nantucket recovered

a Holbrook fumble on the visitors' first possession. A few plays later, Hughes connected with DuVaughn Beckford on a silky 50-yard touchdown reception down the left sideline. Beyond the goalpost, a swollen pink moon hung low against the darkening blue sky. With the help of three interceptions, the hosts drove the score up to 33–0 before the end of the second quarter.

At halftime, the Whalers crowded into the field house, where they sat on benches and cracked the lazy jokes of a team in complete control. While Mike Molta remained on the field to accept his crown as homecoming king, Aloisi addressed the rest of his team. He knew they were getting used to his spiel: "I'm a broken record," he said. "We go all out until that clock says zero." Not that they wanted to embarrass their opponent, but the coach would not accept a lack of focus in the second half. Second-team players and some JVs would have plenty of opportunity to show what they could do.

"I want nobody sulking," said Aloisi, looking purposefully around the room. "Everyone is going play, so make the most of your reps. Show us you should be in there." Above the doorway hung the words WHALER PRIDE. As the players shuffled through the logjam on their way back out to the field, each one reached above the door frame and tapped the words for good luck.

The second half was all but pointless. The final score was 33–14. Now, after weeks of lesser competition, the Nantucket coaches could finally set their sights on their rematch with West Bridgewater. If they could come out with a win, it was highly likely the two teams would share the Mayflower Small title for the season. And if that scenario played out, it would be a colossal boost for a program that had been on the verge of utter collapse not much more than a year ago.

"I'm getting chills," Aloisi said, barely able to maintain his usual reserve, when he spoke to his team in the on-field huddle after the game. The rematch was, in effect, their championship game. He made sure he left his players with a sobering thought.

"Let's make some smart choices," he said, using one of his favorite phrases. "You can't be a party animal and a champion. You can't."

As the players loped in happy clusters across the parking lot to the locker room, Aloisi bantered with the *Inky*'s sports reporter, who said he was heading out to celebrate an anniversary with his girlfriend. The normally stoic coach teased his visitor, unable, for once, to suppress a smile.

*Chapter Ten*

# AN AURA OF INVINCIBILITY

THE BOYS FROM Nantucket trudged off the garish green of the artificial turf at Boston University's Nickerson Field. A couple of hours before, Tim Ostebo had been sacked for a 9-yard loss on the first play of the 1982 Eastern Massachusetts Division 5 Super Bowl. It was still 6–6 in the third quarter, but the team from Manchester was stronger, quicker. They hit hard. Steve Visco, Rocky Fox, and John Bartlett (who would go on to play in the all-state Shriners game and then at Cornell) each needed to recuperate on the Whaler bench after bone-jarring collisions with opposing players. Manchester's hellacious defense held the Whalers to a paltry 38 yards on the ground for the game. An ill-fated quick kick in the third quarter, called while Nantucket was pinned back at its own 1-yard line, resulted in a critical safety for Manchester, but by then the outcome was hardly in doubt. In the end, the Whalers' superb 1982 season came to a close against a clearly superior team. "They were psyched, they were physical, and they were ready," said Coach Capizzo after his team's 28–6 loss. Fran York, the first-year Manchester coach, said his team knew at halftime that it was going to win: "We realized there was no mystique out there."

Yet that's what Vito excelled at, year in and year out—creating an aura of invincibility around his teams. Like a lot of coaches, he padded the numbers. Rob Mooney, a tackle who played both ways in those years, says he was listed as 220, though he probably didn't weigh more than 185. More so than in most towns, winning became a community obsession on Nantucket. The school accommodated the coach's every request. Capizzo recruited volunteers to scout upcoming opponents' games each week off-island. He even had a student trainer, a four-foot-seven-inch kid named Eric Mailloux, who began learning to treat injuries when he realized he was too small to play. Mailloux, who was class president his senior year, answered to the nickname "the Squirt." "Ninety percent of the time, he diagnoses what's wrong with the kids before the doctor sees them," Capizzo told the *Boston Globe*.

After shutting out Madison Park, their season-opening opponent for a third straight year, the 1983 Whalers came from behind for a 14–7 win over Blue Hills, the preseason favorites in the Mayflower League. Ostebo, who separated his shoulder in that game, would have to sit a few weeks. So Capizzo installed a page ripped straight from the old Pop Warner playbook—a single-wing formation with direct snaps to his running backs. The next week, Richard Perry shredded an unprepared West Bridgewater defense for 163 yards and three touchdowns on a dozen carries. A week later, Capizzo added another wrinkle: Perry, a lefty, and fullback Nicky Duarte, a righty, took turns rolling out to either side of the field on the option. Duarte threw for more than 100 yards in a 20–0 win over Southeastern. Years later, when the Miami Dolphins sprang the wildcat offense on the Patriots, Chris Warner, a Patriots blogger who'd been a six-five Nantucket tight end one year behind Perry's class, had to laugh. "We did that twenty-five years ago," he said to himself.

Perry and Duarte combined for nearly 300 yards in the next game, a 16–13 squeaker over Apponequet in a battle of the Mayflower League's two undefeated leaders. Early on Chris Marks (whose father, Phil, was the coach-tackling linebacker in the 1950s) took out the Warriors' key offensive threat, a halfback who was averaging over 7 yards a carry, with a crushing hit that crumpled the runner with injuries to his knee and ribs.

One week later, Nantucket confirmed that this would be another memorable season. Losing 26–8 at halftime against Norton, the team scored three unanswered touchdowns with less than five minutes to play to pull out a stunning victory. Days later, when the weekly *Inky* was published, "the miracle [was still] being relived and recounted from 'Sconset to Madaket," as the newspaper's reporter gushed.

There had been plenty of ill omens. Marks was already out with a concussion from the last game, and Perry sustained one of his own during the comeback. But with less than a minute remaining, Ostebo hoisted the team up onto his six-foot-three-inch frame. First he executed a nerve-racking, tackle-breaking scramble, pushing ahead for 15 yards. From the 30, the quarterback rolled to his left and speared tight end Pete Gillies with a completion that was good for 17 more. On the next play, Ostebo rolled right and found Gillies again, this time in the end zone.

For once, Vito was speechless. And was there something in his eye? The kid had lost his older brother earlier in the year in a drowning mishap in Vermont. Here he was playing like a hero, playing his broken heart out.

From there, the 1983 team became marauders. They trounced

Tri-County at home, 55–0, with Perry running for 131 yards before sitting out the entire second half. They blanked Bristol-Plymouth, 28–0. Following another shutout, this one over Old Colony, a gasping program that had canceled the remainder of its schedule the previous year, the Whalers held sole possession of second place in the statewide Division 5 standings.

In Capizzo's two decades on the rock, his teams had sworn by their dictator's offensive rule of thumb. There are only three things that can happen when you pass the football, he often said, and two of them are bad. The team's sudden reliance on Ostebo's arm was due in large part to the unique presence of David Cantrell, a Methodist minister who was then new to the island. While attending Trinity College Cantrell, a soccer player and onetime Top-10-ranked junior tennis player, walked onto the football team and became its kicking and punting specialist. He was good enough to get considerable interest from NFL teams. When he signed as an undrafted free agent with the New York Jets in 1967, coach Weeb Ewbank handed him a signing bonus of $2,000 cash.

On a day that summer when big cuts were scheduled, Cantrell sat eating scrambled eggs in the cafeteria at Peekskill Military Academy, where the Jets held camp. When he felt a hand on his shoulder, he assumed that he was about to be released. Instead, he turned to find Joe Namath, who handed the rookie a newspaper clipping featuring a story about a European soccer payer who'd been struck by lightning. It was the star quarterback's unique way of showing his support. Though the kicker was flattered, it didn't occur to him to keep the odd memento. "I just threw it in the trash," he says.

Despite the welcome, Cantrell was dismayed by the reckless-
ness of the pro football lifestyle. This was, after all, Joe Willie's
Jets. It was only a matter of days before he turned in his playbook. Twelve grand a year wasn't nearly enough to convince him
to turn a blind eye. After a stint in training camp with the Philadelphia Eagles the following summer, he gave up the game for
good and began working toward becoming a minister.

While working on the Vineyard some years later, Cantrell was
asked to come to Nantucket, where the sole Methodist church
needed a new pastor. Hearing about the prominence of football
in the community, he offered his help to Capizzo shortly after
his arrival.

The newcomer specialized in refining athletic skills. He
taught Ostebo, a high-achieving student who would win a
Bausch + Lomb Science Award, to throw passes using timing
patterns. He taught Chris Warner, the big tight end who would
go on to play at Yale, the proper way to catch a pass, with his
thumbs together. He attempted to teach a Swedish exchange
student who'd never seen a football—Capizzo's latest special-
teams guinea pig—to step into a punt without getting obliter-
ated by onrushing linemen.

Cantrell's association with the team was brief. He was not
exactly in tune with Vito's overriding emphasis on physical
toughness. There was always a little friction between the two
men, he admits: "I didn't really fit the mold, and I didn't really
want to. I did things under my own auspices." When middling
players felt Capizzo's wrath, Cantrell made it his business to take
them aside and help them improve some specific aspect of their
game. "Some people respond well to being battered," says the

former minister, who now runs a Main Street inn. "God knows why. I was the 'others don't' part."

IT TOOK ALL sorts of islanders to build the Whalers legend. En route to Oak Bluffs that November, Nantucket fans and families could gloat over the assurance that, with a victory, their team would be going to its second consecutive state Super Bowl, its third in four years. While a Vineyard win would mean a three-way tie for the Mayflower Legaue championship among the two islands and Apponequet, few Nantucketers bothered to entertain the possibility.

An estimated one thousand Nantucket fans made the excursion from their island to the other, some by jet, many more on the steamship *Uncatena*, named after an old sidewheel steamer that had been retired in 1928. "There were no casks of dried meat nor earthen vessels of water aboard," wrote one rather florid *Inky* reporter of the exodus, "but there were picnic lunches, crossword puzzles, and cases of beer." The trip back after the Whalers' 30–20 win over the Vineyard—the team's twenty-third consecutive regular-season win, sealing a perfect 10–0 record on the season—was much more festive yet. Under "a full Beaver moon," as the paper noted, students took barely concealed gulps of beer while a few concerned adults wondered aloud where their parents were.

Once again, the statistical deficit Nantucket suffered when playing teams from much larger school systems was exposed when the team returned the following week to Nickerson Field. Its opponent, West Roxbury, had made its presence felt on the Vineyard, where the team's coach brought some of his bigger players—"try six-foot-three and six-foot-four," the

*Inky* fretted—on an ostensible scouting mission that doubled as a bit of theatrical intimidation. For the second consecutive season, the Whalers sustained the only blemish on their year-end record in the Super Bowl, losing 14–0. Though Perry ran for his customary 100 yards and the team managed to squeeze inside the red zone four times, they could not break the plane of the goal line. Chris Warner knew the Whalers were in trouble when a defensive end who'd been knocked to his knees by a Duarte block got up and chased down Perry at the 10. "Only time I remember him getting caught from behind," Warner says.

Some began to question whether there was some kind of BU curse to blame for the Super Bowl losses. But Capizzo had no alibis, he said afterward. No complaints.

THE MOST ILLUSTRIOUS run of the Whaler dynasty was destined for at least one more top-shelf season in 1984. Perry, Ostebo, offensive lineman Jonathan Vollans, and defensive sparkplug Gary Yates—described by the *New Yorker* as "barely cabin-boy size" but sporting "a full set of captain's muttonchop whiskers"— were among the many well-tested starters returning for their senior year. After poor Madison Park made the queasy trek over on the ferry in high seas for the home opener, the visitors were subjected to some ugly taunting "not exactly endorsed by the Chamber of Commerce," as the *Inky's* writer noted. Nantucket won, 20–0.

The darlings of the year-round islanders, however, had a rude awakening of their own the following week, when they were toppled by Blue Hills, 14–8, on two big plays by a tailback named Rich Sass, including an 80-yard punt return with a minute left in the game. Capizzo and his team took it out on West

Bridgewater on their own home field, 34–0, before stinging Apponequet in a key league matchup a week later. That game was played in gale-force winds, the residual effect of Hurricane Josephine. It was 6–3 late in the fourth when the home team broke loose for three unanswered touchdowns, making the final score a deceptive 27–3.

A few weeks later Ostebo received honorable mention as a *Boston Globe* player of the week for his three-touchdown performance against Tri-County. He was effectively operating as the team's offensive coordinator, making almost all of the play selections from the huddle and calling audibles at the line of scrimmage. In one game that season, Capizzo trusted him to run a no-huddle offense.

Ostebo and his teammates carried Dick Herman off the field after the win against Tri-County. It was the assistant's one hundredth with the team. By the week of the Vineyard game, Ostebo was on a tear, having thrown for nine touchdowns in three weeks.

With Nantucket destined to finish in second place, behind the only team to beat them that season (Blue Hills), Capizzo's seniors were especially determined to keep the Island Cup in their own trophy case. A Gull Air CASA and a smaller Cessna took off from the Martha's Vineyard airport in the early morning hours of the Saturday before Thanksgiving. The first plane carried twenty-three Vineyard players and coaches; the second, nine more. After the pilots deposited their charges, they flew back for a second round of passengers.

With time running out in the second quarter, Nantucket clung to a shaky 6–0 lead. Bob Tankard made a risky decision to go for the first on fourth down, and it backfired. The play was stuffed, and Nantucket took the ball in great field position, setting up a backbreaking score, with Perry carrying, just before the half.

When they returned for the second half, the lionhearted Scotty Dario, one of Tankard's favorite players, gamely tried to will his team back into the contest, with the coach calling his number eight straight times. The feisty little back moved the ball all the way down to the 9-yard line, but that was as close as the Vineyarders would come to sniffing the end-zone grass. Sophomore Brian Ryder, a brawny kid who had emerged as Capizzo's latest defensive anchor, made two spectacular plays in succession, tossing Dario for a 1-yard loss, then sacking Vineyard quarterback Richie Packish to squelch the drive. Late in the game years of Vineyard frustrations boiled to the surface, with the team taking several penalties for unnecessary roughness.

"Just ancient rites of fertility," observed one teacher, surveying the festive hostility.

Fittingly, in his last game for the high school, Perry accounted for all three of his team's touchdowns. McGrath, the *New Yorker* correspondent, saw in him the deceptive grace of "those truly gifted runners—like Gayle Sayers and O. J. Simpson—who don't *look* particularly fast. He seemed to slide along, hardly moving his legs—like someone doing the moonwalk." With more than 100 yards rushing, "it was the kind of afternoon," wrote the visitor, "that makes for a Nantucket legend."

AFTER GRADUATION, OSTEBO went on to become the starting quarterback and shortstop for the Middlebury Panthers in Vermont. In college the kid who played everything well skied with friends who were training for the U.S. ski team. During those first few summers he returned to the island and his job at Young's, the three-generation bike shop near the ferry landing. Eventually he moved on from the island, as so many of the boys do, though he took the place with him. Almost ten years later, studying for his dual master's at the University of Idaho, he lined the walls of his living space with photos from his upbringing on the rock.

What he didn't take with him, says Ted Anderson, his stepfather, was a disproportionate attitude about his high school glory years. "One of the things I'm most proud of with Timmy was that he was able to leave football behind," says Anderson, who still lives on Nantucket with Ostebo's mother, Gretchen. "There was a time for doing that, and there was a time for grad school and other things.

"He was not one whose greatest moment was going to be on the football field. His greatest moment was still somewhere up ahead."

BOB MOONEY, THE Nantucket lawyer and onetime state representative who'd played back in the early days of island football, was on hand at the Vineyard game that year to watch his son, one of Ostebo's best friends from childhood. Rob Mooney was a tackle who would become one of Capizzo's cocaptains the following year. The elder Mooney pulled up to the game with a license plate that read WHALE.

After the game, he felt the fizzle immediately.

"For the next few months around here," he said, "it's all downhill."

WITH OSTEBO GONE, Coach Capizzo needed a new quarterback. There was no heir apparent, so he created one. He had a high school junior living under his own roof.

Scott Capizzo had plenty of friends in high school. He was funny, and a bit of a wild man. And his father, of course, was the larger-than-life Vito.

But even Scott's closest friends were aghast when his old man began putting him in the most important position on the field during practices in August 1985. Scott was the first to admit he was not an exceptional athlete, and he was no wizard with a playbook, either. Truth be told, he was more interested in the Grateful Dead than football.

The coach had been struggling with his son's excessive partying, and he figured maybe giving the kid such a responsibility would straighten him out. But after a few double sessions it was clear to everyone—most especially Scott—that he had no business running the Whalers offense.

It took several years for the father and son to come to terms with their relationship. Capizzo's friend Sam Aloisi once found himself trying to explain Scott's resentment to the coach. "Scott had to share you with a lot of other guys," he said. "You've been a father to a thousand kids."

"I think they had probably had every great film moment between a father and son at home," says Donick Cary, who was a senior that year. "All the *Great Santini* moments."

Cary, a small but effective lineman who would be named to the All Cape and Islands team that season, moved to the island as a child with his parents, who were looking for a retreat. It was the tail end of the sixties; the Carys took over the community theater. But for all the artistic talents he'd inherited, the only thing Cary wanted to do when he grew up was play for the Whalers.

"We used to play Kill-the-Guy for five hours every day," he says.

Eventually he came to appreciate his creative side, becoming a successful television comedy writer. For years he wrote for David Letterman. The host, assuming Cary's Nantucket upbringing was a privileged one, loved to call him "Mr. Silver Spoon." The writer once nearly sold a pilot to Fox for a comedy series about off-season life on Nantucket.

He also worked on dozens of episodes for *The Simpsons*. It was Cary's concept that drives the episode "Bart Star," in which Bart Simpson becomes the quarterback of his Pee-Wee football team after his father, Homer, takes the coaching job. The program even featured a cameo appearance by Joe Namath, Capizzo's old roommate.

Bizarrely, Cary says he was unaware of the Capizzo-Namath connection at Alabama until much later.

IN SEPTEMBER 1985, Hurricane Gloria forced the postponement of an on-island game against Norton, which took home the win on a Monday. Norton was the team to beat that year, with several players destined for Division I college programs. The school would win the Mayflower League title and a state Super Bowl before moving up to Division 4 for the following season.

Though a cocaptain, Rob Mooney was declared academically ineligible for the Vineyard game that year. He'd elected to take physics in his senior year, and he was struggling with it. Capizzo was not pleased. Linemen don't take physics, he told the kid.

Capizzo wasn't the only one who made the Island Cup a top priority. Chris Warner, who'd moved to Nantucket with his family from the Boston area when he was in sixth grade, missed most of the season with a broken ankle. The following September he began a postgraduate year at Phillips Exeter Academy, where he played on a team good enough to supply Harvard with a future captain. The attention on the team helped Warner draw some recruitment of his own, and he chose Yale.

The experience gave the tight end the rare privilege of playing in three classic rivalry series—Vineyard-Nantucket, Andover-Exeter, and Harvard-Yale. The Yale Bowl holds seventy thousand. "I take the Nantucket-Vineyard series much more personally," says Warner.

THE 1986 ISLAND Cup game capped a return to excellence for Capizzo's boys, who rebounded from a mediocre 6–4 mark the previous year with a 9–1 campaign.

Of thirty-plus graduating senior boys from the class of 1987, twenty-four of them played football for Capizzo. "Nobody wanted to let the town down," recalled Brian Ryder, watching a Whalers game from beyond the end zone during John Aloisi's second season as head coach. As Ryder talked, he watched his daughter climb a tall mound of freshly turned dirt, a remnant of the work to install the high school's new wind turbine. "Don't get dirty," he called to her. "Your mother's away."

After graduating from high school, Ryder took his penchant for hitting people in pads to Division I, accepting a scholarship to Tulane. In 1990, his senior year, he led the Green Wave with 107 tackles, 57 of them unassisted. Tulane's longtime rivalry with Louisiana State University was instituted in 1893. Their annual contest, which was suspended in 2009, was traditionally fought over a satin victory flag, known to the LSU Tigers as the "Tiger Rag." Though the games in Ryder's years sometimes drew crowds of seventy thousand—Tulane played its home games in the Superdome, while Tiger Stadium in Baton Rouge is one of the largest college football stadiums in the country—the rivalry had nothing on the Island Cup. Maybe it had something to do with the fact that the "Battle for the Rag" had grown lopsided in LSU's favor by the time he arrived in New Orleans. Or maybe he just missed Capizzo. Whatever the reason, "you just didn't feel it the same" as the Island Cup, he said.

Other than Almodobar, Ryder came closest to the NFL of any of Capizzo's players over the years. In 1991 he was one of the last men cut from the Patriots' preseason camp. Friends and family urged him to try to sign with another team as a free agent, but he declined. Though he did play some semipro ball, the NFL had never been his ultimate goal. That was getting a top-quality education, and if it weren't for football, he never would have been able to afford it. He moved home and started his own business as an electrician. Now that he's started a family, he has become a Boys Club coach. Ryder's son, Cory, was already playing his fifth season of full-contact football at age eleven.

"He's a menace out there," said his father, grinning.

NOVEMBER 2010

M IKE MOLTA POUNDED the grass. He knew his ankle
was hurt badly enough to keep him out of the rest of the
game. His teammates, taking a knee on the West Bridgewater
field while a trainer fetched a cart, sagged. Molta was their on-
field leader.

Lying on the field, Molta glared at his fellow Whalers. "It's
just my leg!" he shouted. "Jesus Christ! *Relax.*"

On the sideline, his father looked for the bright side. At least
it was the left ankle. His son had wrecked his right ankle in the
Cape Tech game that ended the 2009 season. The doctor had
inserted a plate and seven pins to fix it.

The rematch with West Bridgewater had barely begun, and
already the tension was thick. Under a sign that declared Coach
Panos's two Super Bowl victories, in 1991 and 2006, the Wild-
cats took the field by running through a tear-away team banner
stretched across the end zone by the cheerleaders. Vineyard coach
Donald Herman, whose team had played the night before, stood
behind a goalpost by himself, making observations into a hand-
held digital voice recorder.

After getting pinned back at their own 5-yard line, Nantucket punted. Already ensured good field position, the host team's return man scampered all the way down to the 15. That set up a bull run by Panos's abusive runner, D. J. Jamieson, straight up the gut and into the end zone for the game's first score. The home team tried an option pitch for a two-point conversion, but Taylor Hughes led a gang of Whalers tacklers to stuff the sweep.

Unlike the Whalers' last few games, which had lacked suspense, there was a feverish intensity on the sidelines for this one from the beginning. Everyone present knew that the winning team would have a strong shot at claiming the Mayflower Small title at the end of the season. A few West Bridgewater parents kept up a steady patter of vaguely ominous heckling directed at the island boys, just as Nantucket's fans had often done to their visitors during Capizzo's boon years. And the Whalers seemed rattled. Working out of their usual no-huddle, shotgun formation, a bad snap pushed them back into their own territory. Hughes completed a nice 15-yard pass, but his next throw was tipped, and the team was forced to punt again.

On second and 5, West Bridgewater ran a misdirection play, a quarterback keeper that netted 4 yards. Third and 1: a stop here would be huge for Nantucket. "Right here! Right here!" screamed Vaughan Machado, the assistant coach. The Nantucket boys met the challenge, jamming the line and stopping Jamieson in first stride. On the sideline, their teammates thrust their fists in the air. It seemed as though they had prevented the first down, but the referee spotted the football generously. The home team retained possession.

A few plays later, DuVaughn Beckford picked off a West Bridgewater pass, but the half ended before the Whalers could get near the red zone. "Yo, this game is far from over," said Tim

Marsh, the scrappy senior lineman with plenty of eye black smeared across his cheeks, as the players trudged to a far corner of the field and flopped on the grass.

Molta, his left foot taped and shoeless, hopped over to join his teammates and rolled onto his side. Cocaptain Kevin McLean, back from his suspension, assumed the role of inspirational speaker. "It's only six-nothing, man," he said. "There's lots of time. Like Coach said, they're running it up our ass. That's all they're doin'. Ain't nothing fancy."

After huddling privately, the coaches walked over to address their players. Manchester, the offensive coordinator, noted that Nantucket was fortunate not to be down 28–0, given the number of opportunities they were handing the home team. If the Whalers ran ten plays of their own, maybe three and a half of them had been successful. "Thirty-five percent is not gonna win it," he said.

Coach Aloisi looked grim. "I see a little bit of adversity and we fold," he said, challenging his team to rise to the occasion.

As the two sides prepared for the second-half kickoff, Aloisi's father gazed out at midfield from the sideline, thinking about his own high school team's simple philosophy. "If they could just get three yards on first down, they're going to score," said the coach's father. "They can't keep going backwards."

But the Whalers were back on their heels from the moment Jamieson received the kickoff. In fact, he almost broke the return wide open. A few plays later, he was in the end zone: 12–0, West Bridgewater.

When Hughes, on the next drive, took a big hit on his way out of bounds, he was slow to get up. "Yup, you're all right," announced the public-address man sarcastically. Junior Wildcat

Michael Toczko broke free for a 78-yard gallop down the left sideline, setting up his own touchdown from the 2. Yet still the Whalers refused to cave, stopping a third straight two-point conversion try. Finally, as the fourth quarter got under way, the visitors mounted their first substantial drive of the afternoon, marching all the way down to West Bridgewater's 3-yard line. Parents, coaches, and reserve players produced the most noise they'd made all day, trying to will the team to an improbable comeback. But Beckford was hauled down for a loss on a sweep play, momentarily defusing the excitement. And then the worst-case scenario unfolded: with Hughes scrambling, a West Bridge-water linebacker stepped up to intercept his pass in traffic in the middle of the end zone. The crowd on the home sideline erupted.

Or was it the worst-case scenario? The defender with the ball advanced out of the end zone, reversed field, and was im-mediately tackled behind the goal line, giving Nantucket a two-point safety. Not only that, but they would get the ball right back. "That's *huge!*" shouted Manchester, who knew right away, unlike some of the confused-looking parents, that the play would give his team a golden opportunity for two unanswered scores. As the teams lined up for West Bridgewater's kickoff, Nantucket's parents pleaded for a little more good fortune. The crowds on both sidelines were by now delirious. The bouncing kick squibbed right through McLean's legs, only to land in the sure hands of junior Andrew Benson, who darted all the way to the 50. Gasping Nantucket fans beamed at each other. *This* was heart-stopping football.

From scrimmage, Codie Perry rumbled for 20 yards, and the Nantucket supporters could visualize a scoreboard showing a one-touchdown deficit. Hughes, riding the high, fired a bullet at Beckford, who met the ball on a crossing pattern right on the goal line at midfield. But the receiver was drilled in the side just as the ball arrived, and it sailed through his hands.

West Bridgewater read a Beckford sweep to perfection, and suddenly it was fourth and 6 with seven minutes to play. And after flirting with a miracle, not just for the game but for a championship season plucked from out of the blue, Nantucket's wild hopes were erased when Hughes's desperation pass into the end zone plummeted to the grass.

The sense of relief was palpable on the home side as West Bridgewater took over on downs. For the Whalers, the game was over long before the clock made it official. In the handshake line, Jamieson reached up and patted Mack McGrath, the big Nantucket lineman, on the head.

"FOURTH. QUARTER. COMEBACK! Fourth. Quarter. Comeback!" squealed Tri-County's cheerleaders.

Given their team's 22–12 loss at home to the Whalers in September, there'd been little hope that the ferry trip to the island on a cold Saturday morning would end with a reason to smile for the Cougars, who were just 2–6. By the third quarter, one week after Nantucket's disappointment in West Bridgewater, the Whalers had assumed complete control over their visitors.

The score was 19–0. DuVaughn Beckford was looking like a true skill player, catching a touchdown pass and making a pretty interception on his fingertips. For one of the first times all year, Whaler cocaptain Kevin McLean was getting plenty of work on the offensive side of the ball. For the team's third touchdown, Hughes and Correia connected on the flare pass they'd been working on into the corner of the end zone. The towering sophomore, who would be the starting center on Almodobar's varsity basketball team in the winter, looked like the old NBA titan George Mikan on the play, effortlessly hauling in the football while two scrawny Cougar defenders bounced comically off his hips. In the stands Joanne Angelastro, Aloisi's mother, banged on her battered old cowbell with a drumstick. It was a family heirloom of sorts; her mother had found it in the barn after buying a house in western Massachusetts decades ago.

But the game, seemingly sewn up, began to unravel late. Tri-County scored easily, then pinned the Whalers deep on a squib kick that squirted past McLean. The home offense floundered, then shanked a punt into the wind, giving the visitors the ball back well within Nantucket territory, at the 29. Tim Marsh, the senior who was coming into his own as an undersized lineman, limped off the field with an injury, and the fading Whalers soon gave up Tri-County's second touchdown, plus the two-point try. Suddenly it was 19–16, and Nantucket's Under Armour–clad coaches and blanket-bundled fans were pleading for the boys to tap some inner resolve.

They found it on the next play. A bounding kickoff careened wildly for an excruciating moment before Beckford, the deep man, finally scooped it up. The slow development of the play had given both sides extra time to engage, and by the time Beckford looked upfield, he was wide-eyed. The middle of the gridiron was parted like a hayfield after the first pass by a harvester. Beckford streaked straight up the path for 75 yards and a touchdown that made the score 25–16.

Forty-five minutes later, after his reenergized teammates had laid out a few Tri-County ball carriers and tacked on two more touchdowns for emphasis, Beckford was one of the last remaining Whalers in the locker room, voluntarily dry-mopping the floor, wearing a do-rag over his braids.

A week later the Whalers' yellow school bus—a far cry from the comfortable commuter coach with tinted windows they'd used in Capizzo's heyday—pulled up to a desolate-looking field alongside the high school in Holbrook. A ramshackle field house had a huge mural of a blue-and-white cartoon bulldog on its back side. The building was of no use to the announcers who would have used it; on the second floor, it was infested with wasps and birds. Less than an hour before game time, two lonely figures, the radio announcers Sandy Beach and Bill Abramson, leaned on Beach's sedan, which he'd driven onto the sideline next to the field house. They were preparing to broadcast the game in the open air.

Bill Manchester walked the length of the field, inspecting its weedy, patchy grass and an abundance of divots and molehills. "Picture a river here last year," he said, recalling Nantucket's soggy last visit. This time, it was a gorgeous sixty-degree fall day, though few would be on hand to enjoy it.

Holbrook started the game without a PA announcer, and the turnout was tiny. An eerie silence hung in the air during the coin flip at midfield.

The lack of urgency clearly affected the visitors. Despite stopping Holbrook twice on ill-advised passes in fourth-and-short situations, Nantucket could muster little momentum of its own. "Will you guys finish a play!" yelled a frustrated Almodobar. Finally, junior Codie Perry, the hockey star who was emerging as a Whaler leader in his first year of football, banged into the end zone for the game's first score.

By then, Donald Herman had appeared, traveling off his

own island for one last round of pre-Cup scouting. Leaning against a goalpost, his voice recorder in hand, he seemed unimpressed. Delmont Araujo, his big two-way end, was going to have a big week against the Whalers, he predicted.

Whether the Nantucket players realized Herman was watching them or not, their minds were evidently on the Vineyard, not Holbrook. "You guys are flat!" barked Coach Machado during a time-out. "Where is it, man?" He called for a sophomore lineman named Joseph Turner, who was about to get some reps. "You hang with me," said the coach. "I'm going to find somebody who wants to play some football around here."

When play resumed, Turner stood on the sideline, awaiting his chance. "Let's go, D!" he shouted into the vacuum.

Machado was Aloisi's rah-rah guy, a football throwback the habitually even-handed coach could count on to stir the troops when the situation called for it. Now, however, Aloisi didn't like the attitude his team was putting on the field. The play was getting chippy. After one skirmish, he marched across the hash marks to confront Beckford, last week's hero. You'll sit if you do that again, the coach hissed, seething. "But I didn't do anything!" the young man pleaded.

Uncharacteristically, Aloisi was also getting on the referees' nerves. "Coach, I'm going to tell you one more time—back off the field, or I'm going to throw a flag," said one official, glaring.

The islanders' frustration finally found a pressure valve when the game began to break their way. Correia rumbled for more than 30 yards on a quick screen pass, setting up an easy Hughes touchdown on an uncontested sweep. Andrew Benson grabbed his second interception of the game and ran it back all the way to the Holbrook fifteen. Popped from his blind side, he covered the ball with both arms as he fell forward. After a testy discussion about the accuracy of the yard marker, Hughes scored again before Correia drew a flag for offensive pass interference on a two-point conversion attempt.

"He was going for the ball!" Aloisi shouted.

"I know he's big," replied the ref, "but he can't go through the player."

At halftime, the team gathered on the grass behind the far goalpost, a field's length from the lone figure of Donald Herman. Machado, the special-teams coach, pulled aside Sam Earle, his skinny kicker, who was distraught over missing his two point-after tries. "You're a football player first and a kicker second," said the coach. He left the long-faced kid sitting on his helmet, on an island of his own outside the tight cluster of his teammates. "Loneliest position on the field," Machado murmured as he walked away.

On the sideline Sam Aloisi, who'd driven over from his home in Plymouth to watch his son's team, spotted a familiar-looking fellow in a denim shirt, cowboy boots, and a Red Sox visor. "Holy crap!" said Aloisi. "That's Brads."

"Brads" was Bob Bradley, an assistant coach at Holy Cross who'd grown close to Aloisi's son during his career there. It was Bradley who traveled to Nantucket in the dead of January, after John's senior football season, to persuade him to sign a letter of intent. "It was cold as shit," he recalled. "I wouldn't have taken that God-dang boat ride if he'd not've accepted." The Holy Cross coaching staff knew they wanted the kid after seeing a videotape of his performance in his last Island Cup game. Bradley promised a full scholarship, but in the end the school offered nothing. "Sons of bitches!" the coach still gripes. Bradley later worked for two years with his former player at Worcester Academy, Aloisi's first coaching job. Out of guilt, he claimed.

Bradley had spent the past several years teaching the spread offense, just as the Whalers were now using, in a European football league. He'd coached it at Holy Cross, too. Over the years he'd brought players from UMass and a few of Aloisi's former Crusaders teammates to Austria to play a season or two. "They were throwing around the Austrians like rag dolls," he said.

In college, Aloisi was primarily a D-back, though he did sometimes carry the ball on offense. The intense young man worked relentlessly in the weight room to get himself up over 200 pounds. "He looks like a frickin' X-ray right now," groused Bradley.

But the coach beamed as he talked about his old player, whose work ethic and seriousness of purpose were unquestionable rarities. "He's a highly ethical kid," said Bradley, watching the field as Sam Earle drilled his point-after kick following Nantucket's first touchdown of the second half. "He defines himself, and he's consistent. What the hell else do you want out of a human being?"

On the field, after all the hand-wringing over the lackluster early play, it was Nantucket in a rout, 25–0. Aloisi was relieved. It wasn't pretty, he told his players afterward, but he wasn't going to harp on it. He congratulated his team on its seven wins—the first time in eight long years the program had won as many.

"This team has seven days of life left," he said. "I hope I've gained your trust a little more each week. We've elevated to a certain point, but I hope you're not happy with that."

They'd clinched second place in the Mayflower Small, but the Island Cup still lay ahead. "You will remember this for the rest of your life," said the coach. "You're staring at a beautiful opportunity. I'm real excited for you." Though he wasn't about to admit it, he was nearly as excited for himself. In just his second year with the program—the one he'd been uncomfortably unconvinced he wanted to take on—Aloisi and his deeply committed staff, former Whalers all, were on the verge of restoring the dignity of the once-dynastic Nantucket football team. He could not wait to get to practice on Monday.

DONALD HERMAN'S NEXT victory would be his 200th as a high school head coach, his 188th on the Vineyard. But cold, spitting rain soured the mood even before Somerset tried an onside kick to open its Friday night game on the island, and the clouds rumbling past to the south looked truly dastardly. These visiting kids were big, and they had yet to lose. Somerset, in fact, had just been listed as the number fourteen team in the state in the *Boston Globe*'s weekly poll. If this is what Herman's team, in its second year of Division 3 play, had to look forward to at the higher level, the coach might have to get used to settling into the middle of the pack.

Midway into the first quarter, the coach was crouching in a deep knee bend, staring balefully at his players on the soggy field. He had his back to the rest of his squad on the sideline, which was just as well. He was clearly struggling to keep his blood from boiling over. Though the Vineyard had drawn a Somerset lineman offside on a fourth and 3, grabbing a first down, that was the closest they'd come to mustering an offense. A personal foul added 15 yards to Somerset's first sustained drive, and after their first touchdown, the visitors tried another onside kick. This time it was successful—the Vineyard fumbled it away—and the home team's desperation was already palpable.

Despite a few big defensive plays—a saving tackle from Jette and a tipped pass at the goal line by Denver Maciel—it was still 18–0 at the half. Herman was irate.Trying to contain himself, he took the whiteboard, propped it against the wall in the field house, and tried to diagram the blocking he'd expected on Somerset's biggest lineman, number 78. When the board began to topple, he stabbed it with the marker, then attempted to kick it as it fell to the floor. Araujo, looking a foot taller than the coach, came to his side, picked up the board, and tried to right it. By then, however, Herman was not about to draw up any plays. Assistant Jason O'Donnell, the last coach off the field, solemnly lowered the metal garage door.

Why wasn't the Refrigerator getting blocked? Herman wanted to know. We can't see him, came the meek, mumbled reply.

*"You can't see him?"* repeated the coach, glaring at Adaaro with his head tilted at a crazy angle. "You can't miss him! He's six-four, two-ninety! I want you to go at him like a bat out of hell. Blow him up! We want the ball outside!"

Mistakes were killing them, he said, stating the obvious. Somerset was very good at controlling the ball. They hadn't punted in two weeks. The coach tried to gather his wits. "You gotta visualize the comeback," he said. As his dejected team prepared to head back out into the rain, he implored them to hit somebody: "Have some friggin' fun out there! If you hit people, you're gonna have fun."

But fun was not forthcoming. Somerset senior Seth DeMello, who would rush for over 1,800 yards on the season—more than 8 yards a carry—scored his second touchdown of three for the night. His backfield partner, Adam LeDoux, scored three of his own. Meanwhile, the Somerset defense, which had practiced forcing turnovers all week, saw their hard work pay off. The wheels fell off completely for the Vineyard after the half. In all, they fumbled the ball away five times and were intercepted twice more. "It's not that I'm at a loss for words," Herman told his team on the field after the clock ran out. "I've just got to watch what I say. If we continue to play like this, we'll be four and six, guaranteed."

"GENTLEMEN, IT'S BETTER to have died a small boy than to fumble this football." The quote, from trophy namesake John Heisman, was one of dozens of lines of coaching wisdom printed on sheets of paper, strewn around the front table at the Vineyard's team dinner the night before the Cape Tech game.

"Sounds like last week," said assistant coach Jason Dyer with a rueful chuckle.

Jack Law, the Touchdown Club president, recalled the year he invited the referees and their wives to the island for a team dinner the night before an Island Cup game. "Vito gave them so much shit, they never came back," he said.

If Donald Herman's team was still brooding over its ugly loss to Somerset, it didn't show. The JVs were getting their Hell Week song together. After dinner the team would move into the library to watch *Varsity Blues*.

In the darkened room with the movie running, a few boys snickered when Jon Voight's Coach Bud Kilmer growled to Mox, the rebellious quarterback, "You have got to be the dumbest smart kid I know."

One player blurted out the name of a teammate, drawing

laughs. The screening was interrupted when Herman's cell phone rang. The ringtone was "Glory, Glory," the Georgia rally song.

The game against Cape Tech the following afternoon was almost as uneventful as the two teams' meeting the previous season, which had been cancelled after the Vineyard high school experienced an outbreak of swine flu. The Vineyard's 35–6 win was just a warm-up for Bishop Feehan, a tough team that had a pitiless schedule, with lots of nonleague games against bigger opponents.

The trees were almost entirely stripped of their leaves as the Vineyard began to warm up on a chilly evening in Attleboro, where the Catholic school was located. Vineyard players had the number 21 stuck discreetly on their helmets in honor of the seventeen-year-old Feehan student who had drowned over the summer. Jamie Felix, still not cleared for contact after suffering a concussion, sat on the bench and tried to teach a cheerleader to roll her tongue.

For the first time since the beginning of the season, big Max Moreis stood by in his uniform. The 265-pounder was "available," if unlikely, to play, said the coaches. During the preseason he'd been fitted with an improvised Velcro harness to stabilize his injured right shoulder. Then he injured the left one. Though he sat out most of the season, unable to comb his hair, he'd postponed surgery until the Monday after the Nantucket game so he could suit up one more time.

"The things we do for the game," said Albie Robinson, Randall's stepfather, looking at Moreis from the stands. Leaning on the front railing of the sparsely populated visitors' grandstand, he jittered on the balls of his feet. It was chilly, but Robinson was also anxious for the game to begin. "I still get butterflies," he admitted.

It didn't help when the Vineyard gave up a 40-yard run on the first play from scrimmage. After grinding deep into Vineyard territory, Feehan decided to take a shot on fourth and 8. The pass was complete to a wide-open receiver wearing the Shamrocks' green and gold in the far corner of the end zone.

Following the point-after kick, Herman strode onto the field to confront the sophomore defensive back who'd missed his assignment. "Do your damn job!" the coach yelled into the kid's face mask. The free hot chocolates a Feehan parent carried over on a tray did little to brighten the mood of the Vineyard fans. The 10-yard holding penalty didn't help, nor did T. J. Vangervan's fumble, or the refs' non-call on a fourth-down pass play that could easily have been flagged. "C'mon, ref!" blurted Robinson. "He ain't playin' the ball! He never even looked."

Vangervan's father, Ted, had driven over from his home in Smithfield, Rhode Island, where he works at a wastewater treatment plant, to watch his son play. He and T.J.'s mother had divorced in 2000, and Ted was awarded custody of his son four years later. But he was working all the time; T.J. "basically raised himself from eleven or twelve," he said. When the boy's mother got her life in order, he moved back in with her. His father sold the big Cape-style house he'd built himself and moved off-island.

The elder Vangervan was the son of an opera tenor from the Netherlands who taught Gregorian chant to Trappist monks but made his living as a mason. The tradesman died of double pneumonia not long after his son was born. Ted kept tapes of his father's singing voice.

"Good stuff," he said, looking out at the football field, where his lanky son was having a tough game. When he dropped a punt, his buddy Jette (whom the public address announcer had called "Jet-tee") gave him a supportive slap on the helmet. Feehan's second touchdown of the third quarter made the score 21–0. On the 12-yard draw play for the score, Delmont Araujo got hurt. He slammed his helmet on the grass.

"Can we forfeit?" one chilly cheerleader mumbled, and her coach caught her. "Watch your mouth!" the coach barked.

With the score 27–0, Feehan looked to pour it on. An onside kick was successfully recovered. "That's bullshit!" assistant Jason O'Donnell yelled, glaring across the field. Another holding penalty on the host team ("Our best defenive play," moaned Albie) led to one more Vineyard opportunity, but an interception on a tipped pass let Feehan run out the clock with a few more hand-offs. "Take the knee!" Herman shouted at the opposing coaches.

Though angry with the Feehan coach, he was mainly disgusted with his own team. They'd lost before they took the field, Herman told his players before they climbed onto the bus. They needed to get meaner. They needed to work on hand strength. The fact was, they were still 5–2. "Your goal is to be eight and two," he said. "Seniors, this is on you guys. This is your team." He didn't want to hear about any shenanigans over the weekend that would jeopardize the remaining weeks.

"We know half the police force on the island," he reminded them. "Half of them played for me."

Many of the Vineyard cops were, in fact, former football players—a good number of them nearly Herman's age. Eric Blake, the Oak Bluffs police chief, played for Tankard, Herman's predecessor. So did Tom Smith, an Edgartown officer whose son, Conor, had just undergone emergency surgery to remove his appendix. David and Dan Rossi were two more of Tankard's players now wearing badges. David Rossi assisted Herman for a time during the 1990s. When the graduates from those teams see him on the street, they still call him Coach. It feels a lot better than the wary reaction he gets from some other young men in the community.

Vineyard play-by-play man Ken Goldberg, who has a knack for bestowing catchy nicknames, dubbed linebacker Ryan Ruley "the Little Imp" when he played on the Vineyard's first undefeated team in 1997. A senior that year, Ruley later became a member of the police force out in Aquinnah, the remote corner of the island formerly known as Gay Head. The Ruley family has perhaps the most unusual perspective on the island rivalry of them all: Ryan's father, Steve, once played quarterback for Vito.

Later, working for the A&P supermarket, the elder Ruley was asked to cover shifts for a fellow meat department manager's vacation on the Vineyard. "I liked it so much, we moved here," says Steve Ruley, who now lives in Florida. Nantucketers, of course, have never let him forget it: "They think I'm a traitor." In truth, he says, he's happy for whichever team wins the Island Cup. Surely he's the only one.

ON THE MONDAY after the Vineyard's next game, Herman and his assistants watched glumly as just twenty boys trotted onto the practice field. The team was ravaged with injuries. The bruised hip Delmont suffered against Bishop Feehan had kept him out of Friday's game against another Catholic school and Eastern Athletic Conference foe, Bishop Stang. Brian Montambault had battled a fluke infection in his leg all week before being cleared for the Stang game. Inside linebacker Mike Montanile was out for the season with a shoulder injury. And Conor Smith, with his appendix trouble, was also finished. On the Saturday after the

Feehan game, he'd driven with his dad to West Point to watch
Virginia Military Institute take on Army in a battle of cadets.
Conor felt sick to his stomach on the trip. Then he started
throwing up. The well-bred young man, who felt the weight of
responsibility more than a lot of boys his age, was distraught
that he would have to miss the rest of the season. "I feel bad
for the kid," said his father. "He doesn't know what to do with
himself."

"To say we had some adversity to overcome this week is a
gross understatement," said Coach Herman. They'd overcome it,
but just barely, in the Bishop Stang game. It was a seesaw strug-
gle throughout. Randall Jette threw for two touchdowns and
ran for two more, including a 65-yard punt return in the first
quarter. Stang countered that score with a 75-yard return for a
touchdown on the ensuing kickoff. Before the half, Stang went
up, 21–20, on a middle screen on third and long that broke for
38 yards. During a time-out just before the play, Herman reminded his team that they'd worked on defending the middle
screen in practice that week. Stang was going to run it now,
he predicted. Duly prepped, the Vineyard defense gave up the
touchdown nonetheless. The coach's halftime performance
made his whiteboard-slamming outburst during the Somerset
game look like teatime by comparison.

He was far happier with his team's effort the following week
against Nauset, an independent team from a regional high school
on the Cape, in the Vineyard's final tune-up before the Island
Cup. The Warriors, wearing travel whites trimmed with black
and gold, posed yet another serious threat. On the ferry from
the mainland, several of their players had milled around the pas-
senger deck of the boat, looking as though they were girding

themselves for a brawl. It was cold out, but a couple of the beefi-
est invaders tucked their sleeves under their pads, exposing upper arms like hams.

At the high school, Herman took one look at the visitors and
whistled low. "These fuckers are huge," he mumbled out of the
corner of his mouth, taking care that none of his own players
heard. Their fullback was a truck—six-four, 240—and they had
several linemen of comparable size. Under a looming half-moon,
the two teams went through their stretching exercises on opposite ends of the field. The adrenaline-pumping music blaring
over the loudspeaker veered crazily from the old *Monday Night
Football* theme to DMX's profane rap "We Don't Give a Fuck."
That barely censored anthem was followed by the Vineyarders'
unofficial fight song, "Purple Haze."

Midway through the first quarter, a contingent of Nantucket
coaches climbed out of a cab in the parking lot and paid for
tickets at the folding table by the fence. They climbed up the
grandstand, past the animated Friday night throng of hundreds
of flirting high schoolers, and squeezed into spaces on the bench
along the back row, up near the press box. If the coaches expected to go unnoticed, Almodobar blew their cover when he
replaced his flat cap with a warmer lid—a blue-and-white
Whalers ski hat with a pom-pom on top.

The Vineyard stands erupted when Tyler Araujo took a handoff from Jette, broke a tackle, and found a huge clearing, lumbering 48 yards into Nauset territory. A few plays later, after the
quarterback converted a risky fourth-and-6 play by gaining
the edge on a sweep, the Vineyard seemed on the verge of a
score. But Araujo was strung out, and then laid out, in the scrum
inside the 5. When the whistle blew and the players rolled off

the pile, the fullback remained on the ground. The trainer brought out the golf cart. At halftime, the team would learn that he'd suffered a concussion. Another player done for the season. In the press box, Bill Belcher lamented the team's relentless injury bug. "That's exactly what we didn't want to happen," he said.

With the score tied at seven apiece just seconds before the half, the Warriors made a last-ditch effort to throw into the end zone. Jette was in position to defend the play, but as he and the receiver twisted in the air, he bent back at the waist, making sure to avoid contact. The pass dropped over the Nauset player's outside shoulder and into his hands. Jette, typically the most composed player on the field, was visibly upset. Reluctant to draw the interference penalty, he had given up a touchdown he'd normally prevent nine times out of ten.

As penance, Jette scored on a 60-yard burst down the near sideline to bring his team within six in the third quarter. They had to bring out the cart a second time when sophomore linebacker Doug Andrade—the player who had taken the brunt of Herman's wrath on a blown coverage during the game at Bishop Feehan—wrenched his back in a pile. Play stopped for ten solid minutes while they tended to the injured player. Montambault, Delmont Araujo, and Dhonathan Lemos all came up with gutsy defensive plays, but it wasn't enough. A Nauset fumble deep in Vineyard territory looked like a sure recovery for the home team, but the Warriors were somehow awarded the ball. With time disappearing, the Vineyard's desperate final series ended in futility. When Jette was run out of bounds on a fourth and 10, Martha's Vineyard turned the ball over on downs. Nauset took a knee.

"You have nothing to hang your head about," Herman told

his team. "Be upset that you lost, yes, but not too upset about the way you played." They'd given everything they had, and that's all their coaches could ask. Now the team, six and three, could finally set its sights on the other island.

"I've been looking forward to this for two years," said the coach.

*Chapter Eleven*

# PURPLE PRIDE

IN EIGHT LONG years as the Vineyard's head coach, Bob Tankard managed to beat Nantucket just once. By the end of his run in 1987, the rivalry was lopsided in the Whalers' favor, 27–11–3. Tankard had his best team in 1985, led by Jimmy Jette, Mike Joyce, Glennie Gonsalves, and a core group of linemen including Eric Blake, the future police chief, and Peter Duart, who once shaved an *M* and a *V* on either side of his Mohawk for an Island Cup game. Duart reminded Charles McGrath of Queequeg. Sadly, comparison with Melville's fictional "savage" would prove uncomfortably apt: during the 2010 football season, several years after stepping down as one of Donald Herman's assistants, Duart was sentenced to ten years in state prison after being convicted of sexual assault.

Over the years Tankard grew accustomed to Capizzo's needling at the Mayflower League coaches' meetings. But on the Monday after the Vineyard's 12–2 win with that 1985 squad, Capizzo didn't show up. Unwilling to subject himself to a taste of his own medicine, that was the day he sent an assistant instead. Order was restored the following year, at least from Vito's perspective, when his Whalers throttled the Vineyarders, 34–0.

When Tankard's replacement arrived for the 1988 season, there was little reason to believe the uneven rivalry would begin to balance out. Donald Herman had amassed an unspectacular 12–18 coaching record in three seasons down in Georgia. His first team on the island went 5–5, squandering a chance at a winning season when it dropped the Cup game, 14–0, on the final weekend. Still, the new-look Vineyarders made an impression on Capizzo's staff when they arrived on the Cape for the Mayflower League's annual jamboree wearing ties. Vaughan Machado was quick to point it out to Capizzo.

"Ah, what's that mean?" scoffed the coach.

"Discipline," replied his assistant.

And the 1989 Vineyarders were better—a lot better. On their first possession of the year, option quarterback Todd Araujo set the tone with a breezy 77-yard touchdown sprint. His father, big Joe, ran all the way up the sideline, cheering. The elder Araujo "was not as quick to recuperate from the dash as Todd was," the *Martha's Vineyard Times* teased.

The Vineyard blanked Pope John, 29–0, in the opener, with Araujo scoring three times. Senior Lou Paciello, a workhorse, had eleven tackles and key yardage from the fullback position. The following week Hurricane Hugo forced a postponement until Sunday, when the Vineyard racked up 480 yards of total offense en route to a thorough demolition of the Holbrook Bulldogs, 41–6. Still, Herman was not happy. At halftime he berated his team for its excessive number of penalties. Against a decent opponent, he said, those penalties would be the difference between winning and losing. Yet the margin of victory gave the coach an early opportunity to grant some of his younger players a little game-time experience. One of the JVs who logged some second-half minutes was a 90-pound freshman. Another ninth grader, Jason Dyer, got a chance to show some of his promise as a kicker. "Purple Pride" awards for the game included a lobster from Edgartown Seafood, ice cream from Katama Farms, and a free tape rental from a local video store.

The island's next game was against an unpredictable West Bridgewater team that had won its opener, 36–0, then laid down for Bristol-Plymouth, 38–0. With Paciello, the "hammering" back, taking 124 yards on the ground by brute force, the Vineyarders were lucky to escape with a 7–0 win. "We needed a little humility," Herman told a reporter, "and now we have it."

Dreams of an undefeated season died on the 45-yard line of Bristol-Plymouth a week later, when a potential game-tying drive was snuffed on fourth and 3 with less than two minutes to play. That was more than enough humility for Herman: from there, his team went on a tear, thumping Southeastern and Cape Tech and intercepting seven passes in another romp over Blue Hills.

In early November, the high school's better half got into the football spirit. Junior and senior girls faced off against each other in the inaugural Powder Puff game, which the juniors— co-coached by John Bacheller, who was back for one more round as an assistant with the varsity—won by a touchdown. The *Times* article on the fund-raiser called them "Violent Femmes." The boys, meanwhile, tuned up for the Island Cup with another easy win, besting Old Colony by 35 points.

Headed into the island clash with more confidence than they'd had in years, the Vineyard boasted two backs, the fleet-footed Araujo and the lumbering Paciello, who'd gained nearly 1,000 rushing yards apiece on the season. In addition to the two stars, receiver John Cataloni and 305-pound lineman Niko

Vega were named to the Mayflower League All-Star team. After nine games, the team's defense, coordinated by first-year assistant David Morris, had given up just 40 points.

Following the loss to Bristol-Plymouth, Coach Herman had promised his players that he would shave his beloved mustache if they could run the table the rest of the way. He was more than happy to oblige when they pulled it off. Nantucket was unable to stop Paciello, who smashed past the 1,000-yard mark with three touchdown runs, giving him thirteen on the season, and in the postgame celebration on the field, the smiling coach buzzed away at his thick mustache with an electric razor. In the locker room, he lathered his upper lip with shaving cream and finished the job. (When he got home, his young son, Eric, didn't recognize him.) The 26–14 victory gave Herman his first taste of the Island Cup. It also gave the Vineyard a 9–1 record, the school's best ever.

There would be no postseason play; Bristol-Plymouth won the league with an undefeated season. Still, it felt strange, having this kind of success. "Donald Herman saved Martha's Vineyard football," declares Paciello, who still savors the joy of his senior season after a high school career marked by futility. Herman was determined to instill a tradition of sustained excellence in a football program that had played second fiddle to its neighbor for decades. At the team's year-end banquet a few weeks after Thanksgiving, he received a standing ovation. Though he'd finished second in the balloting for Mayflower League Coach of the Year, Vineyard fans were sure he'd gotten robbed. They knew they had a keeper. It felt damn good to beat Nantucket, and to look down on them in the standings for once. "It is certain that the trophy will spend a lot more time on the Vineyard as the '90s begin," the *Times* predicted.

Of course, success in high school demands a continuous flow of new talent, and many Vineyard footballers were graduating. After getting his diploma, Paciello went off to Springfield College, where he became close buddies with former Whaler Bill Manchester. Todd Araujo left the island for Worcester, where he suited up in another purple uniform for the Holy Cross football team. He went on to become a lawyer, commemorating the Wampanoag side of his family's heritage by specializing in American Indian law and policy. He would work for the Department of Justice as a deputy director of the Office of Tribal Justice before moving to Juneau, Alaska, to practice law and raise his family.

There was something about this Dyer kid that made the coach feel he might be leadership material. He was never without a ball in his hands. He was headstrong, too. The more Herman got to know him when the new season got under way, he realized he'd said "Damn it, Dyer!" so many times it had become a nickname—Dammit Dyer. The fair-haired boy was born in western Massachusetts, where his young mother was raised. Seven weeks after his birth, his mother died of a mysterious case of cardiac arrest. To this day, Dyer says, none of his relatives knows exactly what happened.

"Everyone tells me she was the light of the family," he said during the 2010 season, gazing out the window of the ferry.

The boy moved to the Vineyard with his father, where Daniel Dyer's own father had been a gym teacher at the old Tisbury High School before becoming a baseball coach in the western part of the state. Dan Dyer was a pretty good football player, a safety and receiver on a top-ranked team. He excelled at basketball and set a high-jump record in high school. "But he can't throw a football to save his life," said the son.

Unlike his father, there's no question that Jason Dyer can throw a football. A sophomore for the 1990 season, he won the job as the Vineyard's starting quarterback and quickly began giving his coaches reasons to revise their offensive strategy. Against Holbrook, Dyer threw twenty-three times—an astronomical number for a team accustomed to the ramrod rushing of Lou Paciello. Dyer was a playmaker, a frantic scrambler who refused to go down or waste a play by throwing the ball out of bounds. In that Holbrook game, he completed ten passes for 98 yards. His receivers were still figuring it out. Behind a tough defensive effort led by John Gonsalves, who had thirteen solo tackles, the team won, 16–0.

But it soon became apparent this was a rebuilding year. The Vineyarders lost a sloppy, penalty-filled overtime game to West Bridgewater. Both teams scored in the extra frame, but Dyer's desperate attempt to complete the two-point conversion that would preserve the tie sailed out of bounds. Before the end of regulation, Herman's team had two scores called back on flags, including a fourth-quarter Dyer pass that would have been the difference. "We lost to ourselves," the coach said after the game. "We got rattled and lost our composure." The team had some soul-searching to do, he said.

They also had their hands full with teams looking to avenge losses they'd suffered the year before, when Herman's team stormed through its schedule. Southeastern won in a battle of haymakers with an 80-yard kick return in the final minutes. A week later, Blue Hills overcame a 6–0 halftime deficit with two unanswered second-half scores. By the time the Nantucket game rolled around, Herman, looking glumly at his team's 4–5 record, was downplaying expectations. "We're not supposed to win," he said. "We have no pressure."

It was the Whalers' turn to host. No Vineyard team had won on the other island since way back in 1972, when a 4–4 Vineyard team stunned an undefeated Capizzo squad. The athletic director's office, taking pains to rally the school, posted a note outside the door reminding students and faculty of the old upset. Despite the strong likelihood of a blowout—Nantucket was coming in once again without a loss—the Vineyarders had come to relish the shot at redemption the Island Cup routinely provided. During down seasons, it was, at the very least, a place to air your frustrations. "This resentment and antipathy, as a Vineyarder knows, comes once a year," wrote an aspiring student reporter in a section of the *Martha's Vineyard Times* called "High School View."

If Dyer and his team were intimidated when the Whalers' public address system at the school's old Burnham Dell Field blared "Another One Bites the Dust" before kickoff, they didn't show it. In the early going, Nantucket fumbled away a punt on its own 26-yard line, and a few plays later Dyer calmly hit his classmate Albie Robinson for a short-yardage touchdown.

But Nantucket's Chris Frame exacted quick revenge for the fumble, taking the ensuing kickoff at the nine and running it back the length of the field. The Whalers never looked back, cruising to a 38–14 win.

In a lopsided Super Bowl matchup, the Whalers hung in with a bigger, stronger team from Greater Lowell, a city school with a much larger student enrollment than the island. They lost by a touchdown.

During Jason Dyer's junior year, his father and stepmother got divorced. She moved away, to the Midwest, where she would remarry after meeting a guy with two sons of his own. Dyer stayed on the island with his father, maintaining a heavy-hearted relationship with his mother's family in western Massachusetts. If kids from broken homes are particularly susceptible to alcohol and substance abuse, the young quarterback refused to open that door.

He got his rush on the football field. For the new season, the Vineyard unveiled some new and improved weapons for Dyer's arsenal. They had a speedster named Sahava Gates. Junior Albie Robinson emerged as a difference-maker on both sides of the ball, registering two interceptions, two fumble recoveries, and two touchdowns in the team's 29–0 drubbing of Old Colony on opening day. By midseason Herman's reenergized team was a perfect 5–0, facing a significant matchup on the mainland with Southeastern's own undefeated group. It was, the *Times* suggested, the toughest game of the season "B.N."—before Nantucket.

But Southeastern rolled over, taking a devastating one-two combination in the opening round when Dyer connected with Gates for a pair of long touchdowns, one for 50 yards, the other for 75. The win pushed the Vineyard to the fourth spot in the *Globe*'s interleague poll for Division 5. In fifth sat Nantucket, with six wins and one loss. With a soft schedule, the Vineyard's biggest obstacle in the way of an all-island Mayflower League championship showdown would be overconfidence, the *Times* declared. The most drama in early November might have come in the girls' Powder Puff game, when Coach Bacheller called his favorite play—Sperm Right, Egg Left.

Four thousand boisterous fans showed up at the MVRHS field on the Saturday before Thanksgiving. One of them wore a costume of purple grapes, like a refugee from a Fruit of the Loom commercial. With nightly news footage still fresh in the public mind from the relentless air attack in the recently wrapped Gulf War, the Vineyard's air assault was inevitably compared to General Norman Schwarzkopf's. If not quite as obliterating, it got the job done. With a contingent on hand to commemorate the twenty-fifth anniversary of Capizzo's unde-feated 1966 team, the Vineyard won the season's island battle in a low-scoring affair. "Viking Air Attack Sinks Whalers," crowed the *Times* headline. The win qualified the school to compete two weeks later for the EMass 5B title (the divisions having been split into two levels apiece) against Jeremiah Burke High School, from the inner-Boston neighborhood of Dorchester.

Taking the bus ride to Boston's Robert White Stadium, the site of the Super Bowl, the islanders might as well have been traveling to the other side of the earth. Located in Franklin Park, the imposing facility had once been the site of a massive protest in the aftermath of the assassination of Martin Luther King Jr. Under the black nationalist flag of Marcus Garvey, organizers for a group called the Black United Front presented a list of twenty-one demands for justice. Now the Vineyard had its own statement to make, of a very different kind.

Melting snow made a mess of the field. Three of the Vineyard's four Mayflower League All-Stars for the season—Robinson,

Gates, and John Gonsalves—were injured during the game. But none of that mattered. Seeing the Vineyard for the first time, rabble-rousing *Globe* sportswriter Dan Shaughnessy, inventor of the "Curse of the Bambino," was reminded of the swarming defense of the Minnesota Vikings' old "Purple People Eaters." Burke star William "Bunny" Jefferson put up a valiant effort, but he could not carry his team singlehandedly. The island interlopers thoroughly dominated in the first half, and the end result was not as close as the final score (24–10) might have indicated.

THE ISLANDS SHARED mirror-image records the following season. Each team bowed in its season opener, then reeled off eight straight wins. The Vineyard's sole loss, by a slim 6–0 margin, came at the hands of Ipswich, a north-of-Boston high school that had won a Division 4B Super Bowl the previous season and would win another that December.

Two months later, the Vineyarders were on a steamroller. The team logged three straight shutouts, engineered a come-from-behind victory against a formidably beefy Southeastern team, and overcame injuries to several key starters. Nantucket, meanwhile, had recovered from a 32–0 drubbing against a strong Central Mass opponent to coast through a "fairly boring" winning season, as the *Inky* had it.

On Nantucket the Saturday before Thanksgiving, Dyer, one of the Vineyard's four captains, shook hands with Capizzo at midfield. A small plane flew overhead, trailing a banner that read GO VINEYARDERS! The Vineyard's TV announcers were as giddy as ever, introducing themselves as "Larry, Moe, and Curly" and noting the electricity in the air: "You could probably put the lights on without plugging in," one of them suggested.

Throughout his high school career Dyer, now a senior, had thrived on broken plays. Chased out of the pocket by an opponent's defensive linemen, he made a habit of evading tacklers until he could find an open man downfield.

On this day, however, the Whalers were relentless. For the first three quarters, Dyer and his receiving corps were frustrated time and again. At the beginning of the final quarter, down 12–0, the quarterback fumbled the ball away as he got sacked. On the sideline, Donald Herman wiped his face. Over the next several minutes Capizzo's team executed a methodical march deep into enemy territory. One more score and the game would be out of reach. "You just feel the mood swing," said an uncharacteristically deflated Ken Goldberg, the play-by-play man.

But a successful goal-line stand rekindled the faint hopes of the hundreds of chilly Vineyarders who'd made the trip. Less than five minutes showed on the electric scoreboard. All his life Jason Dyer had demonstrated a knack for making something out of nothing on the football field. Now a strange sense of calm washed over him. Surrounded by high emotion, he had no doubt he could do it again.

Scrambling, he found his friend Jason O'Donnell streaking up the right sideline for a huge gain. A roughing-the-passer call added 10 yards, putting the ball on the 11-yard line. Two plays later, Dyer lofted a perfectly placed toss into the corner of the end zone to Albie Robinson, who stood on his toes as he cradled the ball, then toppled stiffly out of bounds. Straight-on kicker Mike Dowd tied his shoelaces just in time to nail the extra point, and the visitors suddenly need just one more big play to steal away with an improbable victory.

Nantucket gained one first down with its ground game but

could not manage another. With the Vineyard burning its time-outs, the team would get one last opportunity to move the ball. There were just over two minutes to play.

Dyer, wearing number 13, returned the Whalers' kickoff to midfield. On the first play from scrimmage, he dropped back and quickly passed into the flat. Two Nantucket defenders sailed past the receiver, Keith Devine, and he sprinted all the way up the left sideline for the go-ahead score. "Unbelievable!" Goldberg cackled. "Can you believe it?"

Nerves jangled on both sides of the field as Nantucket's coaching staff plotted what was perhaps the team's last series of downs of the season. When the Vineyard broke up a screen pass from Whaler quarterback Dennis Caron (the assistant coach's son), the ball wobbled to a stop on the ground behind the line of scrimmage. While players and referees milled around, Aaron Fox, a feisty player whose older brother, Rocky, had been another standout for Capizzo, astutely scooped up the ball and galloped all the way to the Vineyard 18 before being shoved out of bounds. The play was ruled a lateral—a live ball.

But after Fox was angled out on a sweep for short yardage, big Greg Belcher ran down Caron on a rollout. Third and 10. Mike Dowd leveled Fox at the line of scrimmage. Capizzo, more confident in his offensive leaders than in his field goal kicker, opted to run one more desperation play. On fourth down, Albie Robinson laid himself out to knock away the potential winning touchdown.

Incredibly, with four seconds left, Nantucket still had one final play, after the Vineyard had been forced to punt out of its own end zone. But Dyer, playing deep in the defensive backfield, plucked Caron's Hail Mary pass out of the sky at the goal line. For the first time in twenty years, the football team from Martha's Vineyard would be going home with a victory from the other island.

Two weeks later, Donald Herman's Vineyarders defeated Latin Academy for the team's second consecutive Super Bowl championship. Yet compared to the frantic victory on Nantucket, which would be remembered by both sides as the true turning point in this storybook rivalry, the championship game in Boston was anticlimactic.

Whatever else he accomplishes in his life, on Martha's Vineyard, Jason Dyer will always remain the young man who refused to let his senior team lose a game they had no business winning. Any superlative you could muster about a high school football game, said Ken Goldberg near the finish of the Vineyard's greatest Island Cup upset, "we've seen it here today."

*Chapter Twelve*

# THE SON EVERYONE
# WOULD LIKE TO HAVE

NANTUCKET JUNIOR MICHAEL Day was the great-grandson of Stuart B. Day, an islander who had covered Whalers football games for the *Inky* decades ago. The high schooler's classmates knew his great-grandfather as the namesake of the annual homecoming game. Michael was not just an island legacy—he was also the front-runner to be Capizzo's next starting quarterback as the 1993 season got under way. The last man taking snaps for the Whalers, Dennis Caron Jr. (the JV coach's son), had graduated that spring. Sophomore John Aloisi, who was already getting plenty of playing time as a defensive back, was another option.

Capizzo was close to the Aloisis. He and Barbara had spent a lot of time socially with Sam and Joanne Aloisi before their divorce. Joanne had even been a gym teacher alongside the coach for a short period, years before. Yet a bit of intrigue had arisen between the two families. Joanne put herself on Vito's bad side when she voiced her disapproval of the coach's preferential treatment for the football team. When she spoke to the school principal about it, Capizzo was indignant.

At issue was the football team's long-standing tradition of

leaving school for Saturday away games at noon on Fridays. After taking the ferry they'd run through a casual practice, then spend the afternoon at the Cape Cod Mall in Hyannis before checking into their hotel. The players, of course, loved it, but Joanne felt there was no reason to take the boys out of school. And she said so.

"They could have left at five o'clock," she says. "Vito had gotten to a point where whatever he wanted, went."

Unfortunately, her middle son took the brunt of the coach's wrath. "I made waves, and he took it out on Matt," says Joanne. "There's no getting around it." The oldest Aloisi boy, Sam, had been a Capizzo favorite; the coach, after all, was Sam's godfather. But Matt, a fullback and defensive lineman who was bigger than his brothers, grew discouraged by what he felt was unfair treatment.

There was more uncertainty than usual as the 1993 season began. A dozen seniors from the previous team were gone, and there were only six juniors committed to return. With such inexperience, this season might prove to be one of the most challenging yet for the three-decade coach, wrote the *Inky*'s sports reporter. "We're not talking green," joked the writer, Chris Worth, a descendant of several whaling captains who had been Capizzo's quarterback in the late 1970s. "How about seeds?"

Capizzo's job got that much tougher when Day came down with a case of mononucleosis, which would keep the junior off the field for the first few weeks of practice. And so the baby of the Aloisi family was pressed into action.

He played a fine game in his first start at quarterback, as the Whalers stuffed Arlington Catholic, 13–0, on the strength of four interceptions. Aloisi willed the team's offense with two key fourth-down conversions. But as the game was winding down, he took an awkward hit as he was tackled out of bounds, and he had to be helped off the field with a muscle strain.

"He took the licks," said Coach Capizzo after the game.

When Day returned, he was converted into a receiver, and he immediately became one of Aloisi's favorite targets. The junior made the play of the game in a high-scoring win over Old Colony, catching a pass on a third-and-long situation for 35 yards. Blanketed by a defender, Day leaped like a ballerina executing a grand jeté, tipping the ball away from the defender and into his own hands. Only Lynn Swann made catches like that.

When West Bridgewater's Bill Panos devised a defensive scheme that would shut off the young quarterback Aloisi's sprint out pass, Capizzo countered with an old-fashioned running game between the tackles. Three ball carriers combined for 148 yards on nineteen rushes to lead the versatile Whalers to a 19–0 shutout victory. Two weeks later, after installing the wishbone offense, Nantucket put six different players in the end zone on its first six possessions. During a 37–6 demolition of Southeastern on the final weekend before the Island Cup, the quarterback executed a fake handoff so perfectly that even the officials were fooled. Running back David Murray was pounded into the ground at the line of scrimmage by the entire opposing defense, and the refs blew their whistles before Aloisi could complete his invisible saunter into the end zone on the naked bootleg. No matter: the Whalers scored again two plays later.

With Aloisi coming into his own running the triple option, the team that had been earmarked for a rebuilding year was starting to look like yet another island juggernaut in the making. At the beginning of the season, when the *Inky* writer wondered whether it might be a trying season for the Whalers, he'd been quick to note that the coach had long since proved he was capable of creating champion-caliber teams out of thin air. How many times had he predicted his team would finish 5–5, then ended up 9–1? "Don't fool us, Capizzo," the columnist wrote.

Coincidentally, a win over the Vineyard that year would mark Capizzo's two hundredth career victory. The milestone would put him in select company across the state, alongside local legends such as Walpole's John Lee, Swampscott's Stan Bondelevitch, and Brockton's Armond Colombo, the winningest coach in state history, who led the Division 1 Boxers to nine Super Bowls and ten straight Suburban League titles and married Rocky Marciano's sister.

But Vito was concerned about a different record: 2–3. That was his mark against the Vineyard since the arrival of Donald Herman, who had, annoyingly, won Super Bowls in each of the past two seasons, just his fourth and fifth on the job. Speculation had begun about Capizzo's potential retirement, but he wanted no part of it. "All I care about is beating the Vineyard," he said.

That year, he got his wish. With nearly a thousand Nantucketers paying twelve bucks apiece to travel over to the Vineyard on a chartered ferry, the Whalers outlasted their archrivals, 7–6. Nantucket's lone touchdown came on "Lonesome Lion," an isolation play to a tight end on the left side of the field, with all the other backs lined up to the right. Shane McWeeny got a hand on the Vineyard's only point-after try for the difference in the ballgame. Mike Maury, the younger son of 1970 team captain Chris Maury, dumped a Vineyard runner for a critical 3-yard loss in the closing minutes. On the other side of the ball Mike Dowd, a

Vineyard stalwart who had been kicking all year, missed a 36-yard field goal attempt, sealing the win for the Whalers.

In hindsight, a lot of Nantucket fans and alumni believed they knew how the dependable Vineyarder missed the field goal. "It was divine intervention," says Rob Mooney. Twenty-six-year-old Tim Ostebo, the fearless quarterback from the Whalers' great teams of the early 1980s, died that day in an accident on a snowy mountain pass in Idaho, where he'd been attending graduate school. Like most everyone else on the island, Mooney didn't learn the sad news until Sunday, the day after the Island Cup.

After the game an elated Mike Maury spoke on behalf of the team. "This is our Super Bowl," he said. "Everything else is gravy. We're headed for the gravy now."

Both teams, in fact, brought heavy hearts to the Division 5B Super Bowl. Boston English was mourning the loss of a sophomore student named Louis Brown, who was shot and killed in the city that week. English, a team strong enough to beat the eventual 5A champions from West Roxbury earlier in the season, held off the islanders for a 16–7 win. Afterward, the teams were gracious to each other in the handshake line. "You'll be back," English captain Michael Massey told Aloisi and his teammates. Massey, who ran for 110 yards and scored both English touchdowns, had a knack for making predictions: before the season he'd promised a Super Bowl win, even though his team had won just two games the previous year. Speaking to a reporter after the game, the captain was emotionally overwhelmed on behalf of his embattled school. "I hope this game puts English on the map for something positive," he said.

Capizzo, who often complained about the standards of all

those vocational schools his teams played, was impressed. "It was a real classy high school," he said.

THE FOLLOWING WEEK, the island football community attended its fallen star's funeral. The service took place in the Unitarian Universalist Church on Orange Street, where Ostebo's step-father, Ted Anderson, was the minister. The young man's mother, Gretchen, asked Capizzo to do a eulogy.

"It was the toughest thing I've ever done," says the coach.

Chris Warner, who caught the first touchdown pass of his life as a sophomore when Ostebo drew up a play for him, sat in front of the Rev. Anderson, awaiting his turn to read. His knees were quaking. Standing, he delivered the opening stanzas of A. E. Housman's poem "To an Athlete Dying Young."

> The time you won your town the race,
> We chaired you through the market-place.
> Man and boy stood cheering by,
> And home we brought you shoulder-high.
> To-day, the road all runners come,
> Shoulder-high we bring you home,
> And set you at your threshold down,
> Townsman of a stiller town.

AS ALOISI'S JUNIOR year began, it was becoming apparent that he was one of the special ones. Whalers fans hadn't seen a quarterback with such talent since Ostebo's heyday, the team's local correspondent declared.

To start the season, Aloisi connected with Day for three touchdowns against Arlington Catholic. A few weeks later he led his team to another crisp 19–0 win over a good West Bridge-water team, which was on its way to a third straight Super Bowl appearance in the newly created Division 6. Next the Whalers took it to a competitive Blue Hills program with some fero-cious tackling in a 20-point victory. Capizzo had dubbed that key matchup the "Scallop Bowl": the loser may as well open scallops for the rest of the year, he said. When Blue Hills was shut out by the Vineyard a few weeks later, the team's coach was asked whether he felt the Vineyarders had any chance of un-seating the Whalers.

"None that I can discern," said the aptly named Bill Moan.

Complacency was becoming an issue for the stocked Nan-tucket program. After taking a 27–0 lead against winless Cape Tech, Capizzo rested his starters, and the Crusaders rallied within a touchdown before the Whalers scored once more to seal the victory. Capizzo insisted he was just being courteous, refusing to run up the score against an opponent he liked well enough. "Those are good people," he said. "I don't think I'll be as nice to Bristol-Plymouth or Southeastern."

Nantucket made good on this promise, pounding Bristol-Plymouth, 37–6. Southeastern was another story. Though the vokies from the southern part of the state would win just two games on the season, their defense knocked first Aloisi, then his sophomore backup, Bobby King, out of the game with injuries. Day, who was by then comfortably settled into his role as a two-way deep man, was forced to fill in until a wobbly Aloisi returned in the fourth quarter to engineer a come-from-behind win. Capizzo's squad was "like the Notre Dame of the Mayflower League," marveled the Southeastern coach. Cocaptain Jake Payne, a 220-pounder, had been wishing for just one victory over Nantucket since his freshman year. At least it was close, he said. A win over the island powerhouse "would've made everything" for his fellow seniors. "All four years."

But Southeastern was just a speed bump for Nantucket on the road to the Island Cup. It didn't much matter that the Vineyard was 7–2, with no chance of catching the undefeated Whalers for the league title. Herman's team had beaten East Boston in their first game of the season, and for a time it seemed that East Boston might be Nantucket's 5B opponent in the Super Bowl.

As the Island Cup approached, the papers wondered whether President Clinton, who was becoming a bit of a Vineyard regular, had spent time thinking about the locals' big game. After all, his beloved Razorbacks hadn't started their basketball season yet.

That week Capizzo took a routine first-aid exam, a periodic requirement for gym teachers. As he climbed out of the swimming pool, he felt dizzy. He was taken to the hospital, where doctors discovered a bleeding ulcer. The fifty-four-year-old coach wasn't taking great care of himself. Much of the community learned for the first time that week that he'd needed three pints of blood during another ulcer attack a few years before.

Regardless of how well the team was playing, 1994 was beginning to seem an ominous year for the future of Whalers football. In September, the big news had not been the start of another football season but the inauguration of another fall sport. "Soccer Arrives!" the *Inky* rejoiced in a front-page headline on an article about a 2–0 win over Chatham. The introduction of Vito's reviled "Commie roundball" surely didn't make his queasy stomach feel any better.

Late in the week, Capizzo lay in a hospital bed, missing the pep rally. But the stubborn coach had no intention of missing the game, too.

"No way I was staying in there," he said after his Whalers handled their island rivals with ease, 23–7, on Nantucket. Day caught five of Aloisi's passes for 132 yards and two touchdowns. The receiver came out for the second half wearing number 11, in honor of his friend and teammate Shane McWeeny, who'd missed most of the season after breaking his leg in the first quarter against Arlington Catholic. With the game over, Mike Maury wanted redemption for the previous season's Super Bowl loss. "It feels great to beat the Vineyard," he said, "but this year we go eleven and oh."

Aloisi agreed. His team had made the mistake of thinking their season was complete after beating the Vineyard in 1993, "but losing the bowl was terrible."

Their opponent in the championship game turned out to be the Tyngsboro Tigers, against whom the islanders had played an ugly, underwhelming scrimmage during the preseason. Still, Nantucket fans were convinced this was the year their boys would avenge the big blemish on Capizzo's record: since the 1980 team capped its incredible season with a Super Bowl win, Vito's teams had lost four straight divisional championships. When the *Inky* asked various islanders who would win the bowl game, seven of nine quoted in the paper's "Voices of Nantucket" feature predicted a hometown win. One resident would only venture to guess that the Whalers would give it their best shot. The final respondent had the gall to say it didn't matter.

Though the team went in with the best of intentions, the signs seemed ominous early on, when key junior David Murray ran into a wall of Tigers defenders. After he struggled for a few moments for no gain, the ball popped out of his grasp, and Tyngsboro recovered. Capizzo argued bitterly that the officials had been too slow to whistle the play dead. The call stood, and the Tigers were soon on the board.

On the third play after halftime, with the Whalers down 17–0, John Beamish broke into the open field with the ball and began chewing up yardage. But he was caught from the blind side, and the ball squirted free again. If Tyngsboro's recovery tamped down the hope that the Whalers could climb back into the game, opposing quarterback Mike Provencher's subsequent sneak play was an absolute backbreaker. Designed to pick up just a few yards and a first down, the play surprised everyone when Provencher scampered 40 yards for a decisive score. When he reached the end zone, the *Inky* reported, he "let out a battle cry that probably reached the ears of the Christmas strollers" back on the picturesque island.

The ride back to the ferry terminal was an unhappy one. Given Capizzo's health concerns and the team's frustrating inability to log another perfect season, was it possible the coach was finally beginning to consider retirement?

"I'm not going out a loser," he growled.

THE VINEYARD TEAM graduated more than a dozen seniors in the spring after the 1994 season, including the irreplaceable "B and B Boys." They were the tag team of 240-pound tackles, Aaron Belanger and Greg Belcher, the assistant's son, who was invited to play in the statewide Shriners Game. Resigning himself to a rebuilding year for 1995, Herman put extra effort into the development of a sophomore running back named Ben Higgins, who had the potential to be a real difference-maker. After a big hit, Higgins had a habit of getting to his feet and shaking it off, like a deer shakes off water. The routine earned the young runner an affectionate nickname: "Bambi."

Across the channel, Aloisi, Nantucket's own difference-maker, was entering his senior year with some unfinished business to attend to. The previous winter he'd torn ligaments on the basketball court—ironically, in a game on the other island, in Oak Bluffs. The injury had ruined his junior year of baseball and given him more time to spend during the spring and summer bulking up and preparing for football season.

After an uneventful start to Aloisi's senior year—two more wins—Capizzo's team was stunned in an upset thriller to a new nonleague opponent, Central Falls. Down 20–0, Aloisi nearly single-handedly conjured a comeback, returning an interception for a touchdown and guiding the offense to two more scores. They fell just short, 20–18.

It might have been the knockdown they needed. Nantucket beat up on Tri-County and West Bridgewater before putting on a near-flawless performance to blank Blue Hills, 21–0. Receiver Bobby King—the "air apparent," as the paper called him, to Tiki Blake and Michael Day—had a big day, and Tim Psaradelis caught four passes for ninety-nine yards.

Psaradelis's father, Frank, was the blue-collar son of a Greek immigrant. He was an island boy who was one of the Whalers' most fearless tacklers in the mid-1960s. Frankie didn't talk about his playing days much. When young Tim, then in eighth grade, heard Capizzo mention his father on a radio program as one of the toughest players he'd ever coached, the boy ran into the living room to ask if it was true.

The younger Psaradelis had grown up a bit more comfortably

than his old man. He took up surfing and would soon spend his summers giving lessons to Cody and Cassidy, the celebrity offspring of talk-show host Kathie Lee Gifford and her husband, NFL Hall of Famer Frank Gifford, during their summers on the island.

Of the 48 points the Nantucket team scored the following week against Cape Tech, Aloisi accounted for 30—two quarterback keepers, two punt returns, and an interception. After two key Bristol-Plymouth linemen were suspended for the week following an egg-throwing incident in school, the Whalers downed that team, 33–0, in seriously muddy conditions.

Though their next opponent, Southeastern, was 6–2, few gave them any chance of an upset. "We're gonna try like heck," the team's coach said gamely, a day before his team was shut out. Nantucket, which would end up winning by 23, was still uncertain of victory when Southeastern, down by just a touchdown, pushed inside the 5. But on fourth-and-goal, a Whaler defensive back shoved the opposing running back out of bounds at the half-yard line, forcing a turnover on downs. The tackler was John Aloisi.

When the Whalers arrived on the Vineyard to play a host team with a disappointing 3–6 record, Nantucket's David Murray grabbed the Island Cup and sprinted past the Vineyarders with it, taunting. The infuriated boys in purple stood with their mouths open, momentarily paralyzed by the interloper's audacity. It would prove to be their one chance to reclaim the series hardware for the year, reporters joked.

Behind more than 300 yards of total offense (including a 75-yard dash by Bobby King, now running out of the tailback position), the Whalers won easily once again, 30–13. Late in the game, set to field a kickoff, a sophomore named Travis Lombardi cut in front of Aloisi on the return team, gathered the ball, and promptly fumbled. In victory, Capizzo could laugh it off. The team was building for the future, he said.

Donald Herman had already put his rebuilding year behind him and was looking forward to the following season. "It'll be a different story" in the Island Cup game, he promised.

Like hell it will, Capizzo replied. Though he'd taken to calling his rival the "snake in the grass," his team would not be getting bitten on its own turf a year from now.

ALOISI SAT IN the locker room at the Massachusetts Maritime Academy athletic facility in Buzzards Bay two weeks later. He was crying softly. His Whalers had lost just three games since his sophomore year—two of them in the last two Division 5B championship games. Now they were preparing to take the field against an East Boston team with a first-year coach who had been an assistant on the Boston English team that beat Nantucket in the 1993 Super Bowl. Maybe more so than Vito himself, Aloisi was determined not to lose this game.

The few teardrops he shed did not affect his play at all. Aloisi had a brilliant game against Eastie, shredding the opponent on the ground for nearly 150 yards on just seven carries, two of them good for touchdowns. He threw for two more scores, and on defense he pulled down two interceptions for good measure, underscoring his selection to the *Globe*'s All-Scholastic team as a safety.

"He destroyed Boston English by himself," recalls Capizzo.

This time the trip off the shores of America would be joyous. The ferry back to the island was acccompanied by two Coast Guard cutters. When the scoreboard read 40–6 as time ran out, the Whalers could finally claim their first division championship since Beau Almodobar's senior year. Aloisi, the intense young man with the close-shaved black hair, might be the best football player Nantucket had ever seen, the gracious former running back wrote in a guest column in the *Inquirer and Mirror*'s next issue.

Like so many star athletes in high school, Aloisi had been facing his share of resentment for the attention he received. He may not have had the classic golden hair of the high school quarterback, but he certainly had the halo.

"He's the son everyone would like to have," said Aloisi's coach.

In his own article in the newspaper, Vito Capizzo pointed out that Eastie had 560 high school boys enrolled in the ninth through twelfth grades. Nantucket, by contrast, had just 89. How is it possible that the smaller school won? he asked, posing a question many of his opponents had been asking for three decades. It had everything to do with island life, he believed—the interlocking support system indispensable to a community cut off from the rest of civilization.

He might have also mentioned the lesson learned from the island-bound boys of *The Lord of the Flies*—the one about the will to power that can emerge in an isolated social structure.

*Chapter Thirteen*

# DOOZIES

B EN HIGGINS WAS a young boy growing up on the South Shore when he was introduced to Aerosmith's Steven Tyler in a home studio. Ben's father, Mark, was a musician himself, and he knew a lot of rock and rollers. To the grade schooler, the famously gaunt, frilly rock singer was a frightening sight.

The Higgins family—Ben was the third of seven—moved out to the Vineyard in late 1984. His dad, who made his living as a carpenter, had a job on the island, and he enjoyed it so much he moved the family there. Mark Higgins began lining up gigs with a band, billed under his own name, on the island nightclub circuit—at the Wharf in Edgartown, the Atlantic Connection in Oak Bluffs, and the old Hot Tin Roof, the nondescript roadhouse out by the aiport where Carly Simon was a partner and John Belushi would bring his *Saturday Night Live* colleagues.

Mark Higgins drowned in a boating accident in Texas when Ben was ten years old. "It was a pretty big shocker," Higgins says.

Mark had played football in high school, and his oldest son was a natural athlete. "He was like a friggin' missile," recalls Donald Herman, who brought the kid up to the Vineyard varsity during his freshman year. Higgins was a junior in 1996, when the Vineyarders made good on their rebuilding season the previous year with an 8–3 record. By then, Herman's star running back and defensive rover was an unstoppable terror on the field. Well over six feet tall and not yet filled out to the 200 pounds he carries in adulthood, Higgins could do almost anything he wanted on the football field. His coach, with whom he lifeguarded at South Beach in the summers, "knew how to pick an individual and make him work to his potential," Higgins says. "I could have stayed being just a little faster and a little stronger than the other guys. But he really knew what to say, how to coach me individually."

The Vineyarders kept pace for most of the season with yet another near-perfect Nantucket team. But on the weekend before the Island Cup, Herman's team suffered a major letdown, a perplexing loss to Bristol-Plymouth. Still, national radio host Don Imus weighed in, boldly predicting a Vineyard win just weeks after *Sports Illustrated* featured a flattering story on Capizzo and his program.

Before the Island Cup game, the public address announcer on Nantucket called for a moment of silence for Ian Araujo, the Vineyard graduate who'd lost his life earlier that week in a car accident on the mainland. Araujo, one of the many cousins of the island's first family of football, was an enormous lineman, a legitimate 300-pounder. When the *National* ran its story on the island game during Araujo's sophomore year, the paper included a photo of the big kid standing under the goal post in his civilian clothes. They shot it from a low angle, making the beefy teenager look positively mountainous. In Donald Herman's weekly pregame chat with Vineyard mouthpiece Ken Goldberg, the coach faced the camera and held up a framed photo of his former player hoisting the Island Cup.

When the game got under way, the Vineyard had the first opportunity to score but missed a chip-shot field goal. Like a stormy ferry ride just before the Steamship Authority decides to cancel the rest of the day's schedule, momentum teetered back and forth. The Whalers leaned heavily on running back Bobby King, the Division 5 scoring leader on the season. The Vineyarders, meanwhile, took advantage of some huge defensive plays to keep the game close. When King completed a long halfback pass to wideout Travis Lombardi—the junior who had cut in front of Aloisi on a kickoff in the last Cup game—the Whalers had the ball inside the 2-yard line. But the visitors recovered a fumble on a quarterback sneak. It would not be the last time that Herman's defense would be asked to rise to the occasion at the goal line.

With Nantucket driving again in the second quarter, King took a handoff at midfield and carried the ball off left tackle, straight into a crowd of purple-trimmed jerseys. He kept churning as his tacklers fell. Suddenly he broke loose and streaked across the wide-open middle. Just as he passed the 5-yard line, Vineyard defender Asil Cash—the only other man within 10 yards—dove at him. Incredibly, while splayed in midair, Cash hooked a right cross around King's waist and punched the ball free. A trailer on the play instantly dove on the ball in the end zone for a touchback.

Though the Vineyard had no luck moving the ball out of its own territory, neither could the Whalers find the end zone. After regaining the ball near their own end zone, Vineyard quarterback Mike Snowden, one of the team's all-time leaders in several offensive categories, tried to clear some space by attempting a pass over the middle. But Lombardi, dropping into coverage, made a spectacular catch over his shoulder for the interception. He made a cut and began sprinting up the sideline. Just as he was about to cross the goal line, a Vineyarder blindsided him with a flying tackle. Lombardi was launched so far off the field that he crashed into the chain-link fence set back several yards from the sideline. Up in the press booth, the Vineyard announcers were beside themselves. "Andrew Nourse knocked him into next week!" shouted Goldberg's partner, Norm Vunk.

Nantucket, however, scored on the next play. The slim lead stood throughout most of the second half, with the visiting islanders growing increasingly desperate.

The fourth quarter was peppered with turnovers. After Nantucket intercepted in the end zone, the Vineyard took the ball back on a fumble recovery. When they were stopped a half yard shy of the first down, the host team took over on downs. The Vineyard got the ball back once again, only to have Nourse fumble it away. This time, they forced Nantucket to punt.

With a minute and three seconds to go, the Vineyard had one last chance from its own 20-yard line. After getting the benefit of a few penalties, including a critical pass-interference call against Nantucket, Snowden hit Ben Connelly on a perfect timing pattern across the middle, right at the goal line. The Vineyard announcers erupted in howls of joy.

"What calm?" shrieked Vunk, the commentator, as the special-teams unit ran onto the field for the extra point. "I ain't keepin' calm!" The kick was good, tying the score as regulation expired.

Each team had one series of downs from the opponent's 10-yard line to score in overtime. Nantucket scored easily, but the Vineyard blocked the extra point. On the Vineyard's second play from scrimmage, Snowden carried the ball inside the five. As he lunged for the end zone, he was hit from the side. The ball was jarred loose, and a defensive back in a navy blue uniform pounced on it.

For Travis Lombardi, who would eventually grow sideburns, marry the daughter of the longtime president of the Nantucket Boosters Club, and become the junior varsity coach on John Aloisi's staff, it was the game of his life. Nantucket's 48–15 destruction two weeks later of Boston English—the team that ruined John Aloisi's first bid for a Super Bowl win in 1993—was, though it took place on Nantucket's own home field, almost an afterthought.

WHEN BEN HIGGINS was featured as a Star of the Week in the *Boston Globe* during the run-up to the Island Cup at the end of his senior year, 1997, he was asked what he liked best about living on an island.

"The isolation from the world," he replied.

Higgins had plenty of time to himself that year. The lanky kid whom the Vineyard announcers had dubbed "the Shark" was running with the football on a level so much higher than the average high school player that his coach was routinely obliged to sit him down, sometimes before the first half was over. The athletic running back made a habit of notching more than 200 yards in a game. Against West Bridgewater, he put the ball in the end zone seven times, though three of those scores were called back on penalties.

If the Vineyard had one Achilles' heel that year, it was their aptitude for drawing penalties. They were confident and aggressive. And Higgins wasn't their only threat. The team featured junior Mike Snowden and senior Ben Connelly, who both played quarterback; two-way end Jake Sylvia, who was tall enough to be nicknamed "the Stork"; and linebacker Ryan Ruley, the future cop known as "the Little Imp," who was starved for contact after missing the previous season due to a knee injury.

Once the team squeaked past Old Rochester, a nonleague opponent from a higher division—a team that featured a pair of 300-pound tackles that year—the Vineyarders began to soar. By their second-to-last game of the season, facing Bristol-Plymouth (just as they had on the same weekend the previous season), the team was still undefeated. This year, the coaching staff was determined to keep the players from looking past the opponent at hand toward the Nantucket game. During practice that week, players were expressly forbidden from using the *N*-word and the *W*-word—"Nantucket" and "Whalers." Only in the last few minutes against the vocational school's Craftsmen, when the outcome of the game was ensured, was the ban lifted.

"Nantucket-Nantucket-Nantucket!" the players chattered excitedly until the clock ran out.

"They wished they could strap it on and go then," said Herman a few days later.

Though the *Globe* hyped the game as the fiftieth in the history of the island rivalry, it was actually the fifty-first, or forty-ninth, if you excluded the two games with the Vineyard all-island team in the early 1950s. Either way, Nantucket was clearly the dominant team: its overtime win the year before had been its thirty-third in the series.

With the forecast calling for rain, Vito Capizzo loudly declared that his team would flush their archrivals "down the toilet bowl." Donald Herman knew that his counterpart was just blustering. Nantucket was 8–2, two games behind the league leaders. For once, Herman was fairly certain he had the better team, though he was quick to acknowledge that it was no longer wise to identify an underdog, from either side, in a rivalry that seemed to get better every year.

Just as their coach expected, the Vineyarders were sky-high for the first quarter. Higgins slashed into the end zone after an efficient drive on the team's first possession, and when Ruley came up with a fumble recovery on the Whalers' first drive, it looked like a potential rout. Nourse, who wore a piece of paper that read "11–0" pinned to his back, bounced up from a helmet-to-helmet collision with a bigger Nantucket runner and got in the kid's face.

But Capizzo's team hung tough, forcing Higgins to fumble twice. With just seven seconds to go in the half, the Vineyard star made up for it, slinging a deep bomb on a halfback pass to Ben Connelly, who caught the ball in stride as he crossed the goal line, leaving two staggering defenders in his trail. "It was kind of like playing catch in the backyard," recalls Higgins.

After a scoreless third quarter Nantucket threw a scare into the home crowd when a wide-open Lombardi caught a touchdown pass in the left corner of the end zone. But late in the game, following a missed Vineyard field goal, a Nantucket fumble popped high in the air. Nourse grabbed it and chugged into the end zone, sealing the win with his fists thrust skyward. Toward the end of the game, Lombardi extended a hand to Higgins, helping the Vineyard workhorse to his feet after he

dived on a bobbled handoff. It was a rare display of sportsman-
ship between the two island teams.

THE WIN, THE Vineyard's first over Nantucket in five years,
dating back to the 1992 thriller, sent the Grapes into another
Division 5B Super Bowl, this time at Bridgewater State. Winning the Island Cup, said Coach Herman, was "bigger than being state champs." Still, he wasn't about to let his kids lie down
after they fell behind early to a Westwood team that was already
appearing in its fourth championship game of the decade. A bad
snap as the Vineyarders tried to punt from deep in their own
territory resulted in a Westwood recovery on the 1, setting up
the game's first touchdown.

But Mike Snowden was up to the challenge. On third and 6
inside the Westwood 20, he scrambled just long enough for Joel
Graves to find a patch of open space in the end zone. Just as
he released the ball, the quarterback absorbed a gang tackle by
three onrushing Wolverines. He didn't get to see Graves haul
in the touchdown pass. "I blanked out," Snowden said later, "but I
never thought of leaving the game." With the score 17–6, Higgins
shut the door on Westwood with a 48-yard touchdown run.

"We have a lot of heart," said Snowden, who was diagnosed
with a mild concussion. "This team's like a family. And we'll go
down as the best team in school history."

It had been a remarkable year. The team finished with twelve
wins, no losses. No team coached by Capizzo had ever won that
many in a single season.

Ben Higgins's name still litters the Vineyard record book. He
retains team marks for most points scored in a career and most
scored in a season—160, in his undefeated senior year. His

twenty-four touchdowns that year remain the most ever for a Vineyarder, and his 1,500-plus rushing yards eclipsed by more than 300 the next-highest numbers, posted by fellow island stand-outs Mike McCarthy and David Araujo. Bambi was invited to play in the Shriners game, the statewide high school all-star showcase that takes place in the spring, in both his junior and senior years. He missed both games to attend the annual National Scholastic track meets in Raleigh, North Carolina, where he competed in the long jump.

At home he compiled two file cabinets full of recruiting letters from Division I and IAA schools around the country, including the University of North Carolina and NC State. He finally decided to accept an offer from the University of Florida to train there as a decathlete. He thought about walking on to try out for the football Gators, but his track training was a tremendous commitment. "It was like a job," says Higgins.

After Florida, he held out hope that he might one day get a shot in pro football, spending parts of two years at an NFL training combine in New Jersey. Higgins fathered a son named Elijah and moved to Jupiter, Florida, with the boy and his mother, though the marriage soon ended in divorce. Moving back north, alone, to the island, the onetime high school hero lapsed into depression. He'd never come to terms with his father's premature death, and he didn't have much of a support network. Given his investment in track and football, he hadn't made many close friends in high school. Though he'd claimed to enjoy the isolation of island life, the loneliness took its toll. He found odd jobs as a carpenter. Most of the time, though, he sat around and drank.

"It was a fear thing," recalls Higgins. "I was this guy everyone looked up to, but on the inside, I had a void. I was always good at what I did, and I was damn good at drinking. And nothing good can come out of that."

His binges were sometimes sadly comical. One time he was picked up by an Edgartown police officer while carrying a stolen television set and trying to hail a cab. Higgins hit bottom in 2008, when he served ten days in the Dukes County Jail in Edgartown on a DUI conviction. When he got out, he went to see his son in Florida, where he turned himself in for delinquency on his child support payments. Trying to do the right thing, he suddenly found himself tossed into a prison cell, "eating breakfast with a murderer," with no way of letting his family or his girlfriend know where he was.

That woke him up. After putting those nightmarish episodes behind him, Higgins finally began to figure out what would make him happy in his life. He started running speed-development clinics for high school athletes, and he began writing rock songs on guitar and piano, just like his father. "When you figure out what you want to do, it doesn't seem like work," says the former running back. He earns his living by doing construction and installing home security systems. The name of his business is New Life.

THE NEXT IN Nantucket's long line of go-to players, Chris Gardner had an impressive season of his own the following year, scoring twenty-four touchdowns and rushing for nearly 1,200 yards. He ran behind an undersized but exceptionally cagey offensive line, a Capizzo specialty. Going into the Island Cup game, determined to avenge the loss to Higgins's team, this edition of the Whalers was undefeated, with one tie. The Vineyarders, meanwhile, were 7–2. On his own home field, Capizzo took his revenge on the snake in the grass with a 27–21 victory.

Two weeks later Nantucket traveled to the South Shore campus of UMass-Dartmouth for the 5B championship, taking on the Greater Lawrence Reggies, who were making their fourth Super Bowl appearance of the 1990s. The Reggies featured their own superb running back, Bo Morales, who led the division that year with 182 points. The team had exceeded expectations, having lost sixteen graduating seniors from the previous year's Super Bowl squad. Still, they were hungry after losing that championship game to East Boston on a late-game punt return.

On the second play of the game in Dartmouth, Gardner broke a 74-yard touchdown run, shedding several tacklers. The Whalers scored another touchdown when Tim Reinemo—son of Karsten, the big lineman from Vito's undefeated 1966 team—scooped up a blocked punt and cradled it into the end zone. The younger Reinemo would later attend the Coast Guard Academy, after his coach put in a good word with Senator John Kerry.

But each time the islanders put numbers on the board, Greater Lawrence responded. With the score tied late in the fourth quarter, Nantucket had an opportunity to win. Quarterback Alex Trebby hit all-purpose player Porter Fraker for a 16-yard reception that set up a 37-yard field goal attempt. But Trebby's kick hooked a bit wide, and the game went into overtime.

Nantucket had first crack at scoring from the opponent's 10-yard line. On fourth down, the team lined up for a field goal try, but Capizzo had something up his sleeve. Trebby took the snap and rolled out, looking to throw into the end zone. But he couldn't find his man, and he was buried beneath half of the

Reggies defense. Greater Lawrence seized the victory a few moments later, on the team's second play from the 10, on a reverse.

"I wasn't looking to have this kind of a team," claimed
Robert Rosmarino, the winning coach. "I was thinking about
rebuilding for next year." His words didn't sit well with Capizzo,
who had now lost in six of the Whalers' nine Super Bowl berths
since 1980.

The coach had earned 248 wins on the island. He was the un-
official mayor of the place. All the young football players at the
Boys Club dreamed of suiting up for Coach Capizzo and his
Whalers.

David Halberstam, the Pulitzer Prize–winning journalist,
was a friend and a fan. The author, who bought a modest summer home on the island in 1969, rewarded himself for complet-
ing his major works of nonfiction by writing shorter books that
drew on his passion for sports, including titles about Michael
Jordan, Ted Williams, and Bill Belichick, Halberstam's fellow
part-time Nantucketer.

Another summer regular, *Philadelphia Inquirer* reporter Buzz
Bissinger, had seriously considered writing a book in the mid-
1980s about Capizzo's reign. Bissinger grew up on the Upper
West Side of Manhattan, vacationing with his family in the
house they bought on the island in 1960. He was well aware of
the Capizzo legend, and when the *New Yorker* published its evoc-
ative feature in 1984, Bissinger thought long and hard about de-
veloping the story into a book. Eventually he decided to go to
Texas instead, where he covered the Permian High School
Panthers during their 1988 season. Bissinger's book, *Friday Night
Lights*, came out in 1990 and quickly became a sports classic.

All this recognition was fantastic. It was undeniably fun for

Capizzo to walk into local spots like the Faregrounds, the Downyflake, or the Even Keel and be greeted like royalty. But Vito was getting tired of the grind. His gout was acting up, and he had a herniated disc that was killing him. Taking one step toward retirement, he decided to step down as gym teacher. He notified Beau Almodobar about his decision, and his former star, who'd been back on the island for a couple of years, working at the Boys and Girls Club, applied for the job.

In hindsight, when Vito removed himself from the school on a day-to-day basis, it was as though he pulled the plug. No sports program can sustain its excellence indefinitely, and Capizzo's was probably overdue for a setback. Just as the heroic whaling industry on the island had collapsed a century and a half before, the Whalers suddenly began to seem vulnerable. Though the 1999 team would be the fastest he'd ever had, Capizzo claimed, they were also the smallest. And they had little experience. "Our offensive line is so green, you could grow potatoes on their heads," he told the *Cape Cod Times*.

Over their next three seasons the Nantucket varsity lost nearly as many games as it won: after compiling an astonishing 177–34 mark in the past two decades (since 1979, Almodobar's junior year), the Whalers limped to a 5–5 record in 1999. They would go 6–4 in 2000, and 5–5 again in 2001.

In the twenty previous years, the team had failed to reach seven wins only twice.

IT DIDN'T HELP matters that Donald Herman was just hitting his stride. Settling into his second decade as coach of the Vineyarders, the transplanted Georgian put together another exceptionally well-rounded team for the 1999 season. Among plenty of others, he had speedster Jade Cash, Asil's younger brother, one of the best receivers the team ever produced; Teddy Bennett, the youngest of Tom Bennett's three sons (and Bob Tankard's godson), a tailback and linebacker who earned the nickname "Teddy Ballgame"; fullback Seth Abbott, a senior cocaptain who had started at defensive end on the 1997 undefeated team; and Jarrett Campbell, a 325-pound lineman they called "Big Worm," after a character in the movie *Friday*. He took on a new nickname, "King," after he was named homecoming king that year.

Jarrett was the younger brother of Jermaine and James "Vamp" Campbell. He'd been in first grade when the family moved to the island. Jermaine and James had both moved to Boston during high school and served some time in prison. "The city got them," Campbell told a reporter from the *Cape Cod Times*. "Stupid stuff."

But Jarrett was a good student, and he loved his mother, Brenda, even though she'd refused to let her baby play Pop Warner football. "He doesn't mind hugging and kissing his mom in public," said his coach. "His feet are grounded." As a junior, the big boy took a role in a contemporary stage version of *The Wizard of Oz*. To the delight of his classmates and the faculty, he played the Cowardly Lion. "He's soft," said Campbell, who struggled with asthma. "But when he got his courage, it fit him just right. It was me."

Herman assigned senior Jordan Baptiste to run the offense, replacing three-year quarterback Mike Snowden. "The personnel around him should make the transition easier," said the coach as the season got under way. Oozing talent, the Vineyarders were odds-on favorites to win the Mayflower League.

They knew they were on the verge of something special the

week they played the Warriors from Blue Hills, who traveled to the island for a Friday night game fully expecting to win behind Moses Curry, a talented running back who had emerged as a statewide standout. The Vineyard kept Curry out of the end zone and humbled his teammates, 35–0.

In mid-October, Herman found himself on the verge of his one hundredth victory as a high school coach. "One hundred is a nice round number," he told the *Cape Cod Times*. "I know for a fact I wouldn't be going for a hundred wins in Savannah." He reached the milestone on his first try. In a shutout win at Southeastern, the Vineyarders held their opponent to 25 yards of total offense. As time ran out, the giddy Vineyarders doused their coach with a tub of water.

That same weekend, another milestone of sorts took place on the other island. Capizzo and his Whalers hosted the varsity team from Enfield, Connecticut, where his former assistant, George Thomas, had been hired as head coach. Thomas, who'd spent a decade on the island, hailed from Brockton, a tough south-of-Boston town where survival is a mode of living. The citywide high school there, the largest in New England, serves more than four thousand students on a sprawling campus consisting of nine buildings. Just making the cut for a varsity sports team is a feat in itself; the football Boxers (named in part because Brockton is home to the late Rocky Marciano and another world-class prizefighter, Marvin Hagler) are a perennial Division I superpower who routinely made *USA Today*'s national Top 25 ranking in the 1980s.

Thomas was a hard-nosed phys ed major when he arrived on Nantucket. Initially skeptical that he'd be coaching strong-willed boys, he learned quickly. The kids were not always big, he says, but they played big for the coach. "Kids wanted to go through the wall for him. He built a tradition, which is not easy to do. He had a great work ethic. Kids would spend time in study hall watching film. Vito accepted nothing less than everything you had."

One of Thomas's assistants in Enfield was Bill Manchester, the crafty part-time player from the Whalers teams of the mid-to-late 1980s. In high school, Manchester wasn't quite a gifted athlete, but Thomas remembered how much his teammates liked to play for him and admired his leadership abilities.

Thomas had thoroughly enjoyed his ten years on Nantucket. On nights before Island Cup games, Capizzo sometimes let him take the trophy home, where he'd put it by his bedside. One year he used it as a centerpiece on the Thanksgiving dinner table. Now here he was preparing to face off against his former boss.

"I never thought I'd be standing on the other sideline," said Thomas before the game. "I want my kids to experience the atmosphere and see a successful program." The out-of-staters had a great time getting a fleeting taste of island football. Whether they witnessed a successful program in action was another matter: Thomas's visitors laid an ugly 33–0 whipping on his former colleague.

THE SCORE WASN'T much different a few weeks later, when the Whalers traveled back from enemy territory nursing the wounds of their 38–12 loss in the year's Island Cup contest. The score in the rivalry games would look very similar the following two seasons, too.

With Island Cup bragging rights secured for another season, the Vineyard purple brought its season to an emphatic close at

BU's Nickerson Field two weeks later with a decisive win over East Boston. Herman's "Piglets"—his nickname for his feisty group of offensive linemen, who were outweighed each week but never overmatched—created yawning gaps all afternoon for Abbott and Bennett, who led the team to 344 rushing yards, nearly 300 in the second half alone. It was Herman's fourth Super Bowl victory of the decade—one more than Vito's total—and the younger coach's second undefeated season in the past three.

As THE NEW millennium began, Vineyard football was running like a clean, perfectly calibrated machine. The team followed its undefeated 1999 season with a 10–1 run the following year, including a win against South Boston in the state's newly created playoff system. That set up the Vineyarders for another Super Bowl appearance.

But the team had some rough days ahead. On the last day of November, Chris Rebello, the high school's junior varsity coach, collapsed of a massive heart attack while deerhunting in the woods of Aquinnah. Attempts to revive him were unsuccessful. A onetime Vineyard player whose oldest son, James, was on the freshman team, Rebello was just thirty-seven years old. "This is going to be a very powerful, emotional time for our students," said Pat Regan, the high school principal, "especially on Sunday."

At eleven in the morning that Sunday, the shaken Vineyarders took the field against Bellingham in the Divison 6 championship game. (In the MIAA's ever-changing alignments, the Mayflower League Large had recently been moved into the newly minted D6.) The team hung the coach's jersey, number 42, on an easel on the sideline, and the players wore patches featuring his initials. But on the field, other than a game-opening 83-yard kickoff return by Travis Baptiste, they were no match for the Blackhawks, bowing 35–6. Late in the game, Herman put James Rebello in the backfield. "It's been a tough three days, and it's been hard to focus," said the coach afterward. "But I'm not making excuses. Bellingham was the better team today."

One year later the Vineyard throttled its island rival, shutting out the Whalers, 35–0, on the way to another playoff game. Led by running backs J. D. Wild and Tim Higgins—Ben's younger brother—and a defense that gave up the second-fewest points in the division, the team picked apart an inexperienced West Roxbury secondary in Oak Bluffs for another easy victory. But for the second consecutive season, the D6 championship proved elusive. Though the Catholic schoolboys of Framingham's Marian High School were undersized and had just two seniors, they won the battles in the trenches. "They killed us up front," said Higgins after his team was downed, 12–0.

CAPIZZO WAS SICK to death of watching the Snake rack up all those postseason appearances. In 2002, for the last time in his remarkable career, he did something about it.

Going into the Island Cup on his home turf, the Whalers were a respectable 6–3. The Vineyard was 9–1; a win would put them in the playoffs yet again. But Capizzo and his staff knew that Herman's teams had been passing the ball with sophistication over the past few years, and they planned well for it. They had an audience: a few moments of the game were featured live on NBC during halftime of a nationally televised Notre Dame game. In the segment, Vineyard defensive stalwart

Zach Mahoney returned a fumble for a touchdown, but it was called back on a clipping penalty.

Nantucket had the football gods on their side more than once that day. When Vineyarder Ben Gunn's field goal attempt into a thirty-knot gust hit a wall at the goalpost and dropped straight down into the end zone, it was clear the weather would not cooperate with the Grapes. The Whalers rushed three men and dropped eight defensive players into pass coverage, and Eric McCarthy, Mike McCarthy's middle son, struggled to throw the ball into the swirling wind. Still, playing from behind all day, the Vineyard mounted a furious comeback, pulling within five points with three minutes to go.

After the Vineyarders forced a turnover on downs, McCarthy was intercepted. But the visiting defense held once again, and Herman's team had one last opportunity to win. With less than a minute to go the team brought the ball all the way to the Nantucket 20. In the stands, hysteria reigned. *"Dee-fense!"* the home islanders roared, stomping in unison.

"Emotionally, it was almost overwhelming," recalled Gunn, who had a sure touchdown pass knocked out of his hands on the 1-yard line. In the end, his team simply ran out of time.

Herman was in a state of disbelief. The only comment he could muster was that the opponents had made more big plays. The loss opened the gate for the Warriors from Blue Hills, who slipped into the playoffs as the league representative. Incredibly, it was the first year since 1989—thirteen seasons—that a team from "America," not the islands, could claim the league title.

Like Capizzo before him, Coach Herman had grown accustomed to championship football, and he made damn sure the 2003 edition of the Vineyarders would become another wrecking crew. Early in the season, they buried Southeastern, 51–0, never allowing the home team to cross midfield. J. D. Wild, by then a senior, justified his nickname—"Running" Wild—by scoring three touchdowns in the game. The Whalers, 7–2 on the last weekend of the season, hoped once again to play the spoiler. "You lose, you go pick cranberries," said Capizzo.

This time, however, Herman and his players would not be denied. Wild, who had pulled a chunk of sod from the Whalers' field at the end of the previous year's loss, still kept it at home for motivation. It must have worked. He ran for 97 yards and a pair of touchdowns, and James Rebello, his fellow graduating senior, had seven tackles and an interception as the Vineyard took home the Island Cup, 20–7. The Whalers' lone touchdown accounted for the only points scored by a league opponent against the Vineyard on the season.

"I can't tell you how much this means to me," said Wild, who would soon be playing Division II football for Merrimack College. "I've seen five of my teammates crying. This is our life. We grow up as kids and look at this game.

"I can't even put it in words," he told the *Martha's Vineyard Times*. "It's unbelievable."

The Vineyard's playoff game against the undefeated East Boston Jets was originally scheduled for BU's Nickerson Field. But Jets coach John Sousa got the MIAA to move the game to his own home field, in the shadow of Logan Airport. The field cover was turf, which augured well for the speedy host team. While some Vineyard supporters complained loudly, Herman tried to downplay the situation.

"Let's play ball," he told the *Globe*. "If they're a little faster because of the turf, then we're a little faster, too."

Wild proved the point immediately, starting the scoring with an 81-yard return on the opening kick. The Vineyard also scored on bulky fullback Kyle Robertson's ramrod 1-yard run and kicker E. J. Sylvia's 33-yard field goal. The Jets, greeted by Boston mayor Tom Menino as they ran onto the field for the second half, responded with a third-quarter touchdown to pull within five.

Late in the fourth quarter, the Jets were driving, logging 56 yards on thirteen plays to get all the way down to the Vineyard 4-yard line. It was fourth down. There were five seconds left in the game. And East Boston had no time-outs left.

Quarterback Aaron Flythe called a quick out pattern for Carmen Ciampa in the corner of the end zone, but a Vineyard defender stepped in and broke up the pass. The player, Seth Coleman, was the same Vineyarder who had given up the Nantucket touchdown that ended his team's scoreless streak. "He's a great athlete, a great kid, and you have to be happy for him," said his coach.

The seniors on the island's 2003 football team went into their final Super Bowl opportunity carrying a 41–7 record over their four years at the high school. Five players would be named to the all-division team, and Rebello was chosen to play in the Shriners game. "The strength of this team is that we play with one heartbeat," said J. D. Wild after the team played a frantic Super Bowl contest in frigid Chelsea against Manchester Essex, which had lost a bowl game to Marian (just as the Vineyard had) the previous year.

Wild would finish the season with twenty-three touchdowns, one shy of Ben Higgins's team record. He completed his high school career trailing only Higgins for most points scored in a Vineyard career, and his forty-one career rushing touchdowns eclipsed Higgins's total of thirty-two. In his last game wearing

the purple, he scored three times to lead the Vineyarders to a
2-point win.

PERHAPS THE WILDEST episode in the wild and woolly history
of the Island Cup took place in 2004. Ironically, it was a rare
season that held no significance for either team. Nantucket,
which had compiled back-to-back 7–3 records after falling off
in the late 1990s, was struggling to another 5–5 mark. And Donald Herman's run of excellence was on temporary hold: for the
first time in almost a decade, the Vineyard would finish with a
losing record. Not since the late 1980s had the outcome of the
Island Cup game held no bearing on the two teams' postseason
prospects.

Not that there was no fanfare surrounding the game. Since
Donald Herman's arrival, the teams were dead even in Island
Cup matches, both winning eight. With the October release of
the movie version of *Friday Night Lights*, Buzz Bissinger was on
Nantucket as the Whalers' honorary team captain. The visiting
islanders came in looking like lunatics, with their hair shaved
off on one side of their heads and Maori-style tattoos drawn in
marker on their faces. Before the game one Vineyard player
vaulted over a fence, fell, and dislocated his shoulder. And Ken
Goldberg, the veteran play-by-play man who loved wordplay
(each game began with "the proverbial *coss* of the *toin*") and kept
an autographed photo of King Kong Bundy in his office, unveiled a bulky purple turtleneck that his elderly mother had
embroidered with an *M* and a *V.*

In the pregame show for the Vineyard television audience,
Goldberg presaged what was to come when he mentioned the
"educated toe" of big junior E. J. Sylvia, who had kicked well

all season. Nantucket's Brennan Dooley, grandson of Jack Dooley, the 1940s star, and his wife, the former Jeannie Jaeckle, gave the visitors a taste of their own medicine on the opening kickoff, running it back 90 yards for the game's first score.

"Bummer," said Goldberg.

But the Vineyarders bounced right back, driving 70 yards in five plays capped by a rushing touchdown from Kyle Robertson, who was playing with an ankle fracture that would require surgery. The invaders drove down the field again on their next possession and took the lead, 12–8. Less than a minute later, senior Whaler captain Adam Goodwin took a handoff inside his own territory and carried it 60 yards for the score.

Once again, the Vineyard responded with a long drive and a touchdown. Once again, they failed to make the two-point conversion. The Grapes went into halftime leading 18–12.

The pace of the game ground down after the break. A Dooley interception as the fourth quarter began set up another Goodwin touchdown: 20–18, Whalers. That's where the score remained until, with under a minute to go and Martha's Vineyard out of time-outs, Nantucket opted to punt on fourth down. The Vineyard blocked the punt and recovered on the Nantucket 33. Three plays later, after a sideline pass for a first down, a Robertson rumble to the 10, and a spiked ball to stop the clock, E. J. Sylvia trotted out to attempt a 28-yard field goal with five seconds on the clock.

Capizzo called a time-out, to plan his strategy and rattle the kicker. Then he called another one. But Mike Shea, the Vineyarder who had blocked the punt, was grateful for the extra time: He was the long snapper, and he'd been so excited after the turnover that he felt like he was going to throw up.

The kick, when it finally happened, was perfect. It was 21–20.

With two seconds to go, the exultant Vineyard still had to kick off. Sylvia purposely booted a midrange pop-up; the receiver instantly lateraled to Goodwin, the deep man. He started to sweep to his left, but a defender grabbed a handful of his jersey and hung on. As the runner was trying to break free he was hit by another tackler, and the cluster of players tumbled to the ground. The Vineyard announcers whooped.

And then the ball popped into view, bounding a few yards behind the pile.

Dooley, the other deep man, scooped it up and barreled toward the right sideline. By this time, however, Vineyard fans, reserves, and coaches had all run onto the field in premature celebration. Dooley, picking up blockers as he stumbled crazily upfield, was forced to cut around a small boy in an untucked Vineyard jersey. It was the team's water boy. After crossing midfield, searching for a seam, and trying not to trip over his own teammates, Dooley was conclusively tackled from behind—by Lucas Landers, the same player who had caused the fumble.

It looked like a junior version of The Play, the legendary five-lateral kickoff return at the end of the 1982 game between archrivals Stanford and the University of California–Berkeley. After the Cardinal took a one-point lead in that game on a field goal with four seconds remaining, Cal's Golden Bears scored the winning touchdown on the madcap return, which featured members of the Stanford band wandering onto the field in the middle of the action.

As the Vineyarders erupted and the officials milled about, conferring about whether to call it a game, players from each side lay on the ground near the final tackle. An ambulance eventually drove out on the field to retrieve the Vineyard's Jimmy Bishop, who was carried off as a precautionary measure. When the Vineyard players took a victory lap around the field with the Island Cup, one enraged Nantucket fan took a punch at a player.

"What a doozy!" said Norm Vunk, Goldberg's announcing partner, a few minutes later.

"It was absolute mayhem and bedlam out there," Goldberg replied.

After twenty-four years of doing Vineyard games together, it was Vunk's last broadcast. Goldberg signed off with his usual tribute to his departing colleague. "Say goodnight, Norm," he said, echoing George Burns.

"Goodnight, Norm," Vunk replied on cue.

*Chapter Fourteen*

## GOING DOWN

I<small>T WAS A</small> hard fall, when the fall finally came. After one of the truly legendary careers in American high school football, Vito Capizzo—once an autocratic presence on the island he had made his home—stumbled aimlessly through his last few years on the field they would soon rename for him. Though Nantucket still led the Island Cup series by a wide margin, the team had won the rivalry game just once since 1999. In 2008, Nantucket played with as few as seventeen boys on the roster, and some of them were injured. They'd run the table on the season, 0–10. Not a single win, just like Capizzo's inauspicious inaugural campaign more than forty years before. One day in May, a tired, dejected coach walked into Chris Maury's office and told the AD he was retiring.

This import named Capizzo once strolled the halls of the high school like a potentate, blatantly smoking his cherry tobacco from a pipe, as no other school figure would dare. But he hadn't been a familiar sight in the hallways for years, having retired long ago from his jobs as the middle school's gym teacher and the high school athletic director. The kids didn't know him very well anymore. The gout was killing him. His thyroid was acting up, and he'd had that bout with shingles. On top of all that, his heart was laboring—he'd had three stents put in over the last few years. And there was that incident on the Vineyard a few years back, when he'd been blindsided and knocked cold as a fast-moving play spilled out of bounds. More and more, he'd been leaving the daily grind of running practices and evaluating opponents to his assistants, some of whom were openly jockeying for his job.

Before the 2008 Vineyard game, making his annual appearance on *The Road to the Island Cup*, an hourlong program hosted by radio man Sandy Beach, Capizzo had uttered the unthinkable. He'd wondered aloud whether the game—this game that had come to mean so much to both islands—should continue.

THE YEARS AFTER the "water boy" game of 2004 were much kinder to Donald Herman and his teams than to Vito Capizzo. After finishing 5–6 that year, the Vineyard took one big step in the right direction, and then another. By 2008, the coach had built another formidable, well-rounded team. For the first time in five years, the Vineyarders won their league title. (By then the Mayflower had been split into two leagues, a Large and a Small.) Late in the season, already 7–1 and undefeated against league opponents, the team earned a satisfying win over a good Blue Hills group, which had bumped the previous season's Vineyarders from the playoffs.

With the Mayflower Large already clinched, the Island Cup was barely a tune-up for the Vineyard. Since the farcical finish of the water boy game four years before, the rivalry had not been competitive. The Vineyarders destroyed the Whalers, 48–6, in 2007, and the outcome of their next meeting was never in doubt. The Vineyard's 43–22 victory in 2008 was even more of a blowout than the score indicated, with Herman making substitutions before halftime.

Like most island teams over the years, the 2008 Vineyarders were stocked with familiar names. There were two Moreises and a deBettencourt, and senior Mike McCarthy was finishing his third season as the starting quarterback. He had put up some outstanding numbers. As a Pop Warner kid, he'd looked up to his older brothers and hoped he might become quarterback by his senior year. But Mikey, six-one and 196 pounds, turned out to be the best of the bunch. A threat both to run and to throw, he set the Vineyard season mark that year for all-purpose scoring. By December, he would account for an amazing forty-one touchdowns—twenty-one on the ground, twenty more in the air. His grandmother, Dan McCarthy's widow, could no longer make it to the games, but she remained Mike's biggest fan. "She calls me after every game," he said. "That means a lot to me."

The Vineyard vaulted to another Super Bowl appearance, their eighth of Donald Herman's tenure, that year with a convincing 42–14 win over South Boston's Monument High School, which specialized in producing firefighters, cops, EMTs, and other public safety officials. On a neutral field in Taunton, McCarthy ran the option to perfection, rushing for 122 yards and throwing for 95 more, including a 36-yard scoring strike to a baby-faced sophomore named Randall Jette.

Five days later, the Vineyarders vyed for the EMass Division 3A Super Bowl championship against the Amesbury Indians, who had never been to a Super Bowl before. Though the late autumn sky was already crystal blue during the early morning ferry ride, it was not to be the islanders' day. At Bentley

University, McCarthy turned the ball over on each of his team's first three possessions, and the Indians capitalized all three times with scoring drives. The final was not close: 40–19.

"You never want to play like that in your last high school football game," said Herman. "It leaves a bad taste."

MUCH TO NANTUCKET'S dismay, their team had been playing like that for some time, and against lesser competition. The Whalers were 1–9 in 2005, by far Capizzo's worst season since his first. They'd managed to win six the following year, but just three in 2007. That gave the coach 293 wins on his career. Though he denied it, everyone knew he was hoping to hang on until he could earn his 300th.

Most felt he deserved it. "Vito earned what he got," says George Vollans, the science teacher who'd been the coach's first assistant on the island. "He worked hard. If there are kudos, he deserved them."

Many of Capizzo's rivals felt the same way. "Without him," says Ron Borges, the sportswriter from the Vineyard, "there would be no Nantucket football."

But pressure for the coach to step down had been building for some time. He wanted the number, but his heart was no longer in it. He'd been working much of the year out at Miacomet, the golf course that Alan Costa managed, since 2000. Now that he wasn't teaching, it gave him someplace to go each day. There was no real expectation or job description when he punched the time clock at the pro shop. Mostly Vito puttered around the grounds. It was almost as though he'd put himself out to pasture.

When Capizzo arrived on the island, he'd transformed the winless program of his first year into the undefeated season of

1966, just two years later. Now the tide for the onetime Alabama player had reversed.

Going into the 2008 Island Cup game at home, Nantucket did not have a single victory on the season. Coaches whose teams the Whalers had been eating alive for years were taking their revenge. The islanders lost to Blue Hills, 38–6, and to Tri-County, 31–6, and they got blanked by Cape Tech, 34–0. It was just plain ugly.

No longer was the coach a god among men. Football players whose fathers or older brothers hadn't played didn't know him at all; he wasn't in the school building every day, calling out to them in the halls. "You could definitely tell there were kids who didn't have the same kind of respect for him," says Jamie Viera, who was a tri-captain as a junior that year. It was an especially tough year for Jamie: his father, Joe, the big Nantucket lineman from the 1960s, died unexpectedly during the season after complications during knee surgery.

At times that season there was open mutiny on the football field. Rebellious players swore at the coaches. On a few occasions Capizzo grew so disgusted that he sent everyone home twenty minutes after practice started. The game wasn't fun on the island anymore, wrote Josh Butler in a blog post. A senior, Josh was the son of Elvis Butler, a one-year Whaler standout back in the 1970s who played at Mississippi State, tried out for the 49ers, and was now assisting Vito. The prospects were clear, wrote the younger Butler in midseason: "Basically, if the Whalers don't come together, I think it will be the end of the football program as we know it." The team went out that weekend and got pummeled by a new league opponent, Diman, a small vokie school from Fall River.

Though the Cup game was on Nantucket, the Vineyard led by 31 at halftime. Mike McCarthy threw for three touchdowns and nearly 100 yards. Herman's second string and the JVs played most of the second half.

It was cold, and the coach was exhausted. After the game Capizzo singled out the few players who had not given up, as dire as the situation had become. "I was proud of them for that," he said. "They didn't quit all year, and they didn't quit today." Would there be an Island Cup game in a year? he was asked.

"We'll have to see," he said.

THERE WAS FAR more heartache on Nantucket that year than a mere few losses on the football field. The high school suddenly found itself in the midst of a perplexing rash of teen suicides.

By the beginning of the year there had been three in eleven months. A fifteen-year-old boy hanged himself in his family home; a seventeen-year-old member of the girls' soccer team poisoned herself with carbon monoxide at her house along Mill Hill; and a varsity baseball player killed himself a week after New Year's Day.

"Everybody's going, 'Is my child next?'" an antiques dealer told the *Globe*. The high school set up grief counseling sessions in the conference room. Outside the door hung a piece of green cardboard bearing a quote handwritten in marker: "One must never, for whatever reason," as Eleanor Roosevelt wrote in her autobiography, "turn his back on life."

It could be difficult growing up offshore, as generations of native-born children on these two islands were only too well aware. Not only were the communities on Nantucket and Martha's Vineyard detached from the mainland, but they were also cramped. Though the population of Nantucket had grown in recent years to about ten thousand, and that of the Vineyard to fifteen thousand or so, they were still very much provincial places. Everyone knew your business, and you knew theirs. It was, in fact, one of the key reasons that football had become such an institution on both islands. Social structure was paramount.

But not in the way that off-islanders often suspect. To this day the year-round residents of both islands remain essentially middle-class communities. They're not all Kennedys, as people in other parts of the country sometimes seem to think. Neither are they Fortune 500 magnates, heads of state, or movie stars and pop singers. The families who pay mortgages on their modest Cape homes, or rent them, are the ones who build those houses. They're the ones who work in the restaurants and the supermarkets, at the oil company and the DPW, for the police department, the toggery shops, and the fish markets. They're the ones who put their children through the public school systems on the islands. And they're the ones whose sons play football.

In August, just before the school season got under way, a fourth child, eighteen-year-old Benjamin Rives, was found dead of an apparent suicide, in the woods behind his house. A recent graduate, he was about to leave the island to attend his first year at Pratt, the art school in Brooklyn.

"It's hard enough being a teenager, but being a teenager on this island was really trying," Jill Page, a twenty-eight-year-old barista at the Bean, a popular downtown coffee shop, told the *Globe*.

WHEN THE COACH stepped down, Chris Maury realized he had a difficult decision to make. Should the Island Cup game, in fact, continue?

The cost of inter-island travel had become prohibitive for the school system, Maury reasoned. In a down economy, the teams were no longer taking chartered jets to travel to the host island for the year's big game. The Steamship Authority, which runs the ferries from Woods Hole to the Vineyard and from Hyannis to Nantucket, has no boats that travel between islands outside of the peak summer season. Chartering a ferry cost the school eleven grand—a big sum that would be impossible to extend to the rest of the athletic programs, which shared the proceeds from Booster Club fund-raisers with the football team.

With so few students signing up for football, he even began floating a more drastic idea still—that the program might have to downgrade to the junior varsity level for a few rebuilding years. But for all his concerns, Chris Maury—a team captain in 1970—was ready to throw one last Hail Mary at his school's floundering football program. There were several leading candidates for Capizzo's job, all of them former Nantucket players committed to the island community.

Beau Almodobar was a great player in his day, good enough, despite his underwhelming size, to earn an improbable stint with the NFL's New York Giants. In high school, before he left for Norwich, there were some games when it seemed like every time he touched the ball, he scored. Vineyard standout David Araujo, a few years younger than Almodobar, called him the second-best high school player he ever saw—nearly as good as Jamie Morris, a nails-tough ball carrier from Ayer who set records at Michigan and later played for the Redskins.

Already coaching the varsity basketball team, Almodobar was eager to take on the football program. "I'd love to have it if it's offered," he told the *Cape Cod Times*. "I'm definitely putting my name in the hat." The former running back worked hard to be seen as a pillar in the community, despite—or perhaps because of—his biological father's criminal record.

Despite Almodobar's laser-eyed passion and the legend of his high school playing days, he had some credible competition for the job. Bill Manchester, who graduated from Nantucket in 1988, was a diagnostic technician who loved nothing better than breaking down game film. He already had valuable coaching experience at several schools, including his stint as George Thomas's assistant in Connecticut, and he'd been a head coach at the high school in Marblehead, a coastal town north of Boston, before returning to the island.

And there was an older islander, Vaughan Machado, who positively craved the head coaching position. For twenty-five years the thickly built former quarterback had been the tennis pro at Sankaty Head Golf Club. A onetime deep-sea diver who wrote bluesy songs on his electric guitar when he wasn't selling real estate, the sixty-five-year-old Machado was an excitable guy, always hungry for life experiences. He spoke in an endearingly old-school mashup of language, as if the Gipper had been a hipster: kids who made excuses or didn't practice to their potential were giving him "jive," and his pep talks invariably came down to the notion of proving your "guts."

Machado's intensity, in fact, once put him at odds with Capizzo. Vito hired him as an assistant coach in the mid-1980s, but they parted ways five seasons later. Capizzo, who joked about his own propensity for busting clipboards over his players' helmets right up until his retirement, when that kind of motivational tactic had long since been renounced by every football program in America, claimed he couldn't abide Machado's hot-headed presence on the sideline.

But that was almost two decades ago. Machado loved football, and he was dying to be involved again.

Chris Maury, however, had one more idea. He made a phone call and asked John Aloisi if he would consider coming back to Nantucket to interview for his old coach's job.

Aloisi had been committed to an austere, almost monkish brand of excellence as far back as anyone in his family could re-member. His appearance never changed—the same close-cropped black hair he'd always had. Before he met Katie, he kept a single table setting in the cupboard at his place in Worcester, which he dutifully washed after every meal. "He needs a little joy in his life," said Bob Bradley, Aloisi's mentor during his college years at Holy Cross. "He's got a very tight mainspring."

A superb basketball player and a quarterback who threw with pinpoint accuracy, Aloisi had that rare ability to see the whole field in front of him. Even in high school he could read defenses much better than Capizzo, as the coach readily acknowledged.

Though too slight for football at the college level when he arrived at Holy Cross ("About damn time he put on a purple uniform," as Donald Herman once joked), Aloisi hit the weight room hard, loading up on carbs and eventually getting his six-foot frame up over 200 pounds. By his junior year, when he'd become a reliable ball carrier as well as a defensive back, he was named a cocaptain—just the second football captain in the school's history who wasn't a senior.

Shortly after graduating from Holy Cross, the preternatu-rally poised young man assumed the head coaching position at

Worcester Academy, a prep school located in the same old industrial city as the college. In Aloisi's second year at the helm, he led the team to the New England prep school circuit's Class A championship game. The contest, played on the same weekend as the infamous water boy game on the Vineyard, featured a rematch with undefeated New Hampton, a seemingly untouchable opponent from New Hampshire that had dealt Aloisi's Hilltoppers their only loss of the season. Down by two touchdowns in the second half, Worcester Academy mounted a furious rally, scoring three times in a span of eight minutes to take the lead. With time running out, New Hampton moved the ball all the way to the 1-yard line. Players and spectators were frenzied: "The sidelines were off the charts," the coach recalls. His Hilltoppers held twice, only to give up the winning touchdown on the opponent's third try.

He'd been in Worcester thirteen years by the time he heard from Chris Maury. He and Katie owned a house there. She was from the area. They had a baby boy, and they were planning for another child. A $7,000-a-year job offer wasn't exactly an enticing lure. He'd need a teaching gig, and there were no openings in the high school at the time. And where would Katie work? The whole thing didn't make much sense.

His mother wouldn't tell him what she thought. Of course she wanted her Johnny and his family back on the island, but she was worried that the program had sunk so far it would only give him nightmares. Her brother Dick, John's uncle, was more blunt: "Are you out of your mind?" he said. "This"—the island's once-glorious football program—"is over." Still, Aloisi stayed awake at night thinking about the offer.

On a tiny island—only about ten thousand residents during

the fall and winter months—football under Vito was much, much more than just a game. It brought the community together, just as everyone was preparing to hunker down for another blustery winter by the ocean. "Everything is really intensified in such a small place," says one former Whaler, now living in California. "Success on the field is magnified. You take a lot of the island's hopes and dreams for that year on your shoulders." The mere mention that his high school alma mater might have to forgo its varsity football program for a few years—or, even more alarming, for good—put a pit in Aloisi's stomach.

And what truly made Nantucket football special, as the former star knew all too well, was the team's rivalry with the island to the west, twelve miles across the passageway known as Muskeget Channel. Charles McGrath wrote eloquently about it in a 1984 edition of the *New Yorker*: The "complex, friendly antagonism" between the two schools, he decided, "thrives despite—or perhaps because of—considerable obstacles." The islands when he visited, "in their battened-down, autumnal phase, seemed lonelier and somehow more serious places . . . Like many fierce competitions, I began to suspect, this one has at bottom some of the qualities of sibling rivalry: primal feelings of inferiority and superiority, love and envy, shared, in this case, by two places that are virtually the same—or are more like each other, at any rate, than they are like any other place on the mainland." The writer also detected an "element of mutual longing for importance, of nostalgia for the bygone whaling days, when the towns of Nantucket and Edgartown were two of the wealthiest and most powerful seaports on the world."

The whaling industry, of course, hadn't been the foundation of Nantucket's economy since the early industrial years of the

1840s. In the early part of the nineteenth century, when there were as many as eighty-eight Nantucket whaling ships criss-crossing the earth's oceans in search of the largest living crea-ture on the planet, the growing island's ten thousand residents made it the third biggest town in the state, after Boston and Sa-lem. Today, although the year-round population has crept back to the ten thousand mark in the aftermath of the real estate boom of the late twentieth century, the school system remains one of the smallest in Massachusetts.

The fog rolled in as Aloisi thought about the offer in front of him. It hadn't been long since a game played by high school boys, who took their team name from their homeland's ghostly ancestors, had been a very important part of island life on Nan-tucket. Under Donald Herman, the football program on Mar-tha's Vineyard had won five Super Bowls, sustaining the kind of consistent success that had once marked Capizzo's career. Not coincidentally, over the last decade the Vineyard had become the dominant team in the rivalry. Could he help restore this tradition to prominence?

FOR YEARS, AS Coach Herman so often said, there had been three certainties in island life: death, taxes, and the Island Cup. Now, with the big game suddenly in jeopardy, the year-round islanders had just the two.

In late July 2009, Herman received an odd email from some-one at the Boys and Girls Club on Nantucket. The Boys Club teams sometimes played young Vineyard teams on the morn-ing of the Island Cup game, just as the two islands' junior varsity football teams did. The correspondent was asking when and where the JV teams would be playing that year.

Puzzled, the coach forwarded the email to Sandy Mincone, then the newest athletic director for the Martha's Vineyard schools. After two weeks of trading phone messages with Chris Maury, Mincone finally learned that the other island had made plans to play another team on the weekend before Thanksgiving.

Vineyarders were outraged. That's bullshit, they grumbled. They felt like they were being cheated once more—even in Capizzo's absence—by the other island. It wasn't Vito's retirement, they said, or concerns for the safety of a team with dwindling enrollment. It couldn't be financial difficulties, said the Vineyarders, whose football team was blessed with its own well-connected booster organization, the Touchdown Club, which was separate from all other sports funding. "They're just tired of getting their asses kicked," snorted one frustrated resident at the counter of Linda Jean's, a popular breakfast joint on Circuit Avenue in the old seaside amusement town of Oak Bluffs, one morning midway through the new season.

A Saturday, the place was packed. The Vineyard boys had beaten Seekonk by a touchdown the night before. When Coach Herman strode in, he stopped at several tables on his way to his booth, greeting parents and former players. The Vineyard had run for 257 yards—two touchdowns for Tyler Araujo, one for Randall Jette. It was the team's first season in the tougher Eastern Athletic Conference after moving up from the Mayflower Large, and it had been a rocky start. Herman's team fell to Old Rochester by a touchdown on opening day before getting throttled by two teams, Somerset and Bishop Feehan, that were likely to remain the Vineyard's stiffest competition in their new conference for years to come. "They were a better football team—a bigger, faster football team," lamented the coach after the 20–0 loss to Somerset. "Plain and simple."

On top of that, the Vineyard had to take its first win by forfeit when a team from Charlestown couldn't field enough eligible players. But there would be bright spots, too. The islanders' four victories to date included a wild overtime decision over Coyle and Cassidy, in which the teams traded touchdowns before the Vineyard stuffed a disputed two-point conversion attempt at the goal line to seal the win. They would go on to win their last four in a row to finish at 7–3.

Yet the whole season felt somehow tainted without the Island Cup at stake. Herman was still struggling to understand. He'd seen Maury three times in the spring—both men coached girls' softball—but there'd been no mention of any potential problem with the Cup game. "I got hold of Chris at his house," he recounted, pushing his plate aside. Maury had offered his concerns about the economy, and the fact that neither side could afford the planes. Unlike the Vineyard, which has its Touchdown Club, Nantucket had one booster club for all its sports programs combined. Maury wanted a guarantee that the Vineyard would put all the Nantucket fall teams—soccer, field hockey—on its schedule for the big day, to consolidate costs. Herman countered that there weren't enough fields at either high school to accommodate that idea: "I'm like, 'Either you have the money to play football or you don't.' He said we have to treat all teams equally, and I said, 'No, you don't.'"

One of Maury's suggestions was that the two sides agree to play the game at a neutral site on the Cape, where they could both take regularly scheduled ferries. Herman dismissed that one out of hand. The host island made good money each year on the concession stand, raffle tickets, and other fund-raisers, he argued. "Plus, we're not gonna get a neutral site for free. So for us, that made absolutely no sense." The owner of Linda Jean's was on the board of the Steamship Authority. The coach knew for a fact that the teams could get a chartered ferry for half the usual cost, which was eleven grand. The bickering between islands had attracted no shortage of rumors: "I heard last week that the Fast Ferry"—the catamaran operated by Hy-Line Cruises— "was offered to Nantucket for free," Herman said.

Through the grapevine, Herman learned that Nantucket had contacted Cape Tech, the team it would play on the last weekend, about its schedule as early as May. The Crusaders hadn't played on the weekend before Thanksgiving in 2008, a season in which they'd buried Capizzo's Whalers, 34–0.

"Chris would deny it," said Herman, "but they knew a long time ago this game wasn't gonna take place. I still get pissed off thinking about it." The game had been a natural incentive for both sides for years. "If we got knocked out of the playoffs, we always had that game at the end of the year for motivation," fumed the Vineyard coach. This year he'd been forced to ask his incoming players a strange, uncomfortable question: "What's our motivation?"

THE WHOLE THING was a case of missed communication, explained Chris Maury, sitting in his office next to the Nantucket High gymnasium in early November. He loved the football team; he'd played for Vito, as had his two sons, both now in their thirties—Chris, who'd earned a master's degree at MIT before following his father into design building, and Michael, who was in L.A. finding work as an actor. Yes, he'd considered the possibility that the football program might have to scale back to JV-level competition until it got back on its feet. Seventeen boys had suited up for the last Island Cup game, and eight of them were graduating seniors. While the Vineyarders were moving up to Division 3, he noted, the Whalers had dropped down, to the recently created Mayflower Small.

There were other factors, too. Just as Donald Herman had once warned Capizzo, the addition of soccer as a varsity sport in the 1990s had eroded the football numbers. Not too many of the Portuguese kids were interested in learning the American contact sport. What was more, the new ice rink had drawn more kids into hockey at a young age, and the Nantucket program had quickly become a good one. With all of the travel teams, it was practically a year-round commitment for kids who skated.

When he first floated the idea of a "rivalry day" with the Vineyard that would include the soccer and field hockey teams, he'd been told that their schedules were already full. That conversation had been with the Vineyard AD at the time, former high school quarterback Mike Joyce, who would soon cede the post to Mincone. According to Maury, Joyce had said he likely would have to suspend the use of jets to get his football team to Nantucket. The school system was undergoing budget cuts. "I let him know we were being pounded pretty hard here as well," said Maury. For the first time, Nantucket had been compelled to ask the parents of student-athletes to pay a user fee to help defray the costs of the athletic program.

With Mincone taking over Joyce's job, both sides had trouble reaching the other over the next several weeks. Finally, Maury said, he received a message from Mincone saying the Vineyard had decided to suspend the Island Cup game, rather than try to work out the details of the proposed rivalry day.

"That message is still on my voice mail," said Maury. "I felt it was important to be saved."

It had become a blame game, and Maury, a stocky, serious fellow with trimmed silver hair and eyeglasses, was feeling beleaguered. In his mind, the Vineyard was unfairly putting the burden on Nantucket. There had been stories in the local papers and the *Wall Street Journal*; another was set to run in *USA Today*. One of the blowhards on WEEI, the top-rated sports-talk station in Boston, had even called out Nantucket for ducking the game. "He's on the air, bashing me, calling the kids wusses," recalled Maury, still bristling. "I really took offense to that." To the athletic director, the only news organization that had gotten it right was the high school's own newspaper.

"We went from having what I thought was a workable solution to, basically, the Vineyard pulling the plug on the Island Cup and trying to blame it on me and my school," said Maury. Though he'd been told the other fall teams had full schedules, he'd spotted a Vineyard listing on the MIAA's Web site looking for soccer and field hockey opponents. According to Maury, when the Vineyard's field hockey team came to Nantucket for a tournament game, the coach had told him her schedule had never been filled.

"In light of everything we try to teach high school athletes, integrity has to come into play," he said. If the Vineyard had taken an honest look, they would have recognized the tough situation Nantucket football was in and tried to help, he felt, "instead of slinging mud back and forth."

As classes let out, the hallway outside Maury's office quickly filled with laughing, hooting students. On the other side of the window overlooking the gym, boys wearing backpacks took lazy shots at the basketball hoops. "Hey, crackhead!" someone teased a friend down the hall. One boy slipped into Maury's office and snagged a caramel from a bowl on his desk, calling a thank-you over his shoulder on the way out. A sign taped to the wall read LIFE IS ALL ABOUT HOW YOU HANDLE PLAN B.

"People on the Vineyard are saying the only reason we're not playing is because we were getting the snockers kicked out of us," said Maury. "The truth of the matter is, the last few years the Vineyard has developed into a very good football program, and our program has gone in the opposite direction. And it is a mismatch. Not to take anything away from our kids—that's not really the factor here. My job as AD is to make sure we're doing the right things for my program, my kids.

"Our hope is that we're going to be able to put things back on board in the coming years," he said, "but some things went on here that the Vineyard has to clarify, too. Somebody's not telling the truth here."

THE HIGH SCHOOL'S front office was situated on the other side of the gym, just inside the main doors. John Aloisi had a temporary cubicle in the anteroom, out past the secretary's desk and the sign-in sheet. The new Nantucket football coach had a copy of the historical biography *John Adams*, written by Vineyard resident David McCullough, in his cubicle. Leaning against the desk was an oversized cardboard cutout of the Island Cup. Hired as a permanent substitute teacher, he'd also taken on the role of freshman advisor. He had his foot in the door.

As he walked through the hallway toward the back of the

school, he clapped the backs of several boys. "Do your homework," he said. One stopped to say he'd be late to practice.
"Have your mom call me or email me," said the coach.

Aloisi had loved playing for Vito, he said as he crossed the
football field to unlock the field house. He'd spoken at Capizzo's
retirement ceremony. "It's amazing—four and a half decades,"
he said. "So much has changed—the numbers, the assistant
coaches, the opponents. Everything. He was the only common
denominator."

Taking over the program was a daunting task. Taking it over
without an Island Cup game to look forward to was not quite
how he would have drawn it up.

"We shaved our heads as a team for the game," he recalled as
he walked back across the field—now rechristened Vito Capizzo
Stadium—where he had once thrown the football with the in-
fallibility of youth. "They used to decorate a path from the
airport with streamers. It was awesome."

He'd already assured Donald Herman that he had little interest in biding time until his program was ready to put up a
fight for the Island Cup again. The game itself could help restore some luster to the program. "I want to get it back, whatever means necessary," he said. "Like I tell my players, if a bad
play happens, you learn from it, and make the next one."

*Chapter Fifteen*

## BROTHERHOOD

*The old Nantucket is a thing of the past. A new Nantucket is being evolved, but what shall be its character no prophet may yet foretell.*

—MARY STARBUCK,
*NEW ENGLAND* MAGAZINE, 1902

SIX DAYS BEFORE Thanksgiving, 2010, hefty Max Moreis watched from the sideline as his teammates wrapped up their last practice of the year. The sun had already set. It was a clear, crisp night. A full moon hung over the field.

"Everyone was off the friggin' wall in school today," muttered Coach Herman.

Though Moreis hadn't played in months because of his two shoulder injuries, he fully intended to suit up the following day. After an excruciating season without the Island Cup, when the bickering got so bad it seemed as though the game might be lost forever, cooler heads had finally prevailed. This great, cockamamie rivalry was set to resume on the clearing in the woods of inner Edgartown.

"I'm *baa-aaack!*" Moreis sang, like a psychotic killer in a B-grade slasher movie. If he had the good fortune to score a touchdown in the Nantucket game, he promised, he would run all the way to South Beach and jump in the water.

A few of his teammates stood nearby in their purple varsity letterman jackets, looking a little more subdued. Linebacker Mike Montanile, who'd missed his first Island Cup game with a concussion during his sophomore year, was scheduled to undergo surgery on his own shoulder Monday. The recovery would probably keep him out of baseball season, too. And Tyler Araujo, who'd sustained a concussion in the game against Nauset the previous week, could only take solace in the fact that he was still just a junior. "If I was a senior," he said, "I'd tell them I'm playing."

Line coach Neil Estrella recalled playing for the Island Cup as a senior with a shoulder injury. "Now," he said with a what-are-you-gonna-do smile, "it's a chicken wing." His young daughter, who'd broken her forearm bones two months earlier, stood with the cheerleaders nearby, practicing cartwheels.

Conor Smith, the junior who'd had emergency surgery on his appendix, cued up some loud music on a boom box attached to amplifiers to get the boys fired up: *I'm a bad motherfucker!*

"Hey!" shouted coach Bill Belcher.

"Whose iPod is that?" Mike Hewitt, another coach, suggested Air Supply as an alternative.

On the field, Coach Herman huddled his players together to say a few last words. The underclassmen, he said, needed to hit the weight room over the winter. "And don't say 'I gotta go get a haircut,'" he said. "That's a bullshit answer."

Then he mellowed, as he'd done considerably since his

wild-eyed arrival on the island more than twenty years before. "Tonight is always bittersweet," he said. "Seniors, on the goal line, please."

It was time for Senior Recognition, an annual tradition in which the graduating team leaders lined up in a receiving line. One by one, the coaching staff and the younger players made their way down the line, wishing the seniors well in the Nantucket game, with the rest of their high school year, and in whatever their future lives held in store. David Araujo, the assistant coach, put a hand on the star shaved into the back of Randall Jette's head and pulled him to his shoulder, speaking softly into the quarterback's ear. James Bagnall, the senior center and saxophone-playing metalhead, did Jette one better: he had the purple Mohawk.

"It's not fair," Jette joked. "He has more hair."

After everyone had gone through the receiving line the players walked around the grandstand and into the shed, where they sat on the benches and listened as T. J. Vangervan read the coach's customary letter to the seniors. Some of the players threw an arm around the shoulders of the teammate they sat next to.

"Whether you know it or not," read the tall young man whose grandfather had been an immigrant mason and opera singer, "you've formed a brotherhood." In life, you will get knocked down, the coach had written. With any luck, their football experience had given these boys some indication of what they would do "when—not if—you get knocked down."

In their last game together, they would be playing for the Vineyarders' unprecedented seventh straight win against Nantucket. If there was anyone in the room who wasn't sure why that mattered, the coach wrote, they should ask Coach Estrella, Coach Dyer, or Coach O'Donnell which football game they remembered most.

The mood was nostalgic at the traditional Touchdown Club steak dinner that took place an hour later in the high school cafeteria. Taking places of honor were nineteen of the twenty-eight members of the original 1960 MVRHS football team, who were celebrating their fiftieth anniversary. All six of the cheerleaders from that season were on hand, too, including Barbara Murphy—the recently retired "Spanish teacher extraordinaire"—and Jeannie Mayhew, one of the many Mayhew cousins, who traveled all the way from Florida. Two of the six wore purple sweaters; all six were unable to stop smiling. They sat together at a table beneath the metallic whale bones, sculpted by a late island metalworker who'd gotten his start on the set of *Jaws*, that dominated the cafeteria.

Ken Goldberg, the play-by-play announcer, asked the ladies if they remembered a cheer. Of course they did: *We are the Vineyarders, the mighty, mighty Vineyarders . . .*

A representative of the Great American Rivalry Series stood up to speak next. The series, a promotional creation of iHigh, an online resource for high school athletics, had for the first time selected the Island Cup as one of its featured games. Kristen Parker had just arrived on the island that day. The winner of tomorrow's game would take home not just the Island Cup, she explained, but also the Rivalry Series' rectangular glass trophy.

"That'll be us," chirped Donald Herman.

After Parker spoke, it was returning athletic director Mark McCarthy's turn. The younger son of the late coach Dan McCarthy, for whom the Vineyard field had been renamed during halftime of an Island Cup game, he'd served a previous stint as AD in the late 1980s before leaving the island for Connecticut. Working as a high school athletic trainer in the Hartford area, he attended to a young hockey player who suffered a broken neck on the ice in 1996. "He was a paraplegic before he hit the ice," McCarthy recalled one day in his office. "It changed my life." He went on to spend several years as the director of a sports concussion program before coming back to the island.

Now McCarthy began to introduce the members of his father's 1960 team. "It's important for you guys back there," he said, gesturing to the back rows of tables, where most of the current players were congregated, "to understand that this is the roots of Vineyard football."

One by one, he called their names. There were Joe Araujo and Tim Downs, the quarterback. Lloyd "Butch" Mayhew, the halfback and punt returner. Tom Bennett, the associate director and senior clinical advisor at Community Services. Tony da Rosa. Roy deBettencourt. Emmett Carroll, who ran the old Texaco station in Menemsha for years. Tackle Tony Medeiros, a court officer living in Foxborough, who'd come over on the ferry earlier in the day. Cocaptains Roy Meekins and Gary Simmons, who would take the field as honorary cocaptains the following day for Goldberg's "coss of the toin."

At the dinner, Simmons made a few brief remarks. "If I don't stick to the script," he joked, "Mr. McCarthy said I wouldn't be asked back to the one hundredth."

They recognized the memory of William Hagerty, Bobby's older brother, who was killed in Vietnam on November 20, 1967, forty-three years to the day before this year's Island Cup.

"We're all brothers," said McCarthy. "This is your family.

You're going to be doing this in fifty years as well," he said, again addressing the boys in the back of the room. As he said it, his voice broke, just a little. Then he gathered himself and waved a hand at the evening's guests, this fellowship of Vineyard men in their late sixties.

"This is what you're going to look like," he said with a laugh.

McCarthy had a special surprise for the fiftieth-anniversary teammates: custom-designed T-shirts, each printed with their own name, to commemorate the event. The T-shirts provided a rare opportunity for the AD to pick on his older brother. Mike McCarthy, who had gone on from his stellar Vineyard career to play, and then coach, in the University of Connecticut's Division I program, received a T-shirt that read "Waterboy." He'd been still in grade school when the 1960 team played.

"I'm proud to be their water boy," he said.


THE VINEYARD'S TOUCHDOWN Club had invited the Whalers to breakfast in the cafeteria on the morning of the game, but Chris Maury declined. Jack Law, the Touchdown Club president, shrugged.

"We weren't going to poison them," he said.

Instead, the Whalers were bused from the ferry landing in Vineyard Haven, where they disembarked from the boat they'd chartered—the *Martha's Vineyard*—to the Harbor View Hotel in Edgartown. There the team and coaches sat down in a white-tablecloth function room for some scrambled eggs and last-minute preparation. With the shades drawn, John Aloisi and Bill Manchester projected game film on the wall.

They felt good about their chances if the Vineyard used a cover-three defense. Manchester predicted they'd have some success throwing into the flat. That would require extra effort on pass protection from their offensive line. "Fight, scratch, claw until the whistle, please," said the head coach calmly.

When Vaughan Machado spoke, his voice was raw and hoarse. "Some get it from whiskey," said the part-time guitar player before he stood up. "I get it from yelling at Nantucket kids."

Surprisingly, the *Globe* had picked the Whalers to win. Despite the program's well-documented struggles and the Vineyard's recent dominance, despite the fact that Nantucket now played two divisions below their archrivals, Nantucket, claimed longtime high school sports reporter Bob Holmes, won the Island Cup every year that dolphins appeared in the island harbor.

"It's true," he claimed. "Look it up."

For the second-year Nantucket coaches, that story wasn't so far-fetched. "We are way beyond *try*," Machado told the team. "Today we *do*."

THAT MORNING JUNIOR high school players from both islands squared off against each other on an open field at the edge of the Vineyard high school grounds. John Aloisi's nephew, James, his brother Sam's oldest son, quarterbacked the visitors to a 16-point victory.

The stands at the Daniel G. McCarthy Memorial Athletic Field filled up well before kickoff. The epic choral music of *Carmina Burana* squawked from the loudspeakers. Humming generators stood behind the snack shack and alongside the Great American Rivalry Series' huge inflatable football. Uniformed members of the U.S. Marines, who were sponsoring the Rivalry Series, manned a Chin-Up Challenge for schoolkids over by the food shed.

Old friends from the Vineyard gathered along the fences, exchanging handshakes and hugs. The Nantucket fans, meanwhile, skulked around the outskirts of the field to the far side, where the visiting team had a much smaller grandstand.

When Randall Jette's name was called during Senior Recognition before the game, the young man, wearing number 1, strode out of the south end zone toward midfield. His smiling mother, Grace, walked beside him to his right. Next to her was her husband, Albie.

On the other side of the group, clasping Randall's left hand and walking proudly beside him was his father, Vamp Campbell.

On the 50-yard line a Marine sergeant presented glass trophies for the Rivalry Series Hall of Fame to the first inductees from either side—Jason Dyer, the quarterback who'd engineered the Vineyard's fairy-tale comeback in 1992, and Vito Capizzo, who was wearing a Nantucket cap and rose-tinted sunglasses. A few of the fans who were paying attention to the brief, barely audible ceremony clapped politely.

Up in the press booth, Ken Goldberg was startled by the sight in front of him. "Does Jason Dyer have his arm around Vito Capizzo?" he asked.

Chris Maury had had to convince the retired coach to make the trip. Few people had seen Vito at the Whalers' home games since his retirement, though he was usually there, at least for the first half. He'd gotten in the habit of parking his pickup along the far lot, watching while he leaned on the fence at the top of the embankment overlooking the field. It was out of the way. When he was still coaching, he'd called the spot "Has-Been Hill."

To be sure that Capizzo showed up, Maury had arranged to

have him and Barbara flown to the island in a chartered jet. Watching her husband grapple with the emotions of his retirement had been difficult for Barbara, who'd spent much of her life trying to bring a measure of refinement to her stubborn husband. She often thought about something a player's mother once said to her: that one of the saddest days of her life was when she'd washed her son's uniform for the last time.

Now the coach was happy he'd decided to come. As the game got under way, he stalked the sideline just like old times, evaluating play calls. This time, however, he was careful to keep himself out of earshot of the players. A state cop stood nearby, just in case.

A few minutes into the action, when junior quarterback Taylor Hughes pounded for the end zone, hoping to tie the score after Jette's opening touchdown, Capizzo strained his neck to see. Every islander from both sides of the rivalry collectively held their breath.


HUGHES HAD UNDERGONE hernia surgery when he was just eleven years old. He was a tough kid, just like his old man.

But Taylor's mother, Kip, still worried about her baby. She made a point of traveling to all the Whalers' away games. It was a superstition with her: if she didn't go, he'd get hurt.

It was the boy's pride that hurt when the ball jarred loose just as he was about to cross into the end zone. His older brother had endured the very worst year of Capizzo's twilight, and Taylor's freshman team had taken a beating at the hands of the Vineyard. He wanted nothing more than to lead his team to victory in the Island Cup game. "I've been nervous all week," he'd said a few nights before the trip.

His teammates picked him up a few plays later when Codie
Perry recovered a Vineyard fumble. Hughes connected with Du-
Vaughn Beckford twice on the ensuing drive. Mike Molta banged
in from the 2, but Sam Earle's kick into a stiff breeze sailed wide
left. Still, they were in this thing. It was 7–6, Vineyard.

On the kickoff, however, Jette showed once again why he
was one of the Vineyard's all-time greats. He caught a seam and
turned upfield. The blocking was there; the hole got wider. In
a flash, he had just one man to beat, and that was Terrel Correia.
The outcome of this footrace was never in doubt. Jette left the
tall boy staggering in his wake. Eighty-five yards after catching
the kick, he had his second touchdown of the day.

Moments later, before the Vineyard fans had stopped cheering, Molta fielded a bouncing kickoff and busted it almost to
midfield. By now it was plenty clear: this year's Whalers were not
about to go quietly.

"Yeah!" shouted Beau Almodobar from up on the tower. "It's
gonna be a long game."

*Chapter Sixteen*

# WHALE OF A GAME

IT BEGAN TO look bleak for Nantucket when the Vine-yarders scored once more. With a little more than five minutes to go in the half, Brian Montambault, who'd received a student-athlete scholarship from the Marines earlier in the day, helped his team capitalize on a Whaler fumble with a 4-yard burst into the end zone. The scoreboard showed the underdogs digging themselves a big hole: 19–6, Vineyard.

But Correia smothered an onside kick, giving Nantucket good position at midfield, and the offense made it count. Hughes capped an eight-play drive when he pushed behind his linemen into the end zone. And after a quick three-and-out for the Vineyard, the Whalers got the ball back once more before halftime.

Standing near the Whalers bench on the far side of the field, Matt Aloisi smiled widely as he watched his little brother's team begin to tap its reserves. "How great would it be to score again before the half?" he yelled. His grin faded when Delmont Araujo sacked Hughes for a loss, effectively killing the Nantucket drive and leaving the score frozen at 19–12 at the end of the second quarter.

At halftime, the Vineyard players were upbeat and anxious all at once. The Whalers were playing with focus. The longer they hung in, the more the visitors seemed to be gorging themselves on confidence. What did it matter that the Vineyard's high school was more than twice the size of theirs?

To kick off the last week of practice, the coaches had held a skull session with their players in Aloisi's social studies classroom that Monday to kick off the last week of practice. Mike Molta sat near the back with a Mountain Dew and a package of goldfish crackers. Junior lineman Jonathan Vollans, grandson of Vito's first assistant, looked like Travis Bickle in a sleeveless orange T-shirt and a new Mohawk. Coach Psaradelis was absent; his wife had just given birth to their second child, a girl named Willow.

Aloisi gave his players a number, then challenged them to ignore it. "The Vineyard's enrollment is nine hundred," he said. Whatever the figure, they'd still be playing with the same number of teammates on the field.

He scanned the classroom with a searing gaze. "They're high school football players, your size," he said carefully. "Period."

Beau Almodobar had another question for the players. "How many of you think you've played your best game this season?" he asked.

If any of them weren't sure, they knew the answer definitively when the second half started on Saturday. After squandering an opportunity to tie the game on their opening drive—Molta, at the end of a nice gain, had the ball ripped from his clutches—the Whalers caused a turnover of their own. Blitzing from his linebacker position, Hughes chased Jette deep behind the line of scrimmage as he dropped back to pass. Jette faked the throw, and his counterpart leaped high over his head, arms up. As the quarterback tried to cut away, he lost control of the football, and Mack McGrath, in pursuit, fell on it instantly.

And then the Whalers took the big gamble. On Nantucket's first play from scrimmage, Hughes caught the shotgun snap and handed off to Beckford, who was in motion from left to right. Beckford pitched back to Kevin McLean, who cradled the ball and tossed it farther still behind the line—back to Hughes. All alone, the quarterback rocked, set, and spun a beautiful arcing spiral deep downfield, just as he'd done hundreds of times on equipment day three months earlier. Sure-handed receiver Andrew Benson angled under the ball, hauled it in, and cruised into the end zone, trailed by a streak of purple jerseys.

It was a dramatic 53-yard double flea-flicker—the old razzle-dazzle. Moments later Sam Earle, the kicker who'd been so distraught about his performance at Holbrook the week before, split the uprights to tie the game at 19 apiece.

"And we have got ourselves a whale of a football game!" Sandy Beach rumbled into his microphone, for the benefit of the Whalers fans who hadn't made the trip.

From there, the game was relentless. Montambault, after carrying what seemed like the entire Whalers defense for a remarkable gain, remained prone on the ground when the pile cleared. He'd injured his wrist and was finished for the day. A few plays later, after a Vangervan catch and a successful draw play, Jette scored his third touchdown of the day from in close. As the two lines clashed, he leaped over the back of James Bagnall, his center, and held out the football as if he were releasing a dove. As the ball crossed the plane, he was pulled to his knees, and then backward, by several Nantucketers on the ground. Scrambling to extricate himself, the Vineyard star braced his hand on the helmet of Whaler lineman Alex Rezendes, who lay beneath him, and pushed himself up.

On its next possesssion Nantucket was forced to punt, but the team took the ball back when Andrew Benson intercepted a Jette pass at the Vineyard 30. The fans in blue rejoiced. A young man from the visiting island grabbed the Nantucket flag and brazenly sprinted up the sideline in front of the Vineyard fans. A student from the Vineyard rushed out from the crowd, lowered his shoulder, and laid one of the nastiest hits of the day on the kid.

On the field, Hughes completed a quick, crisp march with a 2-yard plunge to make the score 26–25, Vineyard. When the coaches decided to forgo the potentially game-tying point-after kick, opting instead for a two-point conversion try, the crowd on both sides of the field whooped and laughed in disbelief. What balls!

The Whalers lined up, for the first time all day, in an un-balanced set—an extra man to the right side of the line of scrimmage. On the field, the Vineyarders didn't adjust. Hughes, lining up under center, quickly realized that the conversion was his for the taking. He might have been a little too pumped. The exchange on the snap wasn't clean, and Nantucket fumbled away its chance to take the lead.

Jette, refusing to rattle, led his team on another purposeful scoring drive. To no one's surprise, he would be named the game's MVP. Inevitably, it was he who took the ball into the end zone, for his fourth touchdown of the day.

And still Nantucket had one last chance. With the clock ticking down under a minute to go, Beckford swept to the right, across midfield, for a 16-yard gain. Benson caught a strike on the sideline and fell out of bounds. Hughes dropped back to pass and turned to look for his receiver. Suddenly he had big Delmont Araujo in his face.

TWO YEARS BEFORE, not a soul who had ever enjoyed a little football between these two islands could have suggested that the Island Cup rivalry—long dominated by Vito Capizzo's dynasty, more recently relegated to a glorified exhibition for Donald Herman's perennial contenders—would ever be this competitive again. One year ago, the game had gone on hiatus, and at the time many feared it was for good.

In the end, it wasn't especially important that T. J. Vangervan intercepted Hughes's fluttering pass attempt. It didn't really matter that it was Donald Herman who was doused with water by two of his injured players.

After the handshake line, several of the Nantucket players were bawling. So was Coach Lombardi.

But John Aloisi—the hometown hero who'd led his high school team to three straight Super Bowls and, perhaps more gratifying, three straight wins over the Vineyard; the ascetic son, brother, and father who lived his life with a furrowed brow—John Aloisi was beaming like he was in heaven.

On the television broadcast, Ken Goldberg declared that he was already looking forward to the following year's trip to his second favorite island.

And Taylor Hughes, still a junior, wiped his eyes as he walked to the bus.

"I can't wait until next year," he said.

# OVERTIME

IN EARLY FEBRUARY of his senior year, with his mother and stepfather at his side, Randall Jette signed a letter of intent to play Division I football at the University of Massachusetts.

Vito Capizzo spent the winter in Florida with his wife.

Fifty-five Nantucket boys signed up to play football during the 2011 season.

And at the end of May, Donald Herman sent a striking text message. His new counterpart on the other island, John Aloisi, was stepping down as the Nantucket football coach.

Just like Capizzo in 1964, Aloisi had promised his wife they'd give it three years on the island, then see where they stood. As it happened, he could give only two. He'd been offered a job teaching history in Shrewsbury, near Worcester, at the high school where he'd worked the year before the Nantucket job opened up. The school had more than a hundred applicants; when the head of the department wished aloud that one of them was John Aloisi, the principal picked up the phone and called him.

Two days later, Katie was unexpectedly contacted about returning to her own former employer, also in the Worcester area.

It was the promotion she'd been hoping to get before John accepted the coaching position.

The veteran football coach in Shrewsbury, who had a couple of Super Bowl wins under his belt, quickly made it clear that he would welcome Aloisi as an assistant. The coach had already hinted that he might be approaching an age when he'd be ready to step down.

Bill Manchester and Beau Almodobar interviewed for the Nantucket position. The school system gave the job to Manchester.

For Aloisi, calling the football team together to tell them he was leaving was the hardest thing he'd ever had to do. Yet coaching, for him, was really like a hobby. His true priorities were teaching and raising his two boys. It was distressing to think that he hadn't given enough of himself to the program, but he felt better about the fact that he was leaving it in good hands.

Though Nantucket had lost the only Island Cup game he would coach, his assistants and players knew they'd accomplished something big. Their friends and families knew it, too. The Monday after the game, on separate occasions, two acquaintances approached Aloisi with tears in their eyes. Each told him how proud they were of the players and their community. They hadn't even been at the game—both were listening on the radio.

The day the Island Cup resumed was a great day, recalled Aloisi as he prepared to move his family back to America.

"It was," he said, "almost like both sides won."

# ACKNOWLEDGMENTS

The first time I sat with the Nantucket coaching staff, they were going over defensive assignments. Coach Aloisi mentioned the linebackers Sam and Will, which happen to be the names of my first two sons. Funny that you've got players with the same names, I blurted without thinking. "Sam," of course, is coach talk for the strong-side linebacker; "Will" covers the weak side.

From that moment, they were stuck with me. To their ever-lasting credit, the coaches, families, boosters, and players past and present—on both islands—never failed to make this "wash-ashore" feel welcome. A wholehearted thank-you, then, to the residents of these two extraordinary places. I can only hope that this book gives an accurate glimpse into the lives, hopes, wins, losses, and moral victories of the working people who truly define Nantucket and Martha's Vineyard.

Islanders deserving of my gratitude are too numerous to mention, but I would be remiss not to thank a few in particular. On Nantucket, these include Vaughan Machado and the very gracious Anne Lanman, the Aloisi family, Beau Almodobar, Bill Manchester, Chris Maury, and Vito and Barbara Capizzo.

On Martha's Vineyard: Donald Herman, Bob Tankard, Ken Goldberg, Mark McCarthy, Grace Jette and Albie Robinson, and Alan and Ellen Bresnick for their considerable hospitality.

Thanks to Ben Adams, my editor, whose great enthusiasm for this story helped me tell it to the best of my ability. Thanks as always to Paul Bresnick, my steady agent, for recognizing another good idea. Thanks to Buzz Bissinger, who confirmed it. And thanks to so many of the editors at the *Boston Globe*, including (but not only) Kerry Drohan, Rebecca Ostriker, James Reed, and Roy Greene, who have made my contributions there a real pleasure.

I'd also like to acknowledge a few old friends who continue to prop me up—Jeremy Cowan, Bill Crandall, and Joel Selvin. My father is a good man, and the Sheehans are good people who sure do love them some football. To Sam, Will, and Owen, the three sons Monica has given me: may you cover plenty of ground. Owen came last, but he might have to play middle linebacker. His middle name is Mike.

# A NOTE ON THE AUTHOR

JAMES SULLIVAN is the author of *Seven Dirty Words*, *The Hardest Working Man*, and *Jeans*. He is a regular contributor to the *Boston Globe* and a contributing editor for RollingStone.com, and he previously served as a feature writer and culture critic for the *San Francisco Chronicle*. He has spent considerable time, including his honeymoon, on the islands. He lives north of Boston.